BANK SECRECY ACT: BACKGROUND, STATUTE AND INTERPRETATION

Bank Secrecy Act: Background, Statute and Interpretation

Lilian B. Klein
Editor

Nova Science Publishers, Inc.
New York

For permission to use material from this book please contact us:
Telephone 631-231-7269; Fax 631-231-8175
Web Site: http://www.novapublishers.com

Library of Congress Cataloging-in-Publication Data
Available upon request

ISBN 978-1-60021-472-1

Published by Nova Science Publishers, Inc. ✣New York

CONTENTS

Preface **vii**

Chapter 1 Bank Secrecy Act/Anti-Money Laundering **1**

Chapter 2 Bank Secrecy Act **61**

Index **157**

PREFACE

The Currency and Foreign Transactions Reporting Act, also known as the Bank Secrecy Act (BSA), and its implementing regulation, 31 CFR 103, is a tool the U.S. government uses to fight drug trafficking, money laundering, and other crimes. Congress enacted the BSA to prevent banks and other financial service providers from being used as intermediaries for, or to hide the transfer or deposit of money derived from, criminal activity. The Office of the Comptroller of the Currency (OCC) monitors national bank compliance with the BSA and 31 CFR 103. Since its passage, Congress has amended the BSA a number of times to enhance law enforcement effectiveness. The Anti-Drug Abuse Act of 1986, which included the Money Laundering Control Act of 1986 (MCLA), strengthened the government's ability to fight money laundering by making it a criminal activity.Before 2005, each regulator used separately developed, but similar, examination procedures to assess compliance with the BSA. However, in 2005, in an effort to establish more consistency in examination procedures and application, the regulators, with participation from the Financial Crimes Enforcement Network (FinCEN), jointly developed and issued an interagency BSA examination procedures manual. The new procedures retain the risk-focused approach of the prior procedures, requiring examiners to apply a higher level of scrutiny to the institution's lines of business that carry a higher risk for potential money laundering or noncompliance with the BSA.

In: Bank Secrecy Act: Background, Statute and Interpretation ISBN: 978-1-60021-472-1
Editor: Lilian B. Klein, pp. 1-59

Chapter 1

BANK SECRECY ACT/ANTI-MONEY LAUNDERING*

INTRODUCTION

Background

The Currency and Foreign Transactions Reporting Act,[1] also known as the Bank Secrecy Act (BSA), and its implementing regulation, 31 CFR 103, is a tool the U.S. government uses to fight drug trafficking, money laundering, and other crimes. Congress enacted the BSA to prevent banks and other financial service providers from being used as intermediaries for, or to hide the transfer or deposit of money derived from, criminal activity. The Office of the Comptroller of the Currency (OCC) monitors national bank compliance with the BSA and 31 CFR 103.

Since its passage, Congress has amended the BSA a number of times to enhance law enforcement effectiveness. The Anti-Drug Abuse Act of 1986, which included the Money Laundering Control Act of 1986 (MLCA), strengthened the government's ability to fight money laundering by making it a criminal activity. The Money Laundering Suppression Act of 1994 (Title IV of the Riegle-Neal Community Development and Regulatory Improvement Act of 1994) required regulators to develop enhanced examination procedures and increase examiner training to improve the identification of money laundering schemes in financial institutions.

Today more than 170 crimes are listed in the federal money laundering statutes. They range from drug trafficking, gunrunning, murder for hire, fraud, acts of terrorism, and the illegal use of a wetlands. The list also includes certain foreign crimes. Therefore, a financial institution must educate its employees, understand its customers and their businesses, and have systems and procedures in place to distinguish routine transactions from ones that rise to the level of suspicious activity.

The reporting and record keeping requirements of the BSA regulations create a paper trail for law enforcement to investigate money laundering schemes and other illegal activities. This paper trail operates to deter illegal activity and provides a means to trace movements of money through the financial system.

* Excerpted from Bank Secrecy Act/Anti-Money Laundering, Comptroller's Handbook dated December 2000.

Money laundering is the criminal practice of filtering ill-gotten gains or "dirty" money through a maze or series of transactions, so the funds are "cleaned" to look like proceeds from legal activities. Money laundering does not have to involve cash at every stage of the laundering process. Any transaction conducted with a bank might constitute money laundering. Although money laundering is a diverse and often complex process, it basically involves three independent steps that can occur simultaneously:

- Placement: The process of placing, through deposits or other means, unlawful cash proceeds into traditional financial institutions.
- Layering: The process of separating the proceeds of criminal activity from their origin through the use of layers of complex financial transactions, such as converting cash into traveler's checks, money orders, wire transfers, letters of credit, stocks, bonds, or purchasing valuable assets, such as art or jewelry.
- Integration: The process of using an apparently legitimate transaction to disguise the illicit proceeds, allowing the laundered funds to be disbursed back to the criminal. Different types of financial transactions, such as sham loans or false import/export invoices, can be used.

OCC Initiatives

The OCC has undertaken a number of anti-money laundering initiatives. In 1997, the OCC formed the National Anti-Money Laundering Group (NAMLG), an internal task force that has embarked on several projects. One such project involves targeting banks for expanded scope money laundering examinations. Experienced examiners and other OCC experts who specialize in BSA compliance, anti-money laundering, and fraud staff the targeted examinations. Banks are selected for examination using a filtering process that focuses on:

1. Locations in high-intensity drug trafficking areas (HIDTA) or high-intensity money laundering and related financial crime areas (HIFCA). (A listing of these areas is found at website www.whitehousedrugpolicy.gov.)
2. Excessive currency flows.
3. Significant private banking activities.
4. Unusual suspicious activity reporting patterns.
5. Unusual large currency transaction reporting patterns.
6. Fund transfers or account relationships with drug source countries or countries with stringent financial secrecy laws.

In addition, the OCC works with the Financial Crimes Enforcement Network (FinCEN) to enhance further its ability to identify banks with money laundering risk. For example, the OCC's fraud, BSA/anti-money laundering specialists, and various other OCC personnel have on-line access to primary FinCEN databases. Those databases house currency transaction reports, suspicious activity reports, other BSA information, and Federal Reserve cash flow data (currency flows between the Federal Reserve banks and depository institutions). This on-line access allows the OCC to analyze data to identify banks with unusual currency or suspicious report activity. The OCC also is working with FinCEN to utilize the agency's "artificial intelligence" capabilities to facilitate the targeting program.

The OCC also conducts targeted examinations based on law enforcement leads. For example, if a U.S. Attorney's Office advises the OCC that a national bank may be involved in a money-laundering scheme, the OCC sends a team of examiners to assess the situation. If the examination process identifies weaknesses in the bank's BSA compliance program or other problems within the OCC's supervisory or enforcement authority, the OCC directs the bank to take appropriate corrective action. In addition, if the examiners discover information that may relate to a possible criminal violation, the OCC directs the bank to file a Suspicious Activity Report and provide appropriate documents and information to the receiving law enforcement agency.

Throughout this handbook, the term "national bank" or "bank" includes all banking units of the financial institution, including functionally regulated subsidiaries and financial subsidiaries under the Gramm-Leach-Bliley Act. This may include private banking, international banking, trust, discount brokerage, and other business units of the institution. It may also include other entities the OCC supervises, such as limited purpose banks (i.e., credit card banks and trust companies), federal agencies and branches of foreign banks operating in the United States, international banking facilities of U.S. banks, and, to some extent, foreign branches of U.S. banks.

Penalties

Penalties for money laundering can be severe. Individuals, including bank employees, convicted of money laundering face up to 20 years in prison for each money laundering transaction. Businesses, including banks and individuals, face fines up to the greater of $500,000 or twice the value of the transaction. Any property involved in the transaction or traceable to the proceeds of the criminal activity, including loan collateral, personal property and, under certain conditions, entire bank accounts (even if some of the money in the account is legitimate) may be subject to forfeiture. In addition, banks risk losing their charter, and bank employees risk being removed and barred from banking.

Asset Forfeiture

Under the provisions of the Controlled Substances Act of 1978, the Money Laundering Control Act of 1986, and the Anti-Drug Abuse Act of 1988, real or personal property traceable to illegal drug sales or purchased with laundered money is subject to government seizure and forfeiture.

Occasionally, seized property is collateral for bank loans. Therefore, a bank must obtain and confirm enough information about its customers to protect its loan collateral from loss due to government forfeiture.

When the government seizes property in a civil or criminal forfeiture, individuals or entities claiming that property (owners, lien holders, or general creditors) may request that a judge determine whether the property is subject to forfeiture and whether the property should be released. The court, in deciding whether to release the property may look at several issues, including whether the claimant is an innocent owner, whether failure to release the property would create a hardship for the claimant, whether there is a "substantial connection" between the property and the offense, and whether the forfeiture is grossly disproportional to the gravity of the offense. The government has the burden of proving that the property is properly subject to forfeiture by a preponderance of the evidence.

Because the risk of loss by forfeiture arises most often when a bank has taken collateral, banks should use caution when accepting collateral to ensure there is no reason to believe the customer or the collateral might be involved in any unusual or suspicious activity. The bank should exercise particular care when it extends loans that appear to be risk free because they are fully secured by cash collateral.

Internal BSA Compliance Programs

Under 12 CFR 21.21, all national banks must develop, administer, and maintain a program that ensures and monitors compliance with the BSA and its implementing regulations, including record keeping and reporting requirements. Such a program can help protect a bank against possible criminal and civil penalties and asset forfeitures.

At a minimum, a bank's internal compliance program must be written, approved by the board of directors, and noted as such in the board meeting minutes. The program must include:

- A system of internal controls to ensure ongoing compliance.
- Independent testing of compliance.
- Daily coordination and monitoring of compliance by a designated person.
- Training for appropriate personnel.

Internal Controls

Senior management is responsible for ensuring an effective system of internal controls for the BSA, including suspicious activity reporting, and must demonstrate its commitment to compliance by:

- Establishing a comprehensive program and set of controls, including account opening, monitoring, and currency reporting procedures, that are approved by the board of directors and fully implemented by bank staff.
- Instituting a requirement that senior management be kept informed of compliance efforts, audit reports, identified compliance deficiencies, and corrective action taken. In other words, internal control systems must enable senior management to ensure ongoing compliance.
- Making BSA compliance a condition of employment.
- Incorporating compliance with the BSA and its implementing regulations into job descriptions and performance evaluations of bank personnel.

Independent Testing of Compliance

The bank's internal or external auditors should be able to:

- Attest to the overall integrity and effectiveness of management systems and controls, and BSA technical compliance.
- Test transactions in all areas of the bank with emphasis on high-risk areas, products, and services to ensure the bank is following prescribed regulations.
- Assess employees' knowledge of regulations and procedures.
- Assess adequacy, accuracy, and completeness of training programs.
- Assess adequacy of the bank's process for identifying suspicious activity.

Internal review or audit findings should be incorporated into a board and senior management report and reviewed promptly. Appropriate follow up should be ensured.

Compliance Officer

A national bank must designate a qualified bank employee as its BSA compliance officer, who has day-to-day responsibility for managing all aspects of the BSA compliance program and compliance with all BSA regulations. The BSA compliance officer may delegate certain BSA compliance duties to other employees, but not compliance responsibility. The bank's board of directors and senior management must ensure that the BSA compliance officer has sufficient authority and resources to administer effectively a comprehensive BSA compliance program.

Training

Banks must ensure that appropriate bank personnel are trained in all aspects of the regulatory requirements of the BSA and the bank's internal BSA compliance and anti-money laundering policies and procedures. An effective training program includes provisions to ensure that:

- All bank personnel, including senior management, who have contact with customers (whether in person or by phone), who see customer transaction activity, or who handle cash in any way, receive appropriate training. Those employees include persons involved with branch administration; customer service; lending, private, or personal banking; correspondent banking (international and domestic); trust; discount brokerage; funds transfer; safe deposit/custody; and vault activities.
- Training is ongoing and incorporates current developments and changes to the BSA, anti-money laundering laws, and OCC and FinCEN regulations. New and different money laundering schemes involving customers and financial institutions should be addressed. It also should include examples of money laundering schemes and cases, tailored to the audience, and the ways in which such activities can be detected or resolved.
- Training focuses on the consequences of an employee's failure to comply with established policy and procedures (e.g., fines or termination). Programs should provide personnel with guidance and direction in terms of bank policies and available resources.

Reporting Requirements

The BSA regulations require all financial institutions to submit five types of reports to the government.

1. IRS Form 4789 Currency Transaction Report (CTR): A CTR must be filed for each deposit, withdrawal, exchange of currency, or other payment or transfer, by, through or to a financial institution, which involves a transaction in currency of *more than* $10,000. Multiple currency transactions must be treated as a single transaction if the financial institution *has knowledge* that: (a) they are conducted by or on behalf of the same person; and, (b) they result in cash received or disbursed by the financial institution of more than $10,000. (31 CFR 103.22)
2. U.S. Customs Form 4790 Report of International Transportation of Currency or Monetary Instruments (CMIR): Each person (including a bank) who physically transports, mails or ships, or causes to be physically transported, mailed, shipped or received, currency, traveler's checks, and certain other monetary instruments in an aggregate amount *exceeding* $10,000 into or out of the United States must file a CMIR. (31 CFR 103.23)
3. Department of the Treasury Form 90-22.1 Report of Foreign Bank and Financial Accounts (FBAR): Each person (including a bank) subject to the jurisdiction of the United States having an interest in, signature or other authority over, one or more bank, securities, or other financial accounts in a foreign country must file an FBAR if the aggregate value of such accounts at any point in a calendar year *exceeds* $10,000. (31 CFR 103.24)
4. Treasury Department Form 90-22.47 and OCC Form 8010-9, 8010-1 Suspicious Activity Report (SAR): Banks must file a SAR for any suspicious transaction relevant to a possible violation of law or regulation. (31 CFR 103.18 formerly 31 CFR 103.21) (12 CFR 12.11) (Refer to the "Suspicious Activity Reporting" section of this handbook for further detail.)
5. "Designation of Exempt Person" Form TDF 90-22.53: Banks must file this form to designate an exempt customer for the purpose of CTR reporting under the BSA (31 CFR 103.22(d)(3)(i)). In addition, banks use this form biennially (every two years) to renew exemptions for eligible non-listed business and payroll customers. (31 CFR 103.22(d)(5)(i))

Record Keeping Requirements

The BSA regulations require banks to maintain a variety of records to ensure, among other things, that transactions can be reconstructed. Two of those record keeping requirements are discussed briefly as follows. Detailed descriptions of these and other record keeping requirements for banks can be found in 31 CFR 103. The retention period for all records required to be kept under the BSA regulations is five years.

- Monetary Instrument Sales Records: A bank must retain a record of each *cash* sale of bank checks, drafts, cashier's checks, money orders, and traveler's checks between $3,000 and $10,000 inclusive. These records must include evidence of verification of the identity of the purchaser and other information. (31 CFR 103.29)

- Funds Transfer Record Keeping and Travel Rule Requirements: A bank must maintain a record of each funds transfer of $3,000 or more which it originates, acts as an intermediary for, or receives. The amount and type of information a bank must record and keep depends upon its role in the funds transfer process. Also, a bank that acts as an originator or intermediary for a funds transfer must pass certain information along to the next bank in the funds transfer chain. (31 CFR103.33 (e) and (g))

Exemptions from the CTR Filing Requirements

The BSA regulations were designed to permit banks to exempt certain types of transactions from the CTR filing requirements. In April 1996, September 1997, and September 1998, exemption provisions were revised to reduce further the reporting burden. Perhaps the largest difference between the new and old exemption procedures is that the new procedures refer to an *exempt person*, whereas the old procedures refer to an *exempt account and an exempt amount.* Banks were allowed to use the old exemption provisions until June 30, 2000. The "new" exemption procedures are detailed in 31 CFR 103.22 (d). These new exemption rules were issued in two parts, phase I and II.

Phase I rules were aimed at large national and regional customers. As of April 30, 1996, banks were not required to file CTRs on large currency transactions conducted by certain "exempt persons" defined as:

1. Domestic depository institutions.
2. Departments and agencies of the United States, the states, and their political subdivisions.
3. Any entity established under the laws of the United States, of any state, or of the political subdivision of any state, or under an interstate compact between two or more states, that exercises authority on behalf of the United States or any such state or political subdivision.
4. Any entity, other than a bank, whose common stock or analogous equity interests are listed on the New York Stock Exchange, the American Stock Exchange, or whose common stock, or analogous equity interests have been designated as a Nasdaq National Market Security listed on the Nasdaq Stock Market (except stock or interests listed under the separate "Nasdaq Small-Cap Issues" heading).
5. Any subsidiary, other than a bank, of any entity described in number four (a "listed entity") that is organized under the laws of the United States or of any state and at least 51 percent of whose common stock is owned by the listed entity. Franchises of listed entities may not be treated as exempt persons, unless they qualify as subsidiaries.

Phase II rules [103.22(d)(2)(vi)-(vii)] allow banks to exempt:

1. Any other commercial enterprise (also known under the new exemption procedures as non-listed businesses), to the extent of its domestic operations, other than those ineligible businesses covered by 103.22(d)(6)(viii).

2. A customer that holds a payroll account that regularly withdraws more than $10,000 to pay its U.S. employees in currency solely for withdrawals for payroll purposes from existing transaction accounts.

The "Designation of Exempt Person" form, TDF 90-22.53, must be filed to exempt customers under phase I and II rules. Under the phase II rule:

- Twelve months of account history must exist before the customer can be exempted. (The months do not have to be consecutive, but should be recent.)
- The customer must engage frequently in large currency transactions (eight or more a year).
- The customer must be incorporated or organized under the laws of the United States or a state, or registered or eligible to do business in the United States.

Annually, banks must verify whether each exemption continues to meet the exemption eligibility requirements. Banks may develop their own methods and procedures for this annual review. Biennially, banks must file the "Designation of Exempt Person" form for each nonlisted business and payroll customer. As part of the biennial filing of the "Designation of Exempt Person" form, the bank must certify that, as part of its BSA compliance program, it has policies and procedures in place for identifying, reviewing, and reporting suspicious activity in accordance with the SAR filing requirements. (31 CFR 103.18 and 12 CFR 21.11)

No exemptions under the old rules were permitted after October 20, 1998. However, banks were allowed to treat exemptions granted prior to October 20, 1998 as exempt until June 30, 2000. All exemptions granted by a bank had to be converted to the new exemption procedures by June 30, 2000. For more information about granting, maintaining, and documenting exemptions under the BSA, see 31 CFR 103.22 (d)(2)-(11).

(Contact OCC's Community & Consumer Policy Department at (202) 874-4428 or review the FinCEN website (www.treas.gov/fincen) about the exemption process. Copies of BSA forms may be obtained by contacting the IRS Distribution Center at 1-800-829-3676.)

Suspicious Activity Reporting Requirements

An effective BSA compliance program includes controls and measures to identify and timely report suspicious transactions. A financial institution must apply due diligence to be able to make an informed decision about the suspicious nature of a particular transaction and whether to file a suspicious activity report (SAR). SARs can be filed on any transaction occurring in any bank department.

In February 1996, the Department of Treasury, the OCC, and the other federal bank regulators enacted suspicious activity reporting regulations. The Treasury implemented 31 CFR 103.18 and the OCC, 12 CFR 21.11. As of April 1, 1996, banks must file a SAR within prescribed time frames following the discovery of:

- Insider abuse involving any amount.
- Violations of federal law aggregating $5,000 or more when a suspect can be identified.

- Violations of federal law aggregating $25,000 or more regardless of a potential suspect.
- Transactions aggregating $5,000 or more that involve potential money laundering or violations of the BSA if the bank knows, suspects, or has reason to suspect that the transaction:
  - Involves funds from illegal activities or is intended or conducted to hide or disguise illicit funds or assets as part of a plan to violate or evade any law or regulation or to avoid any transaction reporting requirement under federal law;
  - Is designed to evade any of the BSA regulations; or
  - Has no business or apparent lawful purpose or is not the sort in which the particular customer would normally be expected to engage, and the bank knows of no reasonable explanation for the transaction after examining the available facts, including the background and possible purpose of the transaction.

Suspicious Conduct and Transactions

The following lists provide examples of potentially suspicious activities that should raise red flags for further investigation to determine whether the transactions or activities reflect illicit activities rather than legitimate business activities and whether a SAR should be filed.

Activity Inconsistent with the Customer's Business

- A customer opens several accounts for the type of business he or she purportedly is conducting and/or frequently transfers funds among those accounts.
- A customer's corporate account(s) has deposits or withdrawals primarily in cash rather than checks.
- The owner of both a retail business and a check cashing service does not ask for cash when depositing checks, possibly indicating the availability of another source of cash.
- The customer engages in unusual activity in cash purchases of traveler's checks, money orders, or cashier's checks.
- A large volume of cashier's checks, money orders, and/or wire transfers are deposited into an account in which the nature of the account holder's business would not appear to justify such activity.
- A customer frequently makes large dollar transactions (such as deposits, withdrawals, or purchases of monetary instruments) without an explanation as to how they will be used in the business, or the purchases allegedly are for a business that generally does not deal in large amounts of cash.
- A business account history that shows little or no regular, periodic activity; the account appears to be used primarily as a temporary repository for funds that are transferred abroad. For example, numerous deposits of cash followed by lump-sum wire transfers.
- A customer's place of business or residence is outside the financial institution's service area.

- A corporate customer who frequently makes large cash deposits and maintains high balances, but does not use other banking services.
- A retail business routinely makes numerous deposits of checks, but rarely makes cash withdrawals for daily operations.
- A retail business has dramatically different patterns of cash deposits from similar businesses in the same general location.
- The currency transaction patterns of a business experience a sudden and inconsistent change from normal activities.
- The amount and frequency of cash deposits are inconsistent with that observed at the customer's place of business.
- The business frequently deposits large amounts of cash, but checks or other debits drawn against the account are inconsistent with the customer's retail business.
- Businesses that do not normally generate currency make numerous currency transactions (i.e., a sanitation company that makes numerous deposits of cash).
- Financial transactions involving monetary instruments that are incomplete or contain fictitious payees, remitters, etc., if known.
- Unusual transfer of funds among related accounts or accounts that involve the same principal or related principals.
- A business owner, such as an owner who has only one store, who makes several deposits the same day using different bank branches.

Avoiding the Reporting or Record Keeping Requirement

- A business or new customer asks to be exempted.
- A customer intentionally withholds part of the currency deposit or withdrawal to keep the transaction under the reporting threshold.
- A customer is reluctant to provide the information needed to file the mandatory report, to have the report filed, or to proceed with a transaction after being informed that the report must be filed.
- A customer or group tries to coerce a bank employee into not filing any required record keeping or reporting forms.
- An automatic teller machine or machines (ATM) are used to make several bank deposits below a specified threshold.
- Unusually large deposits of U.S. food stamps (often used as currency in exchange for narcotics).
- A customer is reluctant to furnish identification when purchasing negotiable instruments in recordable amounts.

Fund (Wire) Transfers

- Wire transfer activity to/from financial secrecy haven countries without an apparent business reason or when it is inconsistent with the customer's business or history.
- Periodic wire transfers from a personal account(s) to bank secrecy haven countries.
- Large incoming wire transfers on behalf of a foreign client with little or no explicit reason.

- Frequent or large volume of wire transfers to and from offshore banking centers.
- Large, round dollar amounts.
- Funds transferred in and out of an account on the same day or within a relatively short period of time.
- Payments or receipts with no apparent links to legitimate contracts, goods, or services.
- Transfers routed through multiple foreign or domestic banks.
- Unexplained repetitive or unusual patterns of activity.
- Deposits of funds into several accounts, usually in amounts of less than $3000, which are consolidated subsequently into one master account and transferred, often outside of the country.
- Instructions to a financial institution to wire transfer funds abroad and to expect an incoming wire transfer of funds (in an equal amount) from other sources.
- Regular deposits or withdrawals of large amounts of cash, using wire transfers to, from, or through countries that either are known sources of narcotics or whose laws are ineffective in controlling the laundering of money.
- Many small incoming wire transfers of funds received or deposits made using checks and money orders, with all but a token amount almost immediately being wire transferred to another city or country, in a manner inconsistent with the customer's business or history.
- Large volume of wire transfers from persons or businesses that do not hold accounts.

Insufficient or Suspicious Information by Customer

- The reluctance of a business that is establishing a new account to provide complete information about the purpose of business, its prior banking relationships, names of its officers and directors, and information about the location of the business.
- A customer's refusal to provide the usual information necessary to qualify for credit or other banking services.
- A spike in the customer's activity with little or no explanation.
- A customer desires to open an account without providing references, a local address, or identification (passport, alien registration card, driver's license, or social security card); or refuses to provide any other information the financial institution requires to open an account.
- Unusual or suspicious identification documents that the financial institution cannot readily verify.
- The discovery that a customer's home/business phone is disconnected.
- No record of past or present employment on a loan application.
- A customer makes frequent or large transactions and has no record of past or present employment experience.
- The customer's background is at variance with his or her business activities.
- The customer's financial statements differ from those of similar businesses.

Bank Employee Activities

- Lavish lifestyle cannot be supported by an employee's salary.
- Absence of conformity with recognized systems and controls, particularly in private banking.
- Reluctance to take a vacation.

Bank-to-Bank Transactions

- Significant changes in currency shipment patterns between correspondent banks.
- Increase in large amounts of cash without a corresponding increase in the filing of mandatory currency transaction reports.
- Deposits with a Federal Reserve bank or its branches are disproportionate to the previous historical volume or volumes of similarly sized depository institutions.
- Significant turnover in large denomination bills that would appear uncharacteristic given the bank's location.
- Inability to track the true account holder of correspondent or concentration account transactions.
- A large increase in small denomination bills and a corresponding decrease in large denomination bills with no corresponding currency transaction report filings.
- The rapid increase in the size and frequency of cash deposits with no corresponding increase in noncash deposits.

Other Suspicious Customer Activity

- Substantial deposit(s) of numerous $50 and $100 bills.
- Mailing address outside the United States.
- Frequent exchanges of small dollar denominations for large dollar denominations.
- Certificate(s) of deposit or other investment vehicle used as loan collateral.
- A large loan is suddenly paid down with no reasonable explanation of the source of funds.
- Frequent deposits of large amounts of currency wrapped in currency straps that have been stamped by other banks.
- Frequent deposits of currency wrapped in currency straps or currency wrapped in rubber bands that are disorganized and do not balance when counted.
- Frequent deposits of musty or extremely dirty bills.
- A customer who purchases cashier's checks, money orders, etc., with large amounts of cash.
- A professional service provider, such as a lawyer, accountant, or broker, who makes substantial deposits of cash into client accounts or in-house company accounts, such as trust accounts and escrow accounts.
- A customer insists on meeting bank personnel at a location other than their place of business.

- Domestic bank accounts opened in the name of a *casa de cambio* (money exchange house), followed by suspicious wire transfers and/or structured deposits (under a specified threshold) into these accounts.
- Suspicious movements of funds from one bank into another bank and back into the first bank. For example: 1) purchasing cashier's checks from bank A; 2) opening up a checking account at bank B; 3) depositing the cashier's checks into a checking account at bank B; and 4) wire transferring the funds from the checking account at bank B into an account at bank A.
- Offshore companies, especially those located in bank secrecy haven countries, asking for a loan from a domestic U.S. bank, or for a loan secured by obligations of offshore banks.
- Use of loan proceeds in a manner inconsistent with the stated loan purpose.
- A person or business that does not hold an account and that purchases a monetary instrument with large denominated bills.
- A customer who purchases a number of cashier's checks, money orders, or traveler's checks for large amounts under a specified threshold, or without apparent reason.
- Couriers, rather than personal account customers, make the deposits into the account.
- Money orders deposited by mail, which are numbered sequentially or have unusual symbols or stamps on them.

Opening and Maintaining Accounts and Customer Relationships

The OCC encourages banks to adopt policies that determine the true identity of customers and help to detect suspicious activity promptly. This is fundamental to ensuring compliance with 12 CFR 21.11 and 21.21 and 31 CFR 103.18. As discussed previously, the SAR regulations require banks to report transactions that have no apparent lawful purpose nor are the sort in which a particular customer normally would be expected to engage. In order to determine what constitutes a normal transaction (or set of transactions) for a customer, a bank must have adequate internal controls and systems. Included in these control systems must be prudent account opening procedures and ongoing monitoring systems. Sound policies and procedures for determining expected or normal activity at account opening, coupled with a check against actual transaction activity, help ensure compliance and protect the financial institution against money laundering activity and other financial crimes.

The objective of gathering customer information is not to compromise established relationships between the financial institution and its customers. Rather, policies, procedures, and practices that require management to know what to expect of its customers increases the likelihood that the bank will be in compliance with the BSA regulations and adhere to safe and sound banking practices.

Identifying the Customer

Banks are encouraged to adhere to the following principles when establishing customer relationships, including those initiated via the Internet. The OCC urges banks to exercise caution and due diligence when opening accounts via the Internet. Internal systems and controls should consider the higher risk nature of those accounts and include evaluation of appropriate customer documentation within a reasonable period of time. Regardless of the method of account opening, banks should establish identification standards depending upon the risk posed by the customer.

Personal Accounts

- Require satisfactory identification, such as a driver's license with a photograph, a U.S. passport, or alien registration card, to open an account. Other acceptable secondary forms of identification include a college photo identification card, a major credit card (verify the current status), an employer identification card, and/or a current utility bill from the customer's present residence (i.e., gas, electricity, telephone).
- Consider the proximity of the customer's residence or place of business to the bank office or branch location. If it is inconvenient, the bank should determine why the customer is opening an account at that location.
- Call the customer's residence or place of employment to thank him or her for opening the account. Discovery of disconnected phone service or no record of employment warrant further investigation.
- Consider the source of funds used to open the account. Large deposits, especially cash, should be questioned.
- For large accounts, ask the customer for a prior bank reference and, if appropriate, write to that bank and request a customer reference.
- Consider using:

    - Third-party references, such as credit bureaus, banks, or other references.
    - Verification services.
    - Telephone, web site, and reverse directories.

Business Accounts

- Ask business principals for evidence of legal status (i.e., sole proprietorship, partnership, or incorporation or association).
- Determine who are the beneficial owners of all accounts in private banking, trust, and other specialized banking departments. The bank should pay particular attention to corporate entities, international business corporations, bearer share companies, or nominee officers, especially if such organizations are based in countries or jurisdictions considered to be secrecy or money laundering havens.
- Check the name of a commercial enterprise with an information-reporting agency and check prior bank references.
- Call the customer's business to thank him or her for opening the account. Disconnected phone service warrants further investigation.
- If appropriate, visit the customer's business to verify its existence and its ability to engage in the business it described.
- Require satisfactory identification for all sub-account holders for payable through accounts with foreign banks. (See section on payable through accounts for additional recommendations.)

- Consider the source of funds used to open the account. Large deposits, especially cash, should be questioned.
- Consider obtaining a:
  - Financial statement.
  - Description of the customer's principal line of business.
  - Description of the customer's primary trade area, and whether international transactions are expected to be routine.
  - Description of the business operations, the anticipated volume of cash and total sales, and a list of major customers and suppliers.
  - Third-party reference, such as a credit report, Dun & Bradstreet report, or Lexus/Nexus information.
  - Verification service.
  - Telephone, web site, and reverse directories.

High-Risk Areas

Although attempts to launder money through a financial institution can emanate from many different sources, certain products and services, types of entities, and geographic locations are more vulnerable to money laundering.

High-Risk Products and Services

International Correspondent Banking Relationships

Correspondent bank accounts are accounts banks maintain with each other on their own behalf in their own names. Correspondent bank account relationships are maintained between domestic banks and between domestic and foreign banks. The relationships between domestic and foreign banks may incur a heightened risk of money laundering.

Banks use international correspondent bank accounts for a variety of legitimate business purposes. Many are used to facilitate international trade and investment activities. Others are used for settlement purposes for funds transfer activity and clearing of foreign items. These accounts are designed to move legitimate funds and assets swiftly and securely around the world.

International correspondent bank accounts may pose increased risk of potential illicit activities, including money laundering. Three of the more common types of activity found in international correspondent bank accounts that should receive heightened scrutiny are funds (wire) transfer, correspondent accounts used as "payable through accounts" and "pouch/cash letter activity." This heightened risk underscores the need for effective and comprehensive systems and controls particular to these types of accounts.

A bank must exercise caution and due diligence in determining the level of risk associated with each of its correspondent accounts. Information should be gathered to understand fully the nature of the correspondent's business. Factors to consider include the purpose of the account, whether the correspondent bank is located in a bank secrecy or money laundering haven (if so, the nature of the bank license, i.e., shell/offshore bank, fully licensed bank, or an affiliate/subsidiary of a major financial institution), the level of the correspondent's money laundering prevention and detection efforts, and the condition of bank regulation and supervision in the correspondent's country. The level of perceived risk in each account relationship, including the availability of the account to third parties, should dictate the nature of risk management. As previously discussed, banks must comply with 12 CFR 21.11 and 21.21 and 31 CFR 103.18 and report transactions that have no apparent lawful purpose or are not the sort in which a particular customer would normally be expected to engage.

Wire (Funds) Transfers

As financial institutions, law enforcement agencies, and financial regulators have increased their scrutiny of cash transactions, money launderers have become more sophisticated in using all services and tools available to launder cash and move funds, including wire transfer systems. Financial institutions use two wire transfer systems in the United States, the Fedwire and the Clearing House Interbank Payments System (CHIPS). A telecommunications network, the Society for Worldwide Interbank Financial Telecommunications (SWIFT), is often used to send messages with international wire transfers. Individual transfers that have a high dollar value, a real time system, and a widely distributed network of users characterize all three systems.

Although money launderers use wire systems in many ways, most money launderers aggregate funds from different sources and move them through accounts at different banks until their origin cannot be traced. Most often they are moved out of the country through a bank account in a country where laws are designed to facilitate secrecy, and possibly back into the United States. Money laundering schemes uncovered by law enforcement agencies show that money launderers aggregate funds from multiple accounts at the same bank, wire those funds to accounts held at other U.S. banks, consolidate funds from these larger accounts, and ultimately wire the funds to offshore accounts in countries, such as Panama.

Unlike cash transactions that are monitored closely, Fedwire, CHIPS transactions, and a bank's wire room are designed to process approved transactions quickly. Wire room personnel usually have no knowledge of the customer or the purpose of the transaction. Therefore, other bank personnel must know the identity and business of the customer on whose behalf they approve the funds transfer to prevent money launderers from using the wire system with little or no scrutiny. Also, review or monitoring procedures should be in place to identify unusual funds transfer activity.

Examiners and bankers should pay close attention to "Pay Upon Proper Identification" (PUPID) transactions as well as transfers to and from high-risk geographies. Those types of wire transactions pose significant risk if not monitored and controlled properly.

Pouch Activity

Pouch activity entails the use of a carrier or courier (either independent or common) to transport currency, monetary instruments, and other documents from outside the United States to a U.S. bank account. Pouches can contain transactions for demand deposit accounts, loan payments, etc., and can come from another financial institution or from individuals.

Examiners and banks should be aware that bulk amounts of monetary instruments purchased in the United States that appear to have been structured to avoid the BSA reporting requirements often have been found in pouches or cash letters received from foreign banks. This is especially true in the case of pouches and cash letters received from foreign countries and jurisdictions with reputations as bank secrecy and money laundering havens. The monetary instruments involved are money orders, traveler's checks, and bank checks that usually have one or more of the following in common:

- The instruments were purchased on the same or consecutive days from different locations.
- They are numbered consecutively in amounts just under $3,000 or $10,000.
- The payee lines are left blank or made out to the same person (or to only a few people).
- They contain little or no purchaser information.
- They bear the same stamp symbol or initials.
- They are purchased in round denominations or repetitive amounts.

Contents of pouches are subject to CTR, CMIR, and SAR reporting requirements. As with all bank products and services, pouch activity should be monitored for any potential suspicious activity as the level of risk dictates.

Payable Through Accounts

Foreign banks use payable through accounts (PTAs), also known as "pass through" or "pass by" accounts to provide their customers, for a fee, with access to the United States banking system. Some U.S. banks offer these accounts as a service to foreign banks. Federal law enforcement authorities have stated that the risk of money laundering and other illicit activities is high in those types of accounts.

Generally, a foreign bank requests PTAs for its customers who want to conduct banking transactions in the United States through its account at a U.S. bank. The foreign bank provides its customers, commonly referred to as "sub-account holders," with checks that enable them to draw on the foreign bank's account at the U.S. bank. The sub-account holders, which may number several hundred for one PTA, all become signatories on the foreign bank's account at the U.S. bank. Thus, individuals and businesses, not subject to the U. S. bank's account opening requirements imposed on U.S. citizens or residents, can write checks and make deposits at a U.S. bank as if they were the actual account holders.

PTA activities should not be confused with traditional international correspondent banking relationships when a foreign bank enters into an agreement with a U.S. bank to process and complete transactions on behalf of the foreign bank and its customers. Under this arrangement, the foreign bank's customers do not have access to its account at the U.S. bank. This differs significantly from a PTA with sub-account holders who have direct access to the U.S. bank by virtue of their independent ability to conduct transactions with the U.S. bank through the PTA.

In some cases, U.S. banks do not exercise the same diligence for PTAs that they exercise with domestic customers who want to open checking and other account relationships directly with them. For example, some U.S. banks merely collect signature cards that a foreign bank has completed abroad and submitted to them in bulk. These banks then process thousands of sub-account holder checks and other transactions, including cash deposits, through the foreign bank's PTAs. These U.S. banks expend little or no independent effort to obtain or confirm information about the individual and business sub-account holders that use their accounts. There are also instances when a U.S. bank sets up a traditional correspondent account with a foreign bank and is not aware, due to inadequate controls and management review, that the foreign bank is permitting some customers to conduct transactions secretively through the U.S. bank account.

The OCC is concerned that foreign bank use of payable through accounts at U.S. banks may facilitate unsafe and unsound banking practices, including money laundering and related criminal activities. The potential for money laundering, OFAC violations, and other serious crimes increases when a bank is unable to identify and understand adequately the transactions of the ultimate users (all or most of whom are offshore) of a foreign bank's account. PTAs used for illegal purposes can cause banks serious financial losses in criminal and civil fines and penalties, seizure or forfeiture of collateral, and reputation damage.

The OCC believes that national banks offering PTA services should develop and maintain adequate procedures to guard against possible illicit activities or illegal use of these accounts. These procedures should enable each national bank to identify the ultimate users of its foreign bank PTAs and include obtaining (or having the ability to obtain) substantially the same information on the ultimate PTA users as it obtains on its domestic customers.

This may require a review of the foreign bank's procedures for identifying and monitoring the transactions of sub-account holders and complying with any anti-money laundering statutory and regulatory requirements existing in the host country, and its master agreement with the U.S. bank. In addition, national banks should have procedures for monitoring transactions conducted in foreign bank PTAs. They should report suspicious or unusual activity in accordance with the SAR requirements. (31 CFR 103.18) (12 CFR 21.11)

In an effort to reduce further the risk inherent in PTAs, banks should consider setting limits on transaction types and amounts, placing restrictions on types of account holders, and/or requiring access to internal foreign bank documents and any audits. In some instances, a bank might find itself in a situation where: (1) adequate information about the ultimate PTA users cannot be obtained, (2) it cannot rely adequately on the home country supervisor to require the foreign bank to identify and monitor its own customers, or (3) it is unable to ensure reasonably that its PTAs are not being used for money laundering or other illicit purposes. In situations like these, the OCC recommends that the bank terminate the PTA relationship with the foreign bank as expeditiously as possible.

International Brokered Deposits

Banks may use international deposit brokers or bank employees/ representatives located overseas to solicit foreign deposit customers. Such relationships are considered high risk because of their international nature and the bank's reliance on the broker or bank representative to perform adequate due diligence for account opening. The obvious danger is the possibility of criminal monies entering the U.S. banking system from sources not fully disclosed to the bank, or even the deposit broker/representative. Banks should not do business with brokers and representatives unwilling to disclose fully customer information or establish and maintain adequate due diligence procedures. Banks should also:

- Verify the legitimacy of deposit brokers and representatives (corporate documentation, references, background checks, verification of prior employment, database searches, etc.).
- Require or provide training or information to brokers/representatives on money laundering risks and bank procedures.

- Define the target market for customer accounts.
- Establish account opening, verification, and internal control requirements.
- Review and verify customer information provided by the deposit broker/representative using call back procedures or conducting meetings with customers.
- Segregate and monitor brokered accounts for unusual activity.

Red flags for which the bank should investigate further include:

- High volume of cash activity.
- Deposit activity followed by lump sum wire transfers.
- Unusual monetary instrument or check activity.
- International wire transfers to known money laundering havens.

Special Use Accounts

Special use accounts (SUAs) are in-house accounts established to facilitate the processing and settlement of multiple or individual customer transactions within the bank, usually on the same day. These accounts have several different names, including concentration, omnibus, suspense, settlement, intra-day, sweep, and collection accounts. SUAs are used widely in private banking, wire transfer, and other bank departments.

Money laundering risk can arise in these accounts because customer-identifying information, such as name, address, and account number can be separated from financial transactions. If that happens, an effective audit trail is lost, and accounts can be misused or administered improperly. Banks that use SUAs should implement adequate procedures and controls covering access to and operation of those accounts, including being able to identify, measure, monitor, and control the associated risks.

The bank must be aware of and understand fully the activities of its customers and report transactions that have no apparent lawful purpose or are not the sort in which a particular customer would normally be expected to engage. This includes those customers whom, for whatever reason, are users of these types of special use accounts.

Private Banking

The financial services industry does not use a standard definition for private banking, but most industry participants agree that the primary market is persons with high net worth and their business interests. U.S. banks manage private banking relationships for both domestic and international customers. Generally, the threshold of client net worth depends upon each institution's market demographics. For instance, the dollar threshold for domestic customers may be considerably higher than for customers residing in other countries or jurisdictions that are less prosperous.

Banks offer a mix of financial services under the umbrella of the private banking relationship that include asset management relationships (such as trust, investment advisory, and investment management accounts), offshore facilities, custodial services, funds transfer, lending services, checking accounts, overdraft privileges, letter of credit financing, and bill-paying services. In addition, some financial institutions offer financial planning services, such as tax and estate planning.

Privacy and confidentiality are important elements of private banking relationships. Although customers may choose private banking services to manage their assets, they may also seek confidential ownership of their assets or a safe, legal haven for their capital. When acting as a fiduciary, banks may have statutory, contractual, or ethical obligations to uphold customer confidentiality.

Fiduciary relationships in which the bank maintains little control (i.e., nondiscretionary trust relationships) over trust assets create the greatest money laundering risk. In these types of accounts, the trustee must follow the customers' directions.

Many private banking departments, and other areas of the bank, establish and manage Private Investment Companies (PICs), which are separate legal entities structured to hold a customer's personal assets. PICs offer confidentiality of ownership, hold assets centrally, and provide intermediaries between private banking customers and the potential beneficiaries of the PICs or trusts. A PIC may also be a trust asset. PICs are incorporated frequently in countries that impose low or no taxes on company assets and operations or are bank secrecy havens. Banks should exercise extra care when dealing with beneficial owners of PICs and associated trusts because they can be misused to camouflage illegal activities. Since PICs issue bearer shares, anonymous relationships should not be maintained.

Past money laundering prosecutions have demonstrated that criminals often attempt to use private banking services to launder the proceeds of their crimes. Private banking services are vulnerable to money laundering, because large amounts of money are managed through confidential private banking relationships, and customers may reside in countries identified as high-risk areas for drug trafficking and money laundering. Effective policies and procedures addressing customer relationships can minimize the risks inherent in private banking relationships.

Banks should establish comprehensive policies and procedures to ensure compliance with the BSA and anti-money laundering laws and regulations in every aspect of the high-risk private banking arena. Especially important are policies and guidelines that address the acceptance and approval of private banking business and provide for confidentiality of customer information.

Effective account opening policies and procedures should address who is accountable and who has the authority for opening and documenting new private banking accounts, reviewing documentation when accounts are opened, maintaining updated documentation, and reviewing documentation and transactions on an ongoing basis. In addition, banks should document the identity and source of wealth of all customers requesting custody or private banking services. Account officers should fully understand each customer's general type and level of expected cash flows and source of wealth. This includes whether the wealth is likely to increase (in the case of a growing business concern) or remain fairly steady (in the case of an inheritance that is likely to grow only by accumulating interest or other investment earnings).

Privately or closely held businesses with private banking or trust relationships may serve as money laundering conduits by distributing illegally derived income from the business to the beneficial owners of the private banking account. Therefore, banks should have processes to verify the legal status of businesses wanting to open private banking accounts. Account opening processes should identify the principal owners, review articles of incorporation filed with a state (or partnership agreements), and obtain financial statements, credit reports, referrals, and other documentation. Banks that accept foreign businesses as private banking customers must determine the types of reliable documentation available in the foreign country that show a business is legitimate.

Banks should ensure, through independent auditors, reviewers, private banking account officers or trust department officers, that they have adequate documentation for accepting new private banking account funds. When customers transfer funds and securities from other financial service providers, such as investment advisors and brokerage firms, into private banking accounts, the receiving bank should verify the origins of the assets or funds. Verification and review of employment, salary, bank references, financial statements, and credit reports may assist in determining fund sources and the private banking customer's overall financial situation.

Private banking departments may provide services (such as custody) to investment advisors or other financial intermediaries. To determine the risk of this account type, the bank should consider the account's location (offshore or domestic), whether it is subject to regulatory oversight, and if its customer has sufficient standards in place to verify the identity and legitimacy of its own customers. Depending on the bank's risk assessment, it may wish to obtain and review these customers' policies and procedures to determine whether it can rely upon them to limit the risk that an investment advisor or other intermediary or their customers are involved in money laundering or other illegal activity. The bank should not establish a relationship with a customer that refuses to provide its own procedures for accepting new customers.

When private banking account officers change employers, their customers may move with them. Banks bear the same potential liability for customers of newly hired officers and, therefore, should review these accounts using its process for establishing new private banking relationships. In addition, banks should investigate the background of newly hired private banking account officers.

Lastly, bank compensation plans should not create incentives for employees to ignore private banking account opening processes or possible suspicious activity. Commissions based on the number of new accounts or an increase of managed assets may provide an incentive for employees to neglect customer documentation requirements or other account opening practices.

Processes that require separate authority levels for accepting new accounts minimize opportunities for employees to overlook appropriate new customer requirements. Some banks use a series of officer sign-offs and approvals for opening new private banking accounts, while others have established new customer committee approval processes.

Foreign Branches and Offices of National Banks

The OCC's ability to conduct on-site examinations of the foreign branches and offices of national banks varies depending on the laws of the country or jurisdiction in which the branch is located. In some locations, financial secrecy and other laws prevent onsite OCC examinations, while others limit review of any customer specific reports or records. As a result, examiners rely largely upon internal audits and the U.S. bank's description of their foreign branches' and offices' anti-money laundering and Office of Foreign Assets Control (OFAC) programs to evaluate compliance.

This issue is of great concern to the OCC because of the vulnerability of branches and offices of U.S. banks located in high-risk financial secrecy havens to abuse by money launderers. To address this concern, the OCC has adopted the following policies and recommendations:

- The guidance provided in this handbook applies to foreign branches and offices to the extent possible.
- U.S. banks must develop a system for testing and verifying the integrity and effectiveness of internal controls and conduct in-country audits to monitor activity in their foreign offices and branches. Senior management should obtain and review copies, written in English, of audit reports and any other reports related to anti-money laundering and internal control evaluations.
- U.S. banks should understand the effectiveness and quality of bank supervision in the host country.
- The OCC will conduct on-site examinations in branches and offices in high-risk countries where feasible, and off-site examinations, focusing on internal control systems, including audit, reporting, and monitoring efforts, in low-risk countries and in high-risk countries where on-site examinations are not feasible. When bank secrecy laws in the host country prohibit OCC on-site examinations, the OCC may require the U.S. bank to engage an external audit firm.

Insider Complicity

Complicity is defined as "the state of being an accomplice, partnership or involvement in wrong doing." When an insider is involved in wrong doing, the detection of the suspicious or unusual activity is difficult. Tests for insider complicity must be incorporated into a bank's internal control systems. The cornerstone of such a process is a stringent employee screening process that alerts management to any potential issues prior to hiring. Many banks use external search firms to aid in this process.

In addition to an effective employment screening process, management should ensure that internal controls address insider complicity on an ongoing basis. Employees assigned to higher risk areas of the bank and higher risk accounts (both discussed elsewhere in this handbook) should be subject to heightened scrutiny. Their accounts should be reviewed routinely for any unusual or suspicious activity. Lifestyle vs. salary should be emphasized. Tests for insider complicity should also be part of a bank's audit program.

High-Risk Entities

Although attempts to launder money through a legitimate financial institution can emanate from many different sources, certain kinds of businesses, transactions, or geographic locations may lend themselves more readily than others to potential criminal activity. The following examples could be a potential source of money laundering:

Businesses

- Nontraditional financial entities, such as:
  - Currency exchange houses, also known as *giros* or *casas de cambio.*
  - Money transmitters.
  - Check cashing facilities.

- Casinos and card clubs.
- Offshore corporations and banks located in tax and/or secrecy havens.
- Leather goods stores.
- Car, boat, and plane dealerships.
- Used automobile or truck dealers and machine parts manufacturers.
- Travel agencies.
- Brokers/dealers.
- Jewel, gem, and precious metal dealers.
- Import/export companies.
- Auctioneers.
- Deposit brokers.
- Pawn brokers.
- Professional service providers (lawyers, accountants, investment brokers).
- Cash-intensive businesses, such as convenience stores, restaurants, retail stores, and parking garages.
- Ship, bus, and plane operators.
- Telemarketers.

Banking Functions and Transactions

- Private banking.
- Trust departments.
- Offshore international activity.
- Deposit-taking facilities.
- International correspondent banking activity.
- Internet banking.
- Wire transfers/cash management functions.
- Transactions in which the primary beneficiary or counterparty is undisclosed.
- Loan guarantee schemes.
- Transactions involving large amounts of traveler's checks, official bank checks, money orders, and stored value cards.
- Pouch activity.
- Electronic transactions that permit the rapid movement of currency (e.g., foreign exchange transactions followed by payment into another jurisdiction).
- Trade financing transactions with unusual pricing features.

High-Risk Countries

- Countries in which the production or transportation of illegal drugs may be taking place.
- Bank secrecy havens.
- Emerging countries that may be seeking hard currency investments.
- Countries identified in FinCEN advisories. (For a list of the advisories, see FinCEN web site www.treas.gov/fincen.)

- Major money laundering countries and jurisdictions identified in the U.S. Department of State's annual *International Narcotics Control Strategy Report*.[2]

Common Money Laundering Schemes

Discussed below are several common money laundering schemes.

Information on other common schemes can be found on the FinCEN website (www.treas.gov/fincen).

Structuring

31 CFR103.63 states, "a person structures a transaction if that person, acting alone, in conjunction with or on behalf of others, conducts or attempts to conduct one or more transactions in currency at one or more financial institutions, on one or more days, in any manner, for the purpose of evading the CTR filing requirements." "In any manner," includes, but is not limited to breaking down a single currency sum exceeding $10,000 dollars into smaller amounts, that may be conducted as a series of transactions at or less than $10,000. The transaction(s) need not exceed the $10,000 CTR filing threshold at any one financial institution on any single day in order to constitute structuring.

All attempts to evade the BSA CTR filing requirements for cash transactions that exceed $10,000 (31 CFR 103.22) are criminal and civil violations of the BSA regulations. Under the BSA, no person shall, to evade the CTR reporting requirements:

- Cause or attempt to cause a financial institution to fail to file a CTR as required under the BSA. (31 CFR 103.22)
- Cause or attempt to cause a financial institution to file a CTR that contains a material omission or misstatement of fact.
- Structure, as defined above, or attempt to structure or assist in structuring, any transaction with one or more financial institutions.

Money launderers and criminals have developed many ways to structure large amounts of cash to evade the CTR filing requirements. Unless cash is smuggled out of the United States or commingled with the deposits of an otherwise legitimate business, any money laundering scheme that begins with a need to convert cash proceeds of criminal activity into more legitimate looking forms of financial instruments, accounts, or investments, will likely involve some form of structuring. Structuring remains one of the most commonly reported crimes on SARs.

Bank employees must be aware of and alert to structuring schemes. For example, a customer may structure cash deposit or withdrawal transactions, so that each is less than the $10,000 CTR filing threshold, purchase official bank checks, money orders, or traveler's checks with cash in amounts less than $10,000 (and, possibly, less than the $3,000 cash purchase of monetary instruments record keeping threshold to avoid having to produce identification in the process), or exchange small banknotes for large ones in amounts less than $10,000.

In addition, structuring may occur before a customer brings the funds to a bank. In these instances, a bank may be able to identify the aftermath of structuring. Deposits of monetary instruments that may have been purchased elsewhere might be structured to evade the CTR filing requirements or the cash purchase of monetary instruments record keeping requirements. These instruments are often numbered sequentially in groups totaling less than $10,000 or $3,000, bear the same handwriting (for the most part), and often the same small mark, stamp or initials, and/or appear to have been purchased at numerous places on the same or different days.

The Black Market Peso Exchange

Colombian cartels use the black market peso exchange (BMPE) to launder illicit drug proceeds. Law enforcement agencies estimate that the BMPE has been in operation for at least 30 years and is responsible for laundering at least $5 billion a year in wholesale drug proceeds. It is one of the largest money laundering systems in the United States.

The BMPE is a convenient process that starts with illegal drug proceeds generated in the United States. The cartel sells the proceeds at a discount to a Colombian peso broker. The cartel eventually receives its funds in pesos in Columbia. The peso broker then tries to place the cash into the U.S. financial system. This usually is accomplished by:

- Using smurfs to open numerous small dollar accounts and structuring cash into these accounts.
- Smuggling the cash out of the United States for eventual return in some form other than cash.
- Commingling the illicit proceeds with seemingly legitimate business proceeds.

Once the dollars have been placed in the U.S. banking system, the peso broker typically contacts a Colombian importer that needs U.S. dollars. The peso broker either will exchange dollars for pesos with the importer by selling the importer checks, with the payee left blank, on the U.S. accounts or, alternatively, the broker may purchase U.S. goods on behalf of the Colombian importer. Colombian importers must pay U.S. suppliers with dollars to smuggle commercial goods into Colombia and avoid tariffs and taxes.

For banks to identify and prevent possible BMPE activity, a manual or automated system and procedures must be in place to:

- Look for cash transactions and deposits (usually of monetary instruments with individual face values of less than $3,000) that appear to have been structured before reaching the bank.
- Look for possible suspicious activity in the accounts of nonresident aliens from countries and jurisdictions considered to be at high risk for money laundering. These accounts are characterized by small cash deposits and checks written to purchase large ticket items, sometimes located in the Florida and Panama free trade zones. These accounts also lack typical payments for housing, utilities, and credit cards, etc.
- Screen wire transfers, especially those that involve any type of import/export business and are to or from Colombia, Panama, Aruba or Mexico, for suspicious activity.
- Analyze and report suspicious activity as required under the SAR regulations. (31 CFR 103.18) (21 CFR 21.11)

- Monitor unusual check activity (e.g., structuring, followed by lump sum payments to U.S. appliance manufacturers or import/export companies in Florida and Panama).

Mexican Bank Drafts and Factored Third-Party Checks

FinCEN has warned the financial industry that “Mexican bank drafts” and “factored third-party check” schemes are crucial parts of the money laundering cycle when criminally derived cash has been smuggled out of the United States.[3] Cash smuggled into Mexico is “laundered” or “recycled” for re-entry into the United States. The funds will appear to be of foreign origin.

The monetary instruments FinCEN calls “Mexican bank drafts” are merely checks or drafts that a Mexican bank draws against its correspondent account with a U.S. bank. Mexican bank drafts and factored third-party checks have long been used to facilitate important legal trade and commerce between the United States and Mexico, and the vast majority of Mexican bank drafts are drawn for legitimate purposes. However, U.S. correspondent bank accounts held by Mexican banks have proven to be vulnerable to abuse by money launderers.

The Mexican bank draft money-laundering scheme involves a customer presenting a large amount of smuggled U.S. dollars (usually more than $10,000 and often more than $100,000) to a Mexican bank for the purchase of a check or draft denominated in U.S. dollars. The Mexican bank accepts the U.S. cash and issues a check or draft in U.S. dollars to the customer drawn against its correspondent bank account at a U.S. bank. The customer then may use the Mexican bank draft in a number of ways. For example, the Mexican bank draft can be transported physically across the U.S. border and negotiated. In this instance, the transporter of the Mexican bank draft is not required to file a CMIR with U.S. Customs, unless the check or draft has been endorsed without restriction or otherwise has been converted to a bearer instrument.

Alternatively, the Mexican bank draft can be endorsed and sent to a third party in the United States who then negotiates it. Or, it might be endorsed to a third party in Colombia, Panama, or other money laundering haven and become part of a much larger and more complicated criminal scheme. In any case, the cartel has laundered its illicit U.S. drug sales proceeds and, ultimately, the check will be returned to the U.S. correspondent bank.

The factored third-party check scheme involves casa de cambios, or currency exchange houses, other financial intermediaries or money laundering operations. These entities purchase deposited U.S. dollar checks from smaller Mexican banks at a premium. Instead of sending the checks to a U.S. bank for clearance, the Mexican bank sells them for cash derived from illicit U.S. drug sales that has been smuggled into Mexico. The purchaser of the factored third-party checks may deposit them into the U.S. bank account of an actual or fictitious currency exchanger, check casher, or other nonbank financial institution, or to any U.S. bank account to which the purchaser has access.

Reporting to Treasury

Treasury’s Financial Crimes Enforcement Network (FinCEN) requires the OCC to report quarterly on national bank compliance with the BSA. These quarterly reports list the number of institutions examined for BSA violations, civil money penalty (CMP) referrals, enforcement actions, and other related BSA supervision information. Examiners who conduct a BSA examination enter this information into the OCC's electronic information systems, and the report is generated at the end of each quarter.

BSA Violations and Enforcement

Examiners should document all BSA violations detected during an examination, regardless of significance, in the workpapers and in the OCC's electronic information systems. Examiners must include a discussion of significant violations of the BSA noted during a supervisory activity in a written communication to the institution. Examiners must also enter narrative summaries in OCC's electronic databases (a Type 70 analysis) for violations of 31 CFR 103.18(a)(1), 103.22(b)(1), 103.23(a), 103.23(b), 103.24(a), and 12 CFR 21.21 and 21.11, and any other BSA violations that are included in the report of examination.

Policy for Referring Violations to FinCEN

It is OCC policy to refer significant BSA violations to FinCEN for review for possible civil or criminal penalties. The authority to assess civil penalties for BSA violations against any domestic financial institution, and any director, officer, or employee of a domestic financial institution rests with FinCEN. (Refer to Appendix C for more information on referring BSA violations to FinCEN.)

OCC Policy for Filing SARs with FinCEN

Known or suspected criminal activity and BSA violations must be referred to FinCEN on a Suspicious Activity Report (SAR) form. Examiners who believe such activity has occurred should discuss the circumstances with management and request that management file a SAR. However, if the activity involves bank insiders, examiners should discuss the matter with OCC supervisory office legal counsel before bringing it to the attention of bank directors and bank management. When a bank fails to file, or is unwilling to file a SAR, the OCC must file it. If the case is serious enough, the EIC should consider CMPs and other administrative action for the bank's failure to file a SAR.

OCC Administrative Action

The OCC has authority to take its own administrative action when it identifies significant BSA violations, even after making a referral to FinCEN. For example, the OCC may assess civil money penalties, impose a cease and desist order or other enforcement document against a bank with inadequate internal controls. In these instances, examiners should always contact district or Washington counsel, as appropriate, before taking action.

The Office of Foreign Assets Control

The Office of Foreign Assets Control (OFAC) of the U.S. Department of the Treasury administers and enforces economic and trade sanctions against targeted foreign countries, terrorism sponsoring organizations, and international narcotics traffickers based on U.S. foreign policy and national security goals. OFAC acts under presidential wartime and national emergency powers and authority granted by specific legislation to impose controls on transactions and freeze foreign assets under U.S. jurisdiction. Many of the sanctions are based on United Nations and other international mandates, are multilateral in scope, and involve close cooperation with allied countries. Through the Secretary of the Treasury, OFAC is responsible for promulgating, developing, and administering the sanctions under eight basic statutes.[4]

OFAC has promulgated regulations for banks to follow to help administer the sanctions.[5] The OCC cooperates by ensuring that national banks comply with these regulations. All U.S. banks, federal branches and agencies, international banking facilities, and overseas branches, offices and subsidiaries of U.S. banks must comply with the laws and OFAC-issued regulations. In general, these regulations:

- Require the blocking of accounts and other assets of specified countries, entities, and individuals.
- Prohibit unlicensed trade and financial transactions with specified countries, entities, and individuals.

U.S. law requires that assets and accounts be blocked when such property is located in the United States, is held by U.S. individuals or entities, or comes into the possession or control of U.S. individuals or entities. The definition of assets and property is broad and literally includes anything of direct, indirect, present, future, and contingent value (including all types of bank transactions).

U.S. banks must block transactions that: (1) are by or on behalf of a blocked individual or entity, (2) are to or through a blocked entity, (3) are in connection with a transaction in which a blocked individual or entity has an interest. For example, if a U.S. bank receives instructions to make a funds transfer payment that falls into one of these categories, it must execute the payment order and place the funds into a blocked account. (A payment order cannot be canceled or amended after the U.S. bank has received it.) Banks must report all blockings to OFAC within 10 days of the occurrence and annually by September 30 (as of June 30) concerning those assets blocked. Once assets or funds are blocked, they should be placed in a segregated, interest bearing account and may be released only by specific authorization from OFAC.

Banks should establish and maintain effective OFAC compliance programs. This program should include written policies and procedures for filtering transactions for possible OFAC violations, designating an individual responsible for day-to-day compliance, establishing and maintaining strong lines of communication between departments of the bank, and an annual in-depth audit of OFAC compliance.

The compliance program should also include procedures for maintaining *current* lists of blocked countries, entities, and individuals and disseminating such information throughout the bank's domestic operations and its offshore branches and offices. New deposit, loan, trust, and discount brokerage accounts should be compared with the OFAC lists prior to being opened, and established accounts should be compared regularly with the current and updated OFAC lists. Wire transfer, letters of credit, and noncustomer transactions, such as security or funds transfers should be compared with the OFAC lists before being conducted.

Note: More information about OFAC regulations and brochures, lists of blocked countries, entities, and individuals, and updates to blocks and sanctions is available at OFAC's Home Page on the Treasury Department's World Wide Web server. All the lists are free to be downloaded in several ways. OFAC's Home Page site is www.treas.gov/ofac. Information also can be obtained by contacting OFAC by mail at Office of Foreign Assets Control, Department of the Treasury, 1500 Pennsylvania Avenue, NW, Washington, DC 20220, or by phone at 1- 800-540-6322. OFAC also operates a free automated fax-on-demand service, which can be accessed 24 hours a day, seven days a week, by dialing (202) 622-0077 from a touch-tone phone and following voice prompts.)

EXAMINATION PROCEDURES

General Procedures

These procedures are intended to determine whether the bank's policies, procedures, and internal controls are adequate with respect to the Bank Secrecy Act, Anti-Money Laundering, and Office of Foreign Assets Control laws and regulations. At a minimum, the examiner should perform the general, quality of risk management, and conclusion procedures. Using these procedures, examiners conduct limited transactional testing to form conclusions about the integrity of the bank's overall control and risk management processes and its overall quantity of risk. If weaknesses or concerns are found, examiners should select quantity of risk procedures to conduct additional targeted testing of specific areas of concern.

Objective: Determine the examination scope for compliance with the Bank Secrecy Act (BSA), Anti-Money Laundering (AML), and Office of Foreign Assets Control (OFAC) laws and regulations.

1. Obtain and review the following information from the examiner assigned the Compliance Management System program to identify any previous or emerging problems that require follow-up:

   - Historical examination findings.
   - Working papers from prior examination(s).
   - Board approved policies and procedures related to BSA, AML, and OFAC.
   - Bank compliance audit reports.

2. Obtain and review Federal Reserve cash flow information, and Suspicious Activity Report (SAR) and Currency Transaction Report (CTR) information to identify any previous or emerging problems that require follow up. This information can be obtained from the district office, the district fraud specialist, or designated district staff. Allow at least four weeks lead time.
3. Review correspondence from the IRS or U.S. Treasury Department about the following and determine whether the bank has implemented the appropriate corrective action:

   - Incorrect or incomplete CTRs, SARs, or Reports of Foreign Bank and Financial Accounts (FBARs) returned to the bank.

- Information requests regarding possible civil enforcement actions.
- OFAC correspondence, including CMPs, warning letters, etc.

4. Through early discussions with management and review of requested materials, obtain a general understanding of:

- Management's supervision of BSA compliance.
- The bank's system of internal controls to ensure ongoing compliance.
- The bank's independent testing program.
- Training programs offered.
- The designation, role, and reporting lines of the BSA Compliance Officer.
- Distribution of BSA, AML, and OFAC compliance responsibilities throughout all areas of the bank.
- Manual or automated SAR and CTR monitoring and reporting systems, policies, and procedures.
- Other anti-money laundering policies, procedures, and systems (e.g., customer identification procedures, high-risk area monitoring, computer reports that filter cash or funds transfer activity, etc.).
- OFAC compliance procedures and systems.
- Significant changes in policies, personnel, or controls.
- Changes in processes, including forms, contracts, software programs, etc.
- Types of products or services offered, including those offered to persons or businesses that do not hold accounts.
- Volume of products or transactions.
- Bank's locations and markets.
- Internal or external factors that could affect BSA, AML, or OFAC compliance.
- Management awareness of the provisions of the applicable laws and regulations.

5. Based on review of the requested materials, the CTR and SAR information obtained from the district office/Large Banks, and understanding of the risk profile of the bank gained through management discussions, select a sample of accounts for transactional review. The sample should include as applicable, private banking, trust, nonresident alien, international brokered deposits, and foreign correspondent accounts from high-risk countries, money service businesses, and private investment company (PIC) accounts. Also include accounts with significant cash activity or significant wire activity involving high-risk countries. For each account, request account opening and credit file information and copies of account statements for a recent three-month period. (This sample should be used when performing the quality of risk management procedures.)
6. Complete the "Quality of Risk Management" procedures.
7. Complete appropriate sections of the "Quantity of Risk" procedures. The procedures performed in the "Quantity of Risk" section should address areas of concern and/or where the bank's compliance management system or internal/external audit function is deficient, as identified during the review of "Quality of Risk Management."
8. Complete the "Conclusion Procedures."

Quality of Risk Management

Conclusion: The quality of risk management is (strong, satisfactory, weak).

These procedures are intended to assess the adequacy of the bank's compliance management system in detecting, correcting, and preventing violations of the BSA, AML, and OFAC laws and regulations.

Policy

Conclusion: The board (has/has not) established appropriate policies to ensure compliance with the BSA, AML, and OFAC laws and regulations.

Objective: Determine whether the bank has appropriate policies and procedures to ensure compliance with the BSA, AML, and OFAC laws and regulations and identify risk appropriately.

1. Determine whether the board has adopted and management has implemented adequate policies and procedures to maintain compliance with the BSA, AML, and OFAC laws and regulations. Where appropriate, they should address:

    - Identifying and reporting money laundering in its different forms (placement, layering, and integration).
    - Potential high-risk activities, businesses, and countries.
    - Requirements of applicable laws and regulations, including:

        - 31 CFR 103 (Financial Record Keeping and Reporting of Currency and Foreign Transactions)
        - 12 CFR 21.21 (BSA Compliance).
        - 12 CFR 21.11 (Reports of Suspicious Activities).
        - 18 USC 1956 and 1957 (Money Laundering Statutes).
        - 18 USC 981 and 982 (Civil and Criminal Forfeiture Statutes).
        - 31 CFR 500 et seq. (Office of Foreign Assets Control).
        - Processes and responsibilities for responding to changes in laws and regulations.

    - Employee consequences for noncompliance.
    - A comprehensive program for opening and maintaining accounts and establishing other customer relationships, including the following procedures:

        - Identification, documentation, and verification of customer information.
        - Monitoring for suspicious activity.
        - Reporting suspicious activity.

    - Coverage of all products and units of the bank, including, but not limited to:

- Teller and currency operations.
- Monetary instruments.
- Lending.
- Credit cards.
- Funds transfers.
- Private banking.
- Correspondent banking.
- Payable through accounts.
- Trust activities.
- International.
- Foreign branches and offices.
- Special use accounts.
- Brokerage operations.

2. Verify that the board approved a written compliance program (as required by 12 CFR 21.21) that ensures compliance with all reporting and record keeping requirements of the BSA (including SAR requirements) and provides for:

    - A system of internal controls to ensure ongoing compliance [12 CFR 21.21(c)(1)].
    - Independent testing for compliance to be conducted by bank personnel or by an outside party [12 CFR 21.21(c)(2)].
    - Designation of a qualified individual(s) responsible for coordinating and monitoring day-to-day compliance [12 CFR 21.21(c)(3)].
    - Training for appropriate personnel [12 CFR 21.21(c)(4)].
    - Reporting to board and management efforts to ensure ongoing compliance, including a listing of SARs filed with the appropriate federal law enforcement agencies and the Department of Treasury [12 CFR 21.11(h)].

3. Determine whether the board or an appropriate committee periodically reviews and approves all BSA, AML, and OFAC compliance policies.

Processes

Conclusion: Management (has/has not) established effective processes to ensure compliance with BSA, AML, and OFAC laws and regulations.

Objective: Determine the effectiveness of the bank's processes in capturing risk and ensuring compliance with the BSA, AML, and OFAC laws and regulations.

1. Determine whether the bank's system for communicating the requirements of, and any subsequent changes to, BSA, AML, and OFAC laws and regulations is adequate to ensure ongoing compliance.
2. Determine whether the bank's system for updating policies and procedures is adequate to ensure compliance with current laws and regulations, and that they are approved properly.

3. Assess the procedures used to ensure compliance when new products are implemented or operational changes occur (e.g., changes in software programs). Determine whether legal, audit, and information technology staffs are involved in new product review.
4. Assess the bank's identification and documentation requirements for establishing all accounts and other customer relationships, including those initiated through the mail, Internet, telephone, etc. Determine whether they include:

- Personal Accounts

  - Social security number or alien identification number (from U.S. residents).
  - Verification of acceptable identification (e.g., driver's license, state issued photo identification, passport, national identity card for nonresident aliens, etc.).
  - Verification of address of residence.
  - Estimation of anticipated account activity and customer's income source and/or profession.
  - Consideration of the source of funds to open the account.
  - Information obtained from a service bureau to determine whether a customer has been reported for overdrawing accounts, potentially conducting check kiting schemes, etc.
  - Third-party references, verification services, and telephone, website, and reverse directories.
  - Other account relationships.

- Business Accounts

  - Taxpayer identification number and legal name of the business entity.
  - Verification of legal status of the business (sole proprietorship, partnership, corporation, etc.).
  - Identification (and other information previously listed for personal accounts) for principals of the business and authorized signers.
  - Verification of the location of the business.
  - A description of the principal line of business and all types of business operations in which the customer engages. (Review the business' website, and if necessary, verify with a reporting agency.)
  - An estimation of anticipated account activity.
  - Consideration of the source of funds to open the account.
  - For large commercial accounts, financial statements, and a list of the firm's major suppliers and customers.
  - For foreign business accounts, proof that the business is registered in the country of origin (e.g., articles of incorporation, license, and registration).
  - Information obtained from a service bureau to determine whether a customer has been reported for overdrawing accounts, potentially conducting check kiting schemes, etc., if applicable.

- Third-party references, verification services, and telephone, website, and reverse directories.
- Other account relationships.

5. For the sampled accounts, review compliance with account opening requirements.
6. Review the account statements for the sampled accounts. Evaluate the transactions in the accounts to determine whether they are consistent with the type and nature of the business or occupation of the customer. Examiners may need to request additional supporting documentation on the transactions to understand account activity fully (e.g., copies of checks, debit and credit tickets, and/or wire advices). Be alert for possible structuring or any other suspicious activity.
7. If the bank uses agency, trustee, nominee, or other substitute names to identify customers on the general ledger or on other documents, ensure that the bank maintains files containing each customer's true name and other identifying information. Determine whether management has knowledge of these customers' activities, and the bank is monitoring the accounts for suspicious activity. (The use of substitute names is found customarily in private or foreign banking departments.)
8. Evaluate the system the bank uses to ensure that CTRs are timely and accurately filed. Evaluate teller and other cash entry systems to determine that it captures all applicable cash transactions, and it is comprehensive for all points of cash entry and exit. The system should cover all applicable areas within the bank.
9. Determine whether the bank has an effective automated or manual system to detect, over a period of time, structured transactions less than the $10,000 CTR reporting threshold. Determine whether the bank conducts appropriate follow up, including filing SARs, when structuring is apparent.
10. Using the sampled accounts, identify cash reportable transactions in excess of $10,000 and verify that a CTR was filed accurately and within the required time frame, or the transaction was exempted properly. 31 CFR 103.22
11. Review Federal Reserve cash flow information obtained from district office/Large Banks for any unusual activity. If unusual activity is noted (such as a material variance in totals of currency shipped or received or large denomination currency exchanged), identify the cause. Determine whether increases and decreases in CTR filings generally correspond with cash flow changes.
12. Review and determine the adequacy of the bank's system for monitoring, identifying, reviewing, and reporting suspicious activity.

    - Determine the departments and products that management monitors for suspicious activity.
    - Review reports management uses to monitor suspicious activity.
    - Review documentation maintained on accounts that have been or are currently being monitored.

13. Through discussions with management as well as review of requested materials and results of the account sample transaction reviews, conclude whether internal controls are adequate to ensure compliance with BSA, AML, and OFAC laws and regulations and

effectively minimize risk. Procedures used daily to prevent errors and violations, identify suspicious activity, ensure data integrity, and maintain record keeping requirements should include, but not be limited to:

- Comprehensive, sound, and fully implemented policies and procedures.
- Monitoring and detection procedures to identify and report suspicious activity.
- Comprehensive requirements for obtaining and verifying identification and documentation when opening accounts and establishing other customer relationships.
- Comprehensive monitoring of the activity in high-risk accounts, products, and services.
- Comprehensive monitoring of accounts and transactions involving foreign bank secrecy and money laundering haven countries or jurisdictions.
- Procedures to compare OFAC sanction lists with new and existing accounts and with transactions (especially funds transfers) to guard against OFAC violations.

Personnel

Conclusion: Bank management and personnel (do/do not) possess the required skills and knowledge to ensure compliance with the BSA, AML, and OFAC laws and regulations.

Objective: Determine whether bank management and personnel possess sufficient knowledge and technical skills to manage and perform duties related to the BSA, AML, and OFAC laws and regulations as well as effectively managing risk.

1. Based on interviews and conclusions developed while performing these procedures, assess the knowledge and technical skills of bank management and personnel (including, but not limited to, those who work in BSA compliance, branches, audit, safekeeping and safe deposit, lending, trust, correspondent banking, private banking, international, and the wire transfer room) with respect to BSA, AML, and OFAC laws and regulations. Also consider:

    - Employee roles and responsibilities.
    - Training and experience.
    - Specific products and services offered by the bank.
    - Violations cited.
    - Concerns noted during audits or examinations.

2. Evaluate the job qualifications of the board-appointed BSA Compliance Officer. Obtain a list of the BSA- and AML-related training courses attended since the last examination.
3. Review the bank's training programs (materials, agendas, rosters, frequency, evaluation forms, etc.) and discuss them with management to determine whether all employees with customer contact or customer-transaction-review responsibility receive training. Review the frequency and quality of the training provided. The training programs for BSA, AML, and OFAC may be tailored to meet the needs of various areas of the bank. Generally, they should include a review of:

- The bank's internal compliance policies and procedures and resources available to assist employees.
- The reporting and record keeping requirements of the BSA and the rules for exempting customers from the cash reporting requirements.
- The crime of money laundering.
- Examples of money laundering cases and methods and how such activities can be identified.
- The bank's suspicious activity monitoring and reporting procedures.
- The types of businesses, bank products, and geographies that can be more susceptible to abuse by money launderers and other criminals.
- The requirements of the OFAC regulations.
- Compliance responsibilities of employees.
- Civil and criminal penalties for violations of the BSA, AML, or OFAC laws and regulations and any other consequences of noncompliance for employees.
- Record retention requirements.

4. Determine whether the person(s) providing the employee training has adequate knowledge and sufficient training related to BSA, AML, and OFAC issues. Determine whether on-going continuing education is provided for all personnel conducting training.
5. Review management's employment screening process for reasonableness and to identify safeguards (e.g., background checks and references) implemented to protect the bank from hiring individuals with questionable or possibly suspicious backgrounds.
6. Select a sample of personnel files for review to determine adherence to established policies and procedures.

Controls

Conclusion: Management (has/has not) established effective control systems to ensure compliance with the BSA, AML, and OFAC laws and regulations.

Objective: Determine the effectiveness of control systems in detecting and correcting violations of the BSA, AML, and OFAC laws and regulations, as well as managing risk effectively.

1. Review the following documents and discuss them with management. Determine whether corrective action and follow up are appropriate and timely.

   - Audit/compliance review reports and management responses.
   - Management reports, especially those provided to senior management and the board of directors.
   - Audit/compliance review procedures and working papers.

2. Review compliance audit working papers to determine whether:

   - Procedures addressed all regulatory provisions and the bank's policies and procedures for complying with the BSA, AML, and OFAC laws and regulations.
   - High-risk areas, products, and services are targeted specifically.

- Steps were taken to follow-up on previously identified compliance deficiencies.
- Sample sizes were adequate and audit coverage included all product types and business areas. The time frame chosen for samples should adequately cover the time frame being reviewed. (Note: the sample should not be limited to one day or one location.)
- Significant deficiencies and the root cause(s) of the deficiencies are included in reports to management and the board.
- Corrective actions are timely, appropriate, and reported to management and the board.
- Audits or reviews are performed at regular and appropriate intervals.
- Work performed by auditors is accurate (examiners should check some of the transactions included in the audit to evaluate the accuracy of audit work).
- Conclusions are drawn about the bank's overall compliance performance for BSA, AML, and OFAC.

3. If, based on the procedures above, it is determined that the compliance audit function is unacceptable or deficient, then additional quantity of risk procedures should be performed. The examiner should conduct procedures that address the identified deficiencies. (See "General Procedures," step 7.)

Quantity of Risk

Conclusion: The quantity of risk is (low, moderate, high).

Objective: Determine the level of compliance with BSA, AML, and OFAC requirements.

Reporting, Record Keeping, and Record Retention

1. Select a sample of international accounts with large cash activity. Review account activity and ensure that a CMIR (U.S. Customs Form 4790) was filed for each shipment, except by common carrier, of currency or other monetary instrument(s) in excess of $10,000 from the United States or into the United States, by, or to the bank. 31 CFR 103.23(a) and (b) (In most cases, this refers to the bank's cash shipments.)
2. Determine whether the bank has a financial interest in, or signature authority over, a bank, securities, or other financial account in a foreign country. Ensure that the bank filed within the required time frame the Report of Foreign Bank and Financial Accounts (FBAR: Treasury Form 90-22.1) (31 CFR 103.24)
3. Select a sample of bank records and determine that the bank retained for at least five years either the original, microfilm, or other copy, or reproduction of the records required by the BSA. 31 CFR 103.22(d), 103.27(a)(3), 103.29(c), 103.33(a)-(c), 103.34(a)(1)(ii), and 103.34(b)(1) -(13)

Exemptions

1. Determine who is responsible for the exemption process and maintaining the exemption information. (See 31 CFR 103.22(d) for definition of exempt persons.)
2. Determine which persons the bank has exempted from CTR requirements and the most recent date the exemption was granted.
3. Determine whether the bank has revoked any exemptions. If so, determine the reason for the revocation and ensure that the bank properly completed and filed Form TDF 90-22.53 ("Designation of Exempt Person").
4. Test a sample of exempt accounts, and determine:

    - Whether information concerning exemptions was reviewed and verified at least annually. 31 CFR 103.22(d)(4)
    - Whether each exemption meets the definition of an exempt person and required documentation is maintained. 31 CFR 103.22(d)(2) and (d)(6)
    - For nonlisted business persons (31 CFR 103.22 (d)(2)(vi)), whether the person:

        - Has maintained a transaction account with the bank at least 12 months prior to being exempted.
        - Frequently engages in currency transactions with the bank in excess of $10,000.
        - Is incorporated or organized under U.S. or state law or is registered and is eligible to do business within the United States or a state. Note: This includes sole proprietorships.)

    - For payroll customers (31 CFR 103.22(d)(2)(vii)), solely for withdrawals for payroll purposes, whether the person:

        - Has maintained a transaction account with the bank at least 12 months prior to being exempted.
        - Operates a firm that regularly withdraws more than $10,000 in currency to pay its U.S. employees.
        - Is incorporated or organized under U.S. or state law or is registered and is eligible to do business within the United States or a state. (Note: This includes sole proprietorships.)

    - Whether the bank properly completed and filed Form TDF 90-22.53 ("Designation of Exempt Person") or used a properly completed IRS Form 4789 (currency transaction report) to designate each person as exempt. If so, review documentation supporting the designation to determine whether the information supports the exemption. 31 CFR 103.22(d)(3)
    - Whether the bank has filed a "Designation of Exempt Person" renewal form biennially for all nonlisted businesses and payroll customers by March 15 beginning the second calendar year following the original designation. 31 CFR 103.22(d)(5)
    - Whether the bank's monitoring of exempt persons for suspicious activity is adequate. 31 CFR 103.22(d)(9)(ii)

Sale of Monetary Instruments

1. Select a sample of transactions involving the sale of monetary instruments for cash in amounts between $3,000 and $10,000 inclusive.
2. For purchasers who have deposit accounts with the bank, determine whether the bank's records include the following required information (31 CFR 103.29(a)(1)):

   - The name of the purchaser.
   - Date of purchase.
   - The type(s) of instrument(s) purchased.
   - The serial number(s) of each of the instrument(s) purchased.
   - The dollar amount(s) of each of the instrument(s) purchased in currency.
   - Method of verification of identity (either at the time of purchase or when the deposit account was opened).

3. For purchasers who do not have deposit accounts with the bank, determine whether the bank's records include the following required information (31 CFR 103.29(a)(2)):

   - The name and address of the purchaser.
   - The social security or alien identification number of the purchaser.
   - The date of birth of the purchaser.
   - The date of purchase.
   - The type(s) of instrument(s) purchased.
   - The serial number(s) of each of the instrument(s) purchased.
   - The dollar amount(s) of each of the instrument(s) purchased.
   - Method of verifying the purchaser's specific identifying information (e.g., state of issuance and number of driver's license).

4. Determine whether the bank has an effective automated or manual system to detect multiple sales of monetary instruments in one day, in amounts totaling $3,000 or more. Determine whether the bank conducts appropriate follow up, including filing SARs, when structuring is apparent and maintains the required documentation. 31 CFR 103.29(b)
5. Evaluate the bank's system to monitor the sale of monetary instruments for suspicious activity and determine whether the bank conducts adequate follow-up, including filing SARs, when appropriate.

Funds Transfer

1. Using a sample of high-risk accounts, review account statements for a three-month period. Analyze wire transfers to determine whether the amounts, frequency, and countries of origin/destination are consistent with the nature of the business or occupation of the customer and be alert for any suspicious or unusual activity.
2. From the wire transfer log, select a sample of wires funded by cash for both customers and noncustomers and verify that the bank appropriately filed CTRs. 31 CFR 103.22
3. Evaluate the bank's system to monitor wire transfers for suspicious activity.

Responsibilities of Originating Banks

4. Using the account sample, check a selection of payment orders of $3,000 or more to ensure that the bank retained either the original or a microfilm, other copy, or electronic record of the payment order. 31 CFR 103.33(e)(1)(i) The bank must retain the following records for each payment order of $3,000 or more (see 31 CFR 103.33(g)(1) for transmittal orders):

   - Name and address of the originator. 31 CFR 103.33(e)(1)(i)(A)
   - Amount of the payment order. 31 CFR 103.33(e)(1)(i)(B)
   - The execution date of the payment order. 31 CFR 103.33(e)(1)(i)(C)
   - Any payment instructions. 31 CFR 103.33(e)(1)(i)(D)
   - The identity of the beneficiary's bank. 31 CFR 103.33(e)(1)(i)(E)
   - As many of the following items as are received with the payment order.

     - Name and address of the originator. 31 CFR 103.33(e)(1)(i)(A)
     - Account number of the beneficiary. 31 CFR 103.33(e)(1)(i)(F)(2)
     - Any other specific identifier of the beneficiary. 31 CFR 103.33(e)(1)(i)(F)(3)

5. From a sample of noncustomer funds transfers of $3,000 or more, determine whether the bank retains:

   - For payment orders made in person, verification that the bank required identification and a record of the information and the type of verification used. 31 CFR 103.33(e)(2)(i)
   - When the bank has knowledge that the person placing the payment order is not the originator, a record of the originator's taxpayer identification number (i.e., social security or employer identification number) or, if none, alien identification number or passport number and country of issuance, if known by the person placing the order, or a notation in the record of the lack thereof. 31 CFR 103.33(e)(2)(i)
   - When the payment order is not made in person, a record of the name and address of the person placing the payment order, as well as the person's taxpayer identification number (i.e., social security or employer identification number) or, if none, alien identification number or passport number and country of issuance, or a notation in the record of the lack thereof, and a copy or record of the method of payment (i.e., check or credit card transaction) for the funds transfer. 31 CFR 103.33(e)(2)(ii)

6. Verify that the information the bank must retain for originators is retrievable by reference to the name of the originator. When the originator is an established customer of the bank and has an account used for funds transfers, determine whether the information also is retrievable by account number. 31 CFR 103.33(e)(4)

Responsibilities of Intermediary Banks

7. From a sample of payment orders for funds transfers of $3,000 or more when the bank is acting as an intermediary bank, determine whether the bank retained the original or a microfilm, other copy, or electronic record.31 CFR 103.33(e)(1)(ii)
8. Using the sample, determine whether the bank forwards the required information to the next receiving financial institution, if received from the sender. 31 CFR 103.33(g)(2)

Responsibilities of Beneficiary Banks

9. From a sample of payment orders from customers and noncustomers of $3,000 or more when the bank accepts as a beneficiary bank, determine whether the bank retained either the original or a microfilm, other copy, or electronic record of the payment order. 31 CFR 103.33(e)(1)(iii)
10. Using the sample of noncustomer payment orders, determine whether:

    - The bank verified the identity of the person receiving the proceeds and obtained and retained a record of that information when proceeds are delivered in person to the beneficiary or its representative or agent. 31 CFR 103.33 (e)(3)(i)
    - The bank obtained and retained a record of the beneficiary's name and address, as well as the beneficiary's identification when the bank has knowledge that the person receiving the proceeds is not the beneficiary. 31 CFR 103.33(e)(3)(i)
    - The bank retained a copy of the check or other instrument used to effect payment, or the information contained thereon, as well as the name and address of the person to which it was sent when proceeds are delivered other than in person. 31 CFR 103.33(e)(3)(ii)

11. Determine whether the information that the bank must retain for beneficiaries is retrievable by reference to the name of the beneficiary, and, if the beneficiary is an established customer of the bank and has an account used for funds transfers, whether the information also is retrievable by account number. 31 CFR 103.33(e)(4)
12. Based on the preceding procedures, form a conclusion about the level of risk associated with the reporting, record keeping, and record retention requirements of the BSA as well as the level of risk associated with funds transfer activities.

Payable upon Proper Identification (PUPID)

1. From PUPID logs or other records, review transactions for a specific time frame. Look for any unusual or suspicious patterns of activity. Consider the amount, frequency, and (if available) purpose of the transactions. Determine through discussions with management whether the transactions appear to be reasonable in nature.
2. Evaluate internal controls used to manage the risks involved, e.g., use of logs, and review and reconciliation processes as well as methods to detect suspicious or unusual activities.
3. Form a conclusion about the level of risk associated with PUPID transactions.

Nonresident Alien Accounts and the Black Market Peso Exchange

1. Select a sample of high-risk accounts owned by nonresident aliens (NRAs) and obtain account opening information and account statements for a three-month period. Determine whether management has:

    - Verified the NRA status of each customer and has viewed the original and included a photocopy of the customer's passport or cedula (nation identification card) in the account file.
    - Documented application of the institution's account opening procedures.
    - Established the identity of the ultimate beneficial owner when the account ownership is not indicated clearly by the account title (e.g., trustee, agency, or nominee accounts).
    - Monitored these accounts for suspicious activity.

2. Review sample accounts for suspicious activity, including:

    - Structured deposits, including frequent deposits in round-dollar amounts, between $2,000 and $10,000.
    - Funds transfer activity to or from high-risk geographies.
    - A large volume of transaction activity with low-average monthly account balances.
    - Checks drawn in large or round-dollar amounts.
    - The absence of ATM and point-of-sale transactions and of checks written for small odd-dollar amounts.

3. If unusual activity is found, request and review a sample of suspect wire transfers and checks written on the account. If checks or wire transfers consist of payments for appliances or other retail goods from the Florida or Panama free trade zones, and there are no checks or wires for customary consumer payments, such as utilities and mortgages, the account may be part of a black market peso exchange (BMPE) scheme.
4. Evaluate methods to detect suspicious or unusual activities associated with NRAs or a BMPE scheme.
5. Form a conclusion about the level of risk associated with NRAs or a BMPE scheme.

International Brokered Deposits

1. Obtain a list of international brokered deposit accounts to evaluate the scope and volume of the accounts (the list should include accounts generated from overseas bank representatives or brokers).
2. Evaluate the bank's process to review and approve international deposit brokers and/or hire overseas representatives, and evaluate their backgrounds and qualifications. Consider corporate documentation, references, background checks, verification of prior employment, database searches, and educational and professional background.
3. Review the contracts/agreements and controls established between the bank and the deposit brokers and determine whether they:

    - Address identification and documentation procedures to control risk.

- Provide the ability to access and review identifying and other information concerning account holders.
- Prohibit, or limit, cash transactions by account holders within U.S. borders.
- Prohibit high-risk entities from opening accounts, including finance companies, funds remitters, or other nonbank financial institutions.
- Establish the target market for brokered deposit accounts.

4. Select a sample of international brokered deposit accounts and obtain account agreements, account opening information, and transaction records for a three-month period.
5. Review transactions to determine whether they are consistent with expectations. Examiners may need to request additional supporting documentation on the transactions to understand account activity fully (e.g., copies of checks, debit and credit tickets, and/or wire advices). Be alert for possible suspicious activity.
6. Evaluate the bank's system to identify suspicious activity associated with international brokered deposit accounts.
7. Form a conclusion about the level of risk associated with international brokered deposit accounts.

Foreign Correspondent Banking

1. Select a sample of high-risk foreign correspondent accounts and obtain account agreements, account-opening information, and account statements for a three-month period.
2. Evaluate the adequacy of the account approval process. Consider information obtained on the sampled accounts, such as the foreign bank's anti-money laundering programs; licensing information; third-party access to the account; and the expected frequency, type, and volume of account activity, and other relevant information.
3. Review the account statements sampled to determine whether the transactions in the account are consistent with expectations. Examiners may need to request additional supporting documentation on the transactions to understand account activity fully (e.g., copies of checks, debit and credit tickets, and/or wire advices). Be alert for possible suspicious activity.
4. Evaluate the bank's system to identify suspicious activity in foreign correspondent accounts.
5. Form a conclusion about the level of risk associated with foreign correspondent banking.

"Pouch" Activity

1. Identify the foreign correspondent accounts in the sample that have incoming or outgoing pouch activity (sometimes called "cash letter") via carrier or courier (e.g., DHL, FedEx).
2. Review logs or other documents maintained by management and witness the opening of a sample of incoming pouches (for a period of several days) and the preparation of outgoing pouches. Review the logs and the pouch contents for currency or monetary instruments, and:

- Determine whether CTRs, CMIRs or SARs were filed, if appropriate.

- Identify suspicious patterns of activity.

3. Evaluate the bank's system to identify suspicious activity in the pouch activity of foreign correspondent accounts.
4. Form a conclusion about the level of risk associated with pouch activity.

Mexican Bank Drafts

1. Review the bank's contracts and agreements with Mexican correspondent banks. Determine whether they address procedures for processing and clearing bank drafts.
2. Select a sample of foreign correspondent accounts in which "Mexican bank drafts" are processed. In choosing your sample, include accounts with high levels of activity and with drafts drawn in large dollar amounts. Obtain a sample of Mexican bank drafts processed through the accounts.
3. Evaluate the adequacy of the account approval process. Consider information obtained on the sampled accounts, such as the foreign bank's anti-money laundering programs; licensing information; third-party access to the account; and the expected frequency, type, and volume of account activity, and other relevant information.
4. Determine whether the bank ascertained whether the home country supervisor of the foreign bank required banks to identify and monitor the transactions of their customers in a manner consistent with the bank's requirements.
5. Review the sample of transactions for repetitive names, addresses, and large groups of similar looking drafts. Investigate any unusual or suspicious bank draft transactions.
6. Evaluate the bank's system to identify suspicious Mexican bank draft activity.
7. Form a conclusion about the level of risk associated with Mexican bank drafts.

Payable through Accounts (PTAs)

1. Obtain a list of foreign correspondent accounts where PTAs are offered and determine:

   - The number of sub-accounts within each PTA.
   - An estimate of the number of transactions per month per sub-account.
   - An estimate of the transaction amount.

2. Determine whether the bank ascertained whether the home country supervisor of the foreign bank required banks to identify and monitor the transactions of their customers in a manner consistent with the bank's requirements.
3. Select a sample of PTAs and obtain account agreements and account opening information. Also, from these accounts, select a sample of sub-account holders and obtain sub-account holder information and transaction records for a three-month period.
4. Review the contracts/agreements with the correspondent, and determine whether they:

   - Address procedures and documentation requirements and whether procedures for identification and documentation are consistent with those used for opening domestic accounts at the U.S. bank.
   - Provide the U.S. bank with the ability to review identifying and other information concerning sub-account holders.

- Prohibit cash transactions by sub-account holders within U.S. borders.
- Require the foreign bank to monitor sub-account activities to detect, investigate, and report suspicious or unusual transactions and report findings to the U.S. bank.
- Clearly state the liability of both the U.S. bank and foreign bank, to which the PTA service is being offered.
- Allow the U.S. bank to audit the foreign bank's PTA operations and have access to PTA documents.
- Require the foreign bank to comply with local AML requirements.
- Provide for dollar limits on each sub-account holder.
- Require financial statements on commercial sub-account holders on large accounts.
- Prohibit sub-accounts from being opened by casas de cambio, finance companies, funds remitters, or other nonbank financial institutions.
- Prohibit second-tier sub-account holders.

5. Review sub-account holder transactions, and determine whether they are consistent with expectations.
6. Identify the control system used to prohibit account openings for individuals or businesses or governments located in countries that are banned from doing business with the United States as determined by OFAC.
7. Evaluate the bank's system to identify suspicious activity associated with PTAs.
8. Form a conclusion about the level of risk associated with PTAs.

Special Use Accounts

1. Obtain a list of special use accounts (SUAs) and identify:

    - The account titles and numbers.
    - Their purpose or department.
    - The employees that have access to them.
    - The employees that review and reconcile them.

2. Review and evaluate the internal controls that have been implemented to ensure the proper use of these accounts. Consider:

    - Who within the bank can access (debit or credit) special use account(s) and whether two signatures are required for access.
    - Whether customers have the ability to access special use accounts.
    - Whether customer transactions also are captured in the customer's account statements.
    - The frequency of reconcilements.
    - The process to resolve discrepancies.
    - How transactions are monitored for suspicious activity.

3. Select for further review a sample of SUAs with significant activity. Obtain account activity reports for these SUAs. Evaluate the activity and select a sample of transactions

passing through different SUAs. Focus on higher risk type activity (funds transfer or monetary instruments, etc.) and transactions from high-risk countries.

4. Review transactions for any suspicious or unusual activity.
5. Evaluate the bank's system to identify suspicious activity associated with SUAs.
6. Form a conclusion about the level of risk associated with SUAs.

Private Banking and Trust

1. Obtain and review the following documents:

    - Business or strategic plans for private banking and trust activities.
    - Recent reports received regularly by management on private banking and trust activities.
    - A description of the method for aggregating customer holdings and activities across business units throughout the organization.
    - A description of account officer and manager positions, the compensation program, and recruitment program.
    - Code of ethics policy.
    - A list of accounts:

        - When the bank's private banking and trust customers are foreign government officials, export/import business owners, money transmitters, private investment companies (PICs), financial advisors, offshore entities, or money managers (when an intermediary is acting on behalf of customers).
        - When account officers introduced the bank's private banking and trust customers to the bank or representatives previously employed by other financial institutions.
        - When a third-party investment advisor referred the accounts to the bank.
        - When nominee names are used.

2. Determine during discussions with private banking and trust management, and through review of the bank's documents obtained in step 1:

    - The organizational structure for providing services.
    - The goals and objectives.
    - The products and services offered and contemplated.
    - The marketing strategies.
    - The strategies for addressing the risks unique to those activities.

3. Determine the volume of policy exceptions for more than several months and evaluate the adequacy of the approval process for them.
4. Verify that written policies, procedures, and systems of internal controls for opening and monitoring private banking and trust accounts provide for:

    - Procedures for opening accounts.
    - Operational procedures.

- Periodic reviews.
- Staff responsibility and accountability.
- Training.
- Monitoring for unusual or suspicious transactions.
- Reporting of unusual or suspicious transactions.

5. Evaluate management information systems (MIS) for private banking and trust activities, as appropriate. Evaluate whether the following reports are adequate, useful, timely, aggregated across departments and products, as needed, and provided to senior management and the board of directors, as needed:

   - Customer aggregation reports (all holdings throughout the institution, including overseas and nominee name holdings).
   - Profitability reports.
   - Policy exception and missing document reports.
   - Customer risk classification reports.
   - Unusual account activity (including cash and noncash, funds transfer, asset management, loan payments, offshore activities, etc.).
   - Suspicious activity reports.

6. Review the private banking and trust employee compensation program and determine whether it includes qualitative measures that provide incentives to comply with account opening and suspicious activity monitoring requirements.
7. Review written job descriptions and determine whether they include compliance with anti-money laundering laws, regulations, policies, and procedures.
8. Select a sample of private banking and trust accounts and obtain account opening information and account statements for a three-month period. Emphasize:

   - Customers who deal in large cash transactions.
   - Customers from high-risk countries.
   - Customers who are foreign clients and government officials from high-risk countries.
   - Customers who have accounts offshore or with offshore entities, including PICs.
   - Accounts from the highest compensated employees, recent high performers, and/or new employees.
   - Customers who have large and frequent funds transfer activity.
   - The grantors of private banking and trust accounts that direct loans from their accounts to other parties or business interests of account principals or beneficiaries.
   - Accounts that appear to act as pass-through accounts with high volumes of credits and debits and low average monthly balances.
   - Customers listed on unusual or suspicious activity monitoring reports as well as customers on whom SARs have been filed.
   - Clients with nondiscretionary accounts (e.g., custodial accounts, investment advisory accounts, and revocable trusts).

9. Review account transactions, and determine whether they are consistent with expectations.
10. Evaluate the bank's system to identify suspicious activity associated with private banking and trust customers.
11. Form a conclusion about the level of risk associated with private banking and trust activities.

Offshore Branches and Offices

1. If the location of the foreign office is considered to be at high risk for money laundering and access to customer records is permitted, conduct an onsite examination. Assess the adequacy of the anti-money laundering compliance program. Evaluate internal controls, policies, procedures, reporting, audit, training, and hiring practices. Refer to "Quality of Risk Management" procedures.
2. Select a sample of high-risk accounts for review. For each account, request account opening and credit file information and copies of account statements for the most recent three months. Review the account statements for the sampled accounts. Evaluate the transactions in the accounts to determine whether they are consistent with the type and nature of the business or occupation of the customer. Examiners may need to request additional supporting documentation on the transactions to understand account activity fully (e.g., copies of checks, debit and credit tickets, and/or wire advices). Be alert for possible structuring or any other suspicious activity and appropriate follow up.
3. For branches and offices in other countries, and when access to customer's records is not permitted, or when the risk for money laundering is considered low, review internal and external anti-money laundering audits of the branches or offices. Review the foreign offices' AML program, including policies and procedures, management reports, SARs, hiring processes, and training programs.
4. Evaluate the bank's system to identify suspicious activity associated with offshore branches and offices.
5. Form a conclusion about the level of risk associated with Offshore Branches and Offices.

OFAC

1. Check for accuracy the bank's current listing of prohibited countries, entities, and individuals.
2. Determine whether the OFAC information is disseminated to all appropriate employees, including foreign country offices.
3. Evaluate the controls used to compare new accounts (e.g., deposit, loan private banking, trust, discount, or other securities brokerage transactions), funds transfers, or other new bank transactions with the OFAC listings prior to opening the account, or conducting the transaction.
4. Determine whether established accounts and other customer transactions are compared periodically with the current OFAC listing.
5. Form a conclusion about the level of risk associated with OFAC requirements.

Lending Function

1. Select a sample of loans focusing on high-risk areas (e.g., loans to PICs and cash secured).

2. Review the sample for loan purposes and appropriate documentation.

    - Review and evaluate the bank's procedures used to detect, investigate, and report suspicious loan transactions.

3. Review the bank's in-house reports to identify unusual loan activity, including:

    - Cash-secured loans.
    - Loans that do not fit the customer's general business profile.
    - Premature cancellation of debt, particularly with cash.

4. If the bank's internal process for detecting suspicious activities is inadequate, perform step 3 by selecting your own sample of loans. Base the sample on loans granted to customers in high-risk countries or to high-risk businesses.
5. Based on the previous procedures, form a conclusion about the level of risk associated with the lending function.

Safe Custody/Safe Deposit Boxes

These activities involve requests by customers and noncustomers to hold items, such as boxes, sealed envelopes, or parcels in safe custody. Examiners should pay particular attention to determining whether management has developed adequate identification procedures for persons or businesses that do not hold accounts.

1. Determine whether management has considered money laundering implications and prevention measures associated with this activity.
2. Determine the appropriate level of testing to verify that adequate processes are in place to ensure that investigators can identify the ultimate owner and address of the owner of the items held in safe custody.
3. Based on the previous procedures, form a conclusion about the bank's exposure to money laundering in the safe custody area.

Conclusions

Objective: To prepare written conclusion comments and communicate findings to management. If necessary, initiate corrective action when policies or internal controls are deficient or when violations of law or regulation are identified.

1. Summarize findings and all violations of law, regulation, or ruling from the preceding procedural steps to assess the bank's level of compliance with the requirements of the Bank Secrecy Act and OFAC rules. Remember to discuss violations of law with OCC legal counsel, as appropriate.
2. For those violations determined to be significant or a pattern or practice, determine the root cause of violation(s) by identifying weaknesses in:

    - Internal controls.

- Audit/independent compliance review.
- Training.
- Management oversight.
- Other factors.

3. If suspicious transactions are found, investigate them based on your own understanding of the customer's legitimate business needs. If the transaction does not appear to meet the legitimate business needs of the customer, contact the EIC and consider obtaining advice from the Compliance ADC to determine how best to proceed.
4. Determine the degree to which management was aware of the suspicious transaction(s). Also, determine whether the bank should have been aware of the suspicious nature of the transaction(s).
5. Determine whether civil money penalties (CMP), suspicious activity reporting, or an enforcement action should be recommended (refer to the CMP matrix).
6. Form a conclusion about the reliability of the compliance management system for the Bank Secrecy Act and provide conclusions to the examiner performing the Compliance Management System program.
7. Identify action needed to correct violations and weaknesses in the bank's compliance system, as appropriate.
8. Determine whether any items identified during this examination could materialize into supervisory concerns before the next on-site examination (considering whether the bank has plans to increase monitoring in the affected area, or anticipates changes in personnel, policy, outside auditors or consultants, or business strategy). If so, summarize your concerns and assess the potential risk to the bank.
9. Determine the impact on the aggregate and direction of risk assessment for any concerns identified during the review. Examiners should refer to guidance provided under the OCC's large and community bank risk assessment programs.

   - Risk categories: compliance, transaction, and reputation.
   - Risk conclusions: high, moderate, or low.
   - Risk direction: increasing, stable, or decreasing.

10. Provide the EIC with conclusions (discussing them with the EIC and, if appropriate, with the supervisory office), including:

    - Summary of violations and recommended CMPs/enforcement actions, if any.
    - Recommended corrective action, including instructing the bank to seek back-filing instructions from the Compliance Review Group at the IRS Detroit Computing Center if there are violations involving unreported large currency transactions.
    - Quality of risk management.
    - Quantity of risk (if this section was not completed during the exam, examiners should base their conclusions on the results of the quality of risk management transactional testing procedures and the quantity of risk as identified by the bank's management information and control processes).
    - Recommended matters requiring attention (MRA). MRA should cover practices that:

- Deviate from sound fundamental principles and are likely to result in financial deterioration, if not addressed.
- Result in substantive noncompliance with laws.

MRA should discuss:

- Causes of the problem.
- Consequences of inaction.
- Management's commitment to corrective action.
- The time frame and person(s) responsible for corrective action.

11. Discuss findings with management. Obtain commitment(s) for corrective action as needed. Include in the discussion:

    - Quality of risk management.
    - Quantity of risk (include a listing of all violations, as well as significant violations).
    - C MRA(s).

12. As appropriate, prepare a brief comment for inclusion in the report of examination.
13. Prepare a memorandum or update the work program with any information that will facilitate future examinations. Update OCC electronic databases with all violations of law or regulation. Examiners must enter narrative summaries in OCC's electronic databases (Type 70 analysis) for violations of 31 CFR 103.18(a)(1), 103.22(b)(1), 103.23(a), 103.23(b), 103.24(a), 12 CFR 21.21, 12 CFR 21.11, and any other BSA violations that are included in the report of examination.
14. Organize and reference working papers in accordance with OCC guidance.

APPENDIX A

FinCEN Policy Statements and Guidelines

Twenty-five Day Extension for Magnetic Filing

For CTRs that are filed magnetically, banks must file the CTRs with the IRS Detroit Computing Center within 25 days following the date on which a reportable transaction occurs.

It is important to emphasize that this exemption applies only to CTRs filed magnetically pursuant to an agreement between a bank and the IRS. If for any reason a bank should withdraw from the magnetic tape program or for any other reason file paper CTRs, these CTRs must be filed within the 15-day period following the reportable transaction as required by 31 CFR 103.27(a)(1).

Monetary Instruments for Account Holders

It has come to Treasury's attention that examiners are citing banks for alleged violation of the Bank Secrecy Act (BSA) regulations concerning compliance with 31 CFR 103.29.

Treasury is aware that many banks have instituted a policy that requires deposit account holders who purchase monetary instruments with currency in amounts between $3,000 and $10,000 to first deposit the currency into their accounts from which a check or withdrawal is then issued in payment.

Treasury has determined that there is nothing within the BSA or its implementing regulations, which prohibits a bank from instituting this type of policy. Further, the implementation of such a policy is within a bank's discretion. Should a bank decide to institute such a policy, however, it must do so in writing and include formal written procedures for implementation. The policy and procedures should apply to all deposit account holders and, as a general rule, contain no exceptions. By selling the instruments to deposit account holders and by requiring them to purchase these instruments from their deposit accounts, banks will have records to reconstruct the transaction should it be necessary to do so, therefore, formal records as required by 31 CFR 103.29 are not necessary.

APPENDIX B

Bank Secrecy Act Databases

Currency and Banking Retrieval System

The primary database for BSA data is the Currency and Banking Retrieval System (CBRS). Bank Secrecy Act (BSA) reports have a high degree of usefulness in criminal, tax, or regulatory investigations and proceedings. The Detroit Computing Center (DCC), Internal Revenue Service, maintains the CBRS and provides automated access to the following BSA reports:

- Currency Transaction Reports (IRS Form 4789).
- Report of Foreign Bank and Financial Accounts (IRS Form 90-22.1).
- Report of International Transportation of Currency or Monetary Instrument Reports (US Customs Form 4790).
- Suspicious Activity Reports (SAR). (While the OCC, FinCEN, and the other federal banking agencies have separate forms and rules for SARs, FinCEN and the federal banking regulators jointly own the SAR.)
- "Designation of Exempt Persons" (TDF 90-22.53).

The CBRS also provides access to other Treasury Department reports, including the Report of Cash Payments Received in a Trade or Business (IRS Form 8300) and Currency Transaction Reports by Casinos (IRS Form 8362). However, the OCC is not authorized to review these forms.

The CBRS is used by regulatory and law enforcement personnel to identify bank accounts, currency transactions, international transportation of currency and monetary instruments, asset holdings, foreign financial accounts, and other useful information. Designated OCC district and Washington staffs also use the database to obtain information for BSA examinations.

The Suspicious Activity Reporting System

In 1991, the OCC and other federal banking agencies entered into agreement with FinCEN to standardize and centralize the criminal referral process. Previously, financial institutions filed CTRs marked suspicious and/or criminal referral forms to alert law enforcement agencies of suspicious transactions.

Although useful, the data was often incomplete, regionally based and inaccessible to certain authorities. In addition, federal regulatory agencies maintained separate criminal referral databases. As a result, information sharing was not timely and created excessive risks to the regulatory enforcement process. Based on these shortcomings, it became clear that a centralized data collection and distribution system would be necessary to utilize SAR information fully. In 1994, the Secretary of the Treasury designated FinCEN as the central repository for SARs. The original SAR query system was released when the form was finalized in 1996.

Currency and Banking Query System (CBQS)

FinCEN piloted the latest SAR system in the fall of 1998. The system is known as the Currency and Banking Query System (CBQS) and gives users a mouse driven, Windows enhanced, query system. The significance of CBQS lies in its sophisticated expanded query capabilities. Unlike CBRS, this new system offers the user one query screen containing virtually all the fields present on the actual SAR form and enables users to search any combination of fields.

One of the most important elements of the SAR is the narrative summary. Although CBRS enabled users to view the narrative, this critical portion of the SAR could not be queried on a multiple form basis. CBQS now enables the user to perform searches on data contained within the narrative summaries. As a result, users of CBQS can make more focused and refined queries of the body of data on the system. Currently, CBQS only enables access to SAR data. However, other BSA data may be accessible through CBQS in the future.

The system is used by several agencies, including IRS, FBI, Customs, Secret Service, Postal Inspection, OCC, and other federal bank regulators. Only regulators and authorized law enforcement personnel can access SARs. Authorized agencies all have query capability to access SAR data through CBRS screens. Several agencies also are approved to receive downloads of files to process in their own computer systems.

Assistance and Information

The Detroit Computing Center (DCC) offers a hot line for anyone experiencing difficulties with the CBRS or CBQS systems. The number is (313) 234-2000. In addition, the Compliance Review Group at DCC has overall responsibility for providing assistance to financial institutions and their bank supervisors on BSA reports. They also correspond with banks on BSA report matters, such as exemptions, incorrect/incomplete forms, and failures to file reports promptly. Whenever applicable, banks should be instructed to contact the Compliance Review Group for guidance on correcting BSA report deficiencies. The group refers more serious BSA deficiencies to FinCEN for disposition. The Compliance Review Group can be reached at (313) 234-1613. BSA forms, news, and information relating to the SAR system and other FinCEN related issues are also available on FinCEN's website at www.treas.gov/fincen.

APPENDIX C

Referring BSA Violations to FinCEN

BSA cases are often complex and subject to a variety of mitigating and aggravating factors. The following factors should be considered before potential BSA violations are referred to FinCEN:

- Number of violations.
- Nature of violations (technical, isolated, systemwide, egregious).
- Longevity of the violations (repeat, short-lived).
- Rate of compliance.
- Basis of discovery (OCC, bank).
- Level of compliance with 12 CFR 21.21.
- Corrective action by bank.

FinCEN has been reluctant to impose a civil money penalty against a bank, unless the violations were numerous, flagrant, and long-standing. The OCC should not refer matters that will not result in any action by FinCEN. CTR violations that involve otherwise exemptible customers under the BSA should not be referred to FinCEN. In addition, FinCEN has never penalized a bank exclusively for record keeping violations.

Content of Referral

A BSA referral should allow FinCEN to make a preliminary judgment on the civil money penalty potential of a case by providing:

- Scope of exam.
- Dates of the review period.
- Number of violations.
- Type (cites) of violations.
- Level of compliance.
- Compliance history and adequacy of compliance program (21.21 elements).

This is normally accomplished by providing the examination report. If FinCEN requires additional information, it will contact the bank or the OCC.

Referral Process

Examiners should continue to send significant BSA violations to district counsel for review of legal sufficiency and compliance with BSA referral standards. The Enforcement & Compliance Division (E&C) performs legal reviews of referrals involving large banks. In cases involving suspected ongoing criminal activity, the EIC should immediately contact the appropriate supervisory office. The supervisory office will then notify E&C and the local IRS/CID office.

Enforcement actions against banks arising from BSA referrals to FinCEN should be entered on the Enforcement Action Reporting System (EARS) by the appropriate supervisory office (district, Large Bank Supervision, or Special Supervision/Fraud). In cases involving individuals, district counsel is responsible for entering delegated enforcement actions on EARS. In nondelegated actions, E&C is responsible for entering BSA actions on EARS.

Sample Cover Letter for Referring Potential BSA Violations to FinCEN

(Name)
Assistant Director, Financial Crimes Enforcement Network
Franklin Court Building
Suite 4500 Washington, D.C. 20220

Re: Bank Name

Dear:

A recent examination of the subject bank revealed significant violations of the Bank Secrecy Act (BSA), 31 USC 5311 et. seq., and its implementing regulations, 31 CFR 103. Specifically, our examination uncovered violations of (list cites).

Based on the level of noncompliance and the type of violations uncovered, we are forwarding this information to you for investigation and consideration of criminal or civil penalties. The BSA violations are detailed further in the enclosed bank examination report.

Please acknowledge receipt of this matter by signing, dating, and returning the extra copy provided in the enclosed self-addressed envelope. If your office requires further information, contact (district office contact person). (district office contact person) should be advised of FinCEN's final disposition of this matter.

Sincerely,

(Name)
District Counsel

____
Signature and Title

____
Date Received

Enclosures

Cc: Community and Consumer Policy

APPENDIX D

Availability of Office of Foreign Asset Control Information

The Office of Foreign Assets Control (OFAC) of the U.S. Department of Treasury is responsible for administering a series of laws that impose economic sanctions against selected foreign countries to further U.S. foreign policy and national security objectives. Every financial institution is required to comply with economic sanctions and embargo programs administered under regulations issued by OFAC.

To keep financial institutions informed, OFAC regularly updates lists that designate countries and specially designated nationals that are prohibited from conducting business with any U.S. entity or individual. To make it easier for banks to get current information, the OCC has made OFAC issuances available on the OCC Information Line at (202) 479-0141. The voice prompted, automated fax on demand system offers the most current issue of the following documents on its issuances and miscellaneous section, using the number to the left as the document number.

1011 "Foreign Assets Control Regulations for The Financial Community" (8/17/99).
1012 "Office of Foreign Assets Control Specially Designated Nationals and Blocked Persons" (A-I - part 1 of 3 (10/22/99).
1013 "Office of Foreign Assets Control Specially Designated Nationals and Blocked Persons" (J-T) - part 2 of 3 (10/22/99).
1014 "Office of Foreign Assets Control Specially Designated Nationals and Blocked Persons" (U-Z + Appendices) part 3 of 3(10/22/99).
1015 "Office of Foreign Asset Control Changes to List of Specially Designated Nationals and Blocked Persons Since January 1, 1999" (10/22/99).

If you need help using the OCC Information Line, please call the Communications Division at (202) 874-4700. Policy or examination-related questions regarding OFAC should be directed to Community and Consumer Policy at (202) 874-4428. Information is also available on OFAC's website, www.treas.gov/ofac.

APPENDIX E

Basle Supervisors' Committee Statement of Principles on Money Laundering

The central bank governors of the Group of Ten industrialized countries established the Committee on Banking Regulations and Supervisory Practices in 1974. The committee's objective is to strengthen collaboration among national authorities in their prudential supervision of international banking. The three U.S. federal bank regulatory agencies are represented on this committee. (Note: This preamble has been summarized.)

Members of the committee have long been concerned about the use of the banking system by criminal elements. Criminals can use the banking system to hide the true ownership of funds through nominees and to make payments and transfers of funds. These activities – when associated with monies derived from illegal activities – are commonly referred to as money laundering.

Each of the bank supervisory authorities represented on the committee has a different role and responsibility in suppressing money laundering. All member countries collectively believe that bank supervisors, regardless of their prescribed role, should ensure that ethical standards of professional conduct are being observed in the banking system. Members also believe that supervisors should encourage the implementation of effective policies and procedures to aid efforts to eliminate money laundering.

The members of the committee have developed and approved the attached "Statement of Principles" in accordance with the principles set out, bank management is encouraged to establish policies and procedures to ensure: (i) the proper identification of all persons conducting business with the bank; (ii) the conduct of bank's business in conformity with high ethical standards; (iii) cooperation with law enforcement authorities within the confines of applicable law; and (iv) proper staff training in all matters concerning this Statement of Principles. Bank management is encouraged to incorporate these principles into the existing procedures that are already required under Subpart C of 12 CFR 21 (12 CFR 21.21), Procedures for Monitoring Bank Secrecy Act Compliance.

Statement of Principles

Purpose

Banks and other financial institutions may unwittingly be used as intermediaries for the transfer or deposit of money derived from criminal activity. The intention behind such transactions is often to hide the beneficial ownership of funds. The use of the financial system in this way is of direct concern to policy and other law enforcement agencies; it is also a matter of concern to banking supervisors and banks' managements, since public confidence in banks may be undermined through their association with criminals.

This statement of principles is intended to outline some basic policies and procedures that banks' managements should ensure are in place within their banks with a view to assisting in the suppression of money laundering through the banking system, national and international. The statement thus sets out to reinforce existing best practices among banks and, specifically, to encourage vigilance against criminal use of the payments system, implementation by banks of effective preventive safeguards, and cooperation with law enforcement agencies.

Customer Identification

With a view to ensuring that the financial system is not used as a channel for criminal funds, banks should make reasonable efforts to determine the true identity of all customers requesting the bank's services. Particular care should be taken to identify the ownership of all accounts and those using safe-custody facilities. All banks should institute effective procedures for obtaining identification from new customers. It should be an explicit policy that significant business transactions will not be conducted with customers who fail to provide evidence of their identity.

Compliance with Laws

Banks' management should ensure that business is conducted in conformity with high ethical standards and that laws and regulations pertaining to financial transactions are adhered to. As regards transactions executed on behalf of customers, it is accepted that banks may have no means of knowing whether the transaction stems from or forms part of criminal activity.

Similarly, in an international context it may be difficult to ensure that cross-border transactions on behalf of customers are in compliance with the regulations of another country. Nevertheless, banks should not set out to offer services or provide active assistance in transactions which they have good reason to suppose are associated with money laundering activities.

Cooperation with Law Enforcement Authorities

Banks should cooperate fully with national law enforcement authorities to the extent permitted by specific local regulations relating to customer confidentiality. Care should be taken to avoid providing support or assistance to customers seeking to deceive law enforcement agencies through the provision of altered, incomplete or misleading information. Where banks become aware of facts which lead to the reasonable presumption that money held on deposit derives from criminal activity or that transactions entered into are themselves criminal in purpose, appropriate measure, consistent with the law, should be taken; for example, to deny assistance, sever relations with the customer, and close or freeze accounts.

Adherence to the Statement

All banks should formally adopt policies consistent with the principles set out in this statement and should ensure that all members of their staff concerned, wherever located, are informed of the bank's policy in this regard. Attention should be given to staff training in matters covered by the statement. To promote adherence to these principles, banks should implement specific procedures for customer identification and for retaining internal records of transactions. Arrangements for internal audit may need to be extended in order to establish an effective means of testing for general compliance with the statement.

Basle, December 1988

REFERENCES

[1] 31 USC Sections 5311-5330 and 12 USC Sections 1818(s), 1829(b), and 1951-1959.

[2] The INCSR, including the lists of high-risk money laundering countries and jurisdictions, may be accessed by OCC employees through Community and Consumer Policy's BSA intranet web site or by internet at the U.S. State Department's web site (www.state.gov) under Bureau of International Narcotics and Law Enforcement Affairs.

[3] In September 1996, FinCEN published Advisory Vol. 1, Issue 6: "Mexican Bank Drafts and Third Party Checks."

[4] (1)Trading With the Enemy Act, 50 USC Sections 1-44. (2)International Emergency Economic Powers Act, 50 USC 1701-06. (3)Iraqi Sanctions Act, Pub. Law. 101-513, 104 Stat. 2047-55. (4)United Nations Participation Act, 22 USC 287c. (5)International Security and Development Cooperation Act codified at 22 USC 2349 aa-9. (6)The

Cuban Democracy Act, 22 USC Section 6001-10. (7)The Cuban Liberty and Democratic Solidarity Act, 22 USC 6021-91. (8)The Antiterrorism and Effective Death Penalty Act, (enacting 8 USC 219, 18 USC 2332d, and 18 USC 2339b.)

[5] 31 CFR 500 et. seq.

Laws

31 USC 5311 - 5330, Bank Secrecy Act
12 USC 1818(s), 1829(b)
12 USC 1951 - 1959

Regulations

12 CFR 21.11, Suspicious Activity Report
12 CFR 21.21, Bank Secrecy Act Compliance
31 CFR 103, Financial Record Keeping and Reporting of Currency and Foreign Transactions

OCC Issuances

Advisory Letter 98-4, "Safe Harbor When Filing SARs"
Advisory Letter 2000-3, "Common BSA Compliance Deficiencies"
OCC Bulletin 2000-19, "Suspicious Activity Report"
Banking Circular 266, "Large Funds Transfer for Money Laundering Purposes"
SMS Tech Bulletin 94-4, "Exam Narrative Report – BSA"

In: Bank Secrecy Act: Background, Statute and Interpretation ISBN: 978-1-60021-472-1
Editor: Lilian B. Klein, pp. 61-155

Chapter 2

BANK SECRECY ACT*

ABBREVIATIONS

AML	anti-money laundering
BSA	Bank Secrecy Act
CAMELS	Capital, Assets, Management, Earnings, Liquidity, and Sensitivity
CIP	Customer Identification Program
CMP	civil money penalty
CSBS	Conference of State Banking Supervisors
CTR	Currency Transaction Report
FDI Act	Federal Deposit Insurance Act
FDIC	Federal Deposit Insurance Corporation
FFIEC	Federal Financial Institutions Examination Council
FinCEN	Financial Crimes Enforcement Network
HIFCA	high-intensity financial crimes area
ICE	Immigration and Customs Enforcement
IG	Inspector General
IRS	Internal Revenue Service
MLCA	Money Laundering Control Act of 1986
MLSA	Money Laundering Suppression Act of 1994
MOU	memorandum of understanding
NCUA	National Credit Union Administration
OCC	Office of the Comptroller of the Currency
OFAC	Office of Foreign Assets Control
OTS	Office of Thrift Supervision
SAR	Suspicious Activity Report

* Excerpted from GAO Report 06-386 dated April 2006.

EXECUTIVE SUMMARY

Purpose

Since 1970, when Congress passed the Bank Secrecy Act (BSA), the United States has been expanding its framework for preventing, detecting, and prosecuting money laundering with new laws and amendments to the BSA.[1] The purpose of the BSA is to prevent financial institutions from being used as intermediaries for the transfer or deposit of money derived from criminal activity and to provide a paper trail for law enforcement agencies in their investigations of possible money laundering. Over the years, the BSA has evolved into an important tool to help a number of regulatory and law enforcement agencies detect money laundering, drug trafficking, terrorist financing, and other financial crimes. The most recent comprehensive enhancements to the BSA occurred in October 2001 under title III of the USA PATRIOT Act (PATRIOT Act).[2] This title is referred to as the International Money Laundering Abatement and Anti-Terrorist Financing Act of 2001. Title III made a number of amendments to the anti-money laundering (AML) provisions of the BSA intended to facilitate the prevention, detection, and prosecution of money laundering and terrorist financing. For example, by requiring every financial institution to establish an AML program, the PATRIOT Act extended AML program requirements to financial institutions that had not previously been subject to federal financial regulation.[3]

In recent years, noncompliance with BSA requirements among depository institutions has raised concerns in Congress about the ability of the federal banking regulators (regulators) to oversee BSA compliance at depository institutions and to ensure, through examinations, that these institutions have the controls in place to identify suspicious activity that could be related to money laundering or terrorist financing.[4] The accurate and timely recording of BSA examinations results is important for ensuring that timely and appropriate federal enforcement actions are taken against noncompliance. In 2004 and 2005, investigations of depository institution customers by various law enforcement agencies and congressional investigators resulted in several highly publicized cases and significant penalties for BSA noncompliance by the institutions. During hearings on BSA oversight and enforcement, congressional committees have focused on the timeliness of regulators' enforcement actions for BSA noncompliance.

The Senate Committee on Banking, Housing, and Urban Affairs asked GAO to undertake a review of the examination and enforcement programs for BSA compliance that the federal banking, thrift, and credit union regulators use at depository institutions in the United States. Specifically, GAO's objectives were to determine how (1) the regulators examined for BSA compliance at the depository institutions they supervise, (2) the regulators have updated examination procedures and trained examiners since the passage of the PATRIOT Act, (3) the regulators identify and track BSA violations to ensure timely corrective actions at the institutions they examine, and (4) enforcement actions are taken for violations of the BSA.

Background

The regulatory system for the BSA involves several different federal agencies. The Department of the Treasury's (Treasury) Financial Crimes Enforcement Network (FinCEN) is the administrator of the BSA and has the authority to enforce the act through the assessment of penalties, including civil money penalties (CMP).[5] In 1994, the Secretary of the Treasury delegated to the Director of FinCEN overall authority for enforcement of, and compliance with, the BSA and its implementing regulations. In the same year, the Secretary also delegated BSA examination authority to the regulators.[6] As part of a reorganization, in 2004, FinCEN created an Office of Compliance to oversee and work with regulators on BSA examination and compliance matters.

The regulators examine a variety of institutions for BSA compliance, including but not limited to national banks, state member banks, state nonmember banks, thrifts, and credit unions. The regulators review depository institutions for compliance with the BSA as part of their safety and soundness examinations or in targeted examinations focused on BSA compliance. Safety and soundness examinations are periodic on-site examinations conducted to assess an institution's financial condition; policies and procedures; and adherence to laws and regulations, such as the BSA. These examinations generally are conducted every 12 to 18 months at institutions, such as community banks, midsize banks, savings associations, and credit unions, on the basis of the regulator's rating of the institution's risk. At large complex banking organizations and large banks, these examinations are conducted on a continuous basis in cycles of 36 months. The Board of Governors of the Federal Reserve System (Federal Reserve), the Federal Deposit Insurance Corporation (FDIC), and the National Credit Union Administration (NCUA) share safety and soundness examination responsibility with state banking departments for state-chartered institutions.[7]

The regulators take a risk-focused approach to safety and soundness examinations, including reviews for BSA compliance. That is, the examination is targeted to the institution's key areas of risk or specific problems. In BSA examinations, the risk-focused approach enables regulators to apply the appropriate scrutiny and devote examination resources to business lines or areas within depository institutions that pose the greatest risk for BSA noncompliance, such as wire transfers, private banking, international correspondent banking, large cash transactions, and other high-risk areas.

Other departments are involved in BSA enforcement. The Department of Justice (Justice) pursues charges against depository institutions for criminal noncompliance with the BSA. The Department of Homeland Security's Bureau of Immigration and Customs Enforcement and the Internal Revenue Service's Criminal Investigation division also investigate cases involving money laundering and terrorist financing activities.

Results in Brief

Before 2005, each regulator used separately developed, but similar, examination procedures to assess compliance with BSA program requirements; however, the application of some examination procedures could vary widely. Examiners reviewed institutions for these requirements as part of safety and soundness examinations, using procedures that generally were similar across all five regulators and that included steps related to planning and scoping; the creation of risk profiles; and supervisory consultation, reporting, and corrective actions, when appropriate. While the regulators specified certain procedures, the overall risk-focused approach they used for BSA examinations required examiners to exercise professional judgment in determining the extent to which certain procedures would be conducted.

According to examiners, differences in product risks, the varying sizes and complexity of the institutions, and other factors could affect how examiners made decisions, such as assessing the scope of the examination and determining the extent of transaction testing conducted. However, under pre-2005 BSA-related examination guidance, the application and documentation of certain procedures could vary widely. For example, GAO's review of the regulators' manuals and guidance for BSA examinations and of a sample of examinations conducted over a 4 1/2-year period found fewer requirements for and less documentation of transaction testing in examinations of smaller institutions. GAO's review indicated more documentation of examination planning procedures for larger institutions. As recently as 2004, about one-third of state banking departments reported that they were not examining depository institutions for BSA compliance; however, as of November 2005, 45 state banking departments reported examining for BSA compliance. In addition, many state banking departments increased their coordination with the regulators and FinCEN, and, as of March 2006, 36 state banking departments had signed memorandums of understanding (MOU) with FinCEN.

During the course of GAO's review, the regulators jointly developed and, in June 2005, issued an interagency BSA examination procedures manual and subsequently conducted nationwide training on the new procedures for examiners and others, in an effort to establish more consistency in examination procedures and application. The new procedures retain the risk-focused approach of the prior procedures, but recognize that, depending on the specific characteristics of the product, service, or customer, the risks vary from one institution to another. The manual also states that as new products or services are introduced, institution management's evaluation of money laundering and terrorist-financing risks should evolve. Thus, the manual requires examiners to apply a higher level of scrutiny to lines of business that carry a higher risk for potential money laundering or noncompliance with the BSA. However, the new procedures also link institutions' risk assessments to risk profiles, introduce more uniformity into the assessment of the BSA independent audit function, and require transaction testing in all examinations regardless of the institution's risk profile. As a result, the new procedures provide a uniform framework that could result in greater consistency in BSA examinations across the regulators. In recent years, regulators also have intensified their focus on BSA-related skills and examiner training relating to BSA compliance. For example, the regulators regularly train examiners on examination procedures and provide them with up-to-date guidance on changes or new requirements, such as those stemming from the PATRIOT Act or the interagency procedures. Following the issuance of the interagency procedures, the regulators held a series of training sessions and other events for federal and state examiners. Additionally, some regulators have increased the number of examiners with BSA specialization, many of whom serve as resources for other examiners in the field.

Recent improvements to one of the primary mechanisms used to monitor BSA examinations allowed regulators to better record and track BSA-related information. However, differences in the terminology that regulators use to classify compliance problems may result in inconsistencies. Although the regulators were recording and tracking BSA-related examination and violation information from 2000 to 2004, recent system improvements have allowed some regulators to better track and cite BSA violations than in the past. For example, systems upgrades currently allow FDIC to distinguish violations under specific categories, rather than one general category. Also, regulator data showed that the number of BSA-related violations generally increased from 2000 to 2004. The systems upgrades also allowed regulators to more readily produce information for other users, such as FinCEN. Under an MOU into which the regulators and FinCEN entered in September 2004, the regulators now share with FinCEN more specific data on BSA examinations and violations data. For example, the regulators provide FinCEN with quarterly reports on the number of examinations conducted and the number and type of violations cited. Furthermore, FinCEN has begun to provide the regulators with analytical reports that help identify compliance problems and trends across regulators and to disseminate information about AML issues. FinCEN plans to provide the regulators with additional reports, such as those on AML issues across industries, in the future. All of the regulators have begun to analyze the violation data internally for their own purposes, but FinCEN and the regulators have not yet discussed whether these data indicate a need for additional guidance to examiners. Despite their enhanced systems and reporting, GAO found differences in the regulators' guidance and the terminology they used to classify BSA problems—with guidance varying in scope and many key terms undefined. In addition, in developing the MOU, FinCEN and the regulators acknowledged that the regulators do not use the same terminology to describe BSA noncompliance. GAO's review of 138 examinations found a variety of terms used to describe BSA noncompliance, and examiners appeared to use different terms for apparently similar problems. For example, in addition to the term "violation," examiners used the terms "apparent violation," "weakness," "deficiency," and "exception" when referring to BSA noncompliance. To avoid any uncertainty over what information was included, the wording in the MOU called for banking regulators to notify FinCEN of "significant BSA violations or deficiencies."

According to regulatory officials, most cases of BSA/AML noncompliance are corrected within the examination framework through supervisory actions, such as bringing the problem to the attention of institution management and obtaining a commitment to take corrective action, or through informal actions, such as letters that document such commitments. Both the regulators and FinCEN can undertake formal enforcement actions, which range from public written agreements with the institution to CMPs. According to the regulators, formal enforcement actions are used to address cases involving pervasive, repeated noncompliance; failure to respond to supervisory warnings; and other factors. For example, from 2000 to 2005, FinCEN assessed CMPs in 11 cases. Starting in 2004, more of these CMPs were assessed in conjunction with the relevant regulator, and the penalties were significantly higher. However, only FinCEN has delegated authority under the BSA to assess CMPs; the regulators do so under separate authorities. In 1994, the Secretary of the Treasury was directed by statute to delegate the authority to assess CMPs under the BSA to the regulators, with such limitations as the Secretary deemed necessary. However, according to FinCEN officials, this was not done, partly because of challenges involved in crafting a delegation that would result in consistent and accountable BSA enforcement. Furthermore, FinCEN officials said that these challenges increased substantially with the addition of new types of institutions subject to BSA compliance requirements under the PATRIOT Act. FinCEN officials said that because of the increased cooperation on BSA compliance with the regulators in recent years, they were not aware that the lack of delegated authority had produced any significant enforcement ramifications. For example, they pointed out that FinCEN now is involved earlier in the regulators' enforcement process and engages in joint actions with the regulators with more frequency than in the years preceding adoption of the MOU. Furthermore, FinCEN officials said they had no plans to pursue this delegation.

While FinCEN and the regulators can take a variety of actions against depository institutions, under federal statute, Justice takes action against depository institutions, for money laundering offenses and certain BSA offenses. From 2002 to 2005, Justice pursued criminal charges against six depository institutions for noncompliance with the BSA. In general, these cases were identified through criminal investigations of the institutions' customers. The criminal cases have raised concerns in the banking industry that depository institutions would be targeted for criminal investigation. However, Justice officials emphasized that willful and pervasive violations by the institutions were important factors in these cases. Some cases resulted in guilty pleas and others resulted in deferred prosecution agreements, contingent on the depository institutions' cooperation and implementation of corrective actions. In each case, the depository institution paid a monetary penalty.

Principal Findings

Regulators Used Similar Procedures for BSA Examinations Pre-2005, but Their Application Could Vary Widely

Before 2005, the regulators used separate examination guidance to review BSA compliance at depository institutions, although the examination procedures generally were similar. However, the ways in which procedures were applied could vary, as could their documentation. In recent years, more state banking departments—which generally use federal BSA examination procedures—have conducted BSA examinations and increased their coordination with the regulators and FinCEN.

Examiners Took Similar Steps to Prepare for, Determine the Scope of, and Report on BSA Examinations

Before 2005, the regulators used separate examination guidance to review BSA compliance at depository institutions, although the examination procedures generally were similar. Examination activities included planning and scoping; creation of risk profiles; and supervisory consultation, reporting, and corrective actions. In addition to undertaking these procedures, examiners also have exercised professional judgment in determining the manner or extent to which certain procedures were conducted. In general, the procedures that examiners have used (and continue to use) to prepare for and report on examinations were similar—planning and scoping activities were to result in the creation of a risk profile for the institution to be examined. Examiners were then to conduct risk-assessment procedures to evaluate an institution's potential for BSA noncompliance, money laundering, or terrorist financing. To perform the risk assessments, examiners were to gather and analyze information from the institutions or other sources about operational procedures or activities that might expose the institution to risk in these areas. Examiners also were to draw on similar sources of information to create the risk profiles, including the institution's internal assessments and information from other federal agencies. In addition, examiners were to assess the institution's internal controls and independent audit function, as well as the institution's BSA/AML program, officer, and training.

Examiners were to use an institution's risk profile to determine the nature and extent of procedures to be performed during the examination. If the institution's risk profile was low, examiners generally were to conduct what are variously referred to as basic, core, or limited examination procedures. In addition to the basic procedures previously mentioned, examiners could perform transaction testing, depending on the regulator's examination requirements. If an institution's risk profile was high or examiners identified BSA compliance problems (e.g., with the institution's BSA/AML policies, procedures, programs, or internal controls), examiners generally were to conduct expanded procedures in high-risk areas or the areas of identified deficiencies.

Finally, in concluding the examinations, examiners were to consult with their supervisors on examinations findings, include recommendations in examination reports, and consult with institutions' management about any corrective actions. Subsequently, examiners were to prepare the report of examination—detailing the scope, compliance risk, findings, recommended corrective actions, and management's commitment to take corrective action. The report of examination is also to indicate any corrective actions completed by management before the end of the examination. Examiners were to perform follow-up activities between examinations, or at the next scheduled examination, to verify compliance with corrective actions.

Under pre-2005 guidance, the regulators did not consistently require or document transaction testing. The regulators required transaction testing in examinations of larger institutions with higher asset levels, but not always at smaller institutions. From each regulator, GAO reviewed about 30 examinations that were conducted between January 2000 and June 2004. This review, when coupled with GAO's review of regulator guidance and examination manuals, showed instances where documentation of examination procedures varied widely and regulators did not consistently require or document transaction testing. Our examination review found less documentation of transaction testing in examinations at smaller institutions with lower assets—such as the community banks and savings associations—than at larger institutions with higher assets. The Office of Thrift Supervision (OTS), FDIC, and NCUA examination guidance permitted examiners to exercise their professional judgment in determining whether to perform transaction testing. The Office of the Comptroller of the Currency (OCC) required transaction testing for large banks, and the Federal Reserve required that some transaction testing be performed in all examinations.

Since 2004, State Banking Departments Have Become More Involved in BSA Compliance

As recently as 2004, about one-third of state banking departments reported not examining for BSA compliance; however, state banking departments since have taken a more active role in conducting these reviews. In some states, federal examiners independently reviewed institutions or reviewed institutions jointly with examiners from state banking departments. According to a Federal Reserve official, the frequency of these examinations and the decision of whether to perform the review jointly depended on the institution's risk level. In addition, during the course of GAO's work and in response to an FDIC Inspector General recommendation, FDIC announced in 2004 that its examiners would conduct reviews for BSA compliance during examinations of FDIC-supervised institutions led by state banking departments that do not cover BSA compliance. The number of state banking departments that conduct these reviews has increased in recent years. According to officials from some state banking departments, because of the increased attention to AML and terrorist-financing issues following September 11, 2001, some state banking departments began examining for BSA compliance or expanded the scope of existing reviews. Results of a Conference of State Bank Supervisors query of its members indicated that, as of November 2005, 45 state banking departments were reviewing for BSA compliance.[8] In general, whether recently examining for BSA compliance or continuing well-established procedures, state examiners used the regulators' examination procedures to examine for BSA compliance.

Beginning in 2004, state banking departments, the regulators, and FinCEN increased coordination on BSA-related examination and information-sharing activities. In addition, the regulators also began training state examiners on reviewing for BSA compliance. As of March 2006, 36 state banking departments had signed MOUs with FinCEN aimed at further improving coordination of BSA/AML activities. According to FinCEN, these agreements provide the framework for enhanced collaboration and information sharing between federal and state agencies that will allow FinCEN to better administer the BSA, while simultaneously assisting state agencies to better fulfill their roles as financial institution departments. In March 2006, FinCEN was receiving data for the fourth quarter of 2005 from the states.

Regulators Have Promoted Consistency in Examinations in Recent Years by Adopting Interagency Procedures and Expanding Training

During the course of GAO's work, the regulators took a number of steps to promote consistency of BSA examinations, including issuing new interagency procedures and revising and expanding examiner training. To disseminate new information and increase knowledge of the BSA and related issues, the regulators have increased training on the BSA and the PATRIOT Act and have coordinated efforts to educate staff on the interagency procedures. Some regulators also have focused on developing more BSA/AML specialist examiners.

New Interagency Procedures Create a Framework for Consistent BSA Examination Processes

In June 2005, the regulators, in collaboration with FinCEN, issued a new BSA/AML examination manual through the Federal Financial Institutions Examination Council (FFIEC).[9] In the regulators' view, the FFIEC *Bank Secrecy Act Anti-Money Laundering Examination Manual (*FFIEC *Examination Manual)* is the product of best practices among the regulators and aims to promote procedural consistency in the conduct of BSA examinations at all depository institutions. In contrast to previous guidance, the FFIEC *Examination Manual* organizes guidance on risk assessment procedures primarily in one place—that is, in the core overview scoping and planning section. The manual also comprehensively describes risk assessments for BSA examinations, taking examiners from the planning stages to using conclusions to develop risk profiles. The manual recognizes that, depending on the specific characteristics of the product, service, or customer, the risks are not always the same. The manual also states that as new products or services are introduced, the institution's management's evaluation of money laundering and terrorist-financing risks should evolve. The FFIEC core examination procedures provide uniform guidance for examiners to follow when validating the independent audit as part of the planning and scoping of the BSA examination. The expanded sections of the manual provide guidance on specific lines of business or products that may present unique challenges and exposures for which institutions should institute the appropriate policies, procedures, and processes.

Furthermore, the FFIEC *Examination Manual* requires transaction testing at each examination, regardless of the institution's BSA risk level, and emphasizes the importance of transaction testing for making conclusions about the integrity of the institution's overall controls and risk management processes. The manual emphasizes the importance of transaction testing for making conclusions about the integrity of the institution's overall controls and risk management processes, and further requires that transaction testing be conducted to evaluate the adequacy of the institution's compliance with regulatory requirements and the effectiveness of its policies, procedures, processes, and suspicious activity monitoring systems. According to the manual, examiners perform transaction testing to evaluate the adequacy of an institution's compliance with regulatory requirements or to determine whether its policies, procedures, processes, and suspicious activity monitoring systems are effective.

Regulators Have Increased Their Focus on BSA-Related Skills and Training

Although each regulator provides BSA/AML training to its examiners, each approaches training differently. OTS and NCUA require all new staff to attend a basic AML training course. OTS and NCUA used regional conferences to train examiners on BSA issues. The Federal Reserve requires all staff seeking to obtain an examiner commission to successfully complete a BSA/AML proficiency test.[10] FDIC requires all examination staff to obtain BSA/AML training through classroom or Web-based training. OCC offers four different training schools as well as specialized BSA/AML training on a voluntary basis to certain staff. In addition to their own training, regulators also used interagency or outside venues to train staff. Regulators also updated their AML training to cover all of the relevant provisions of the PATRIOT Act.

After the issuance of the new procedures on June 30, 2005, FFIEC coordinated a far-reaching effort to train examiners and the industry on the new procedures, holding a series of training events across the country.

State banking departments also participated in training on the FFIEC *Examination Manual.*

Although safety and soundness and compliance examiners primarily perform BSA/AML examinations, some regulators use examiners with specialized skills to provide training, serve as a resource to other examiners, or assist on complex examinations. All of the regulators offer career paths and options for becoming a BSA subject matter expert.[11] More recently, some regulators have planned to train or increase substantially the number of subject matter experts they have to help meet PATRIOT Act requirements and address the increasing complexity of BSA examinations.

Regulators Improved Tracking of BSA Examination and Violations Data, but Differences in Terminology Could Result in Inconsistencies

The regulators use various internal control mechanisms to monitor BSA examinations, and recent improvements in their automated examination and enforcement data systems have enabled them to better track and report BSA information. The regulators are able to more readily share BSA-related information, a particularly important ability in light of the MOU regulators signed with FinCEN in September 2004. However, the regulators differ on how they classify and define some BSA compliance problems.

Changes to Regulators' Data Systems Have Enabled Them to Better Track BSA Data

Regulators use automated data systems to store and track examination data and information on supervisory and enforcement actions. Since 2000, all of the regulators have changed or upgraded their data systems to improve their recording and monitoring capabilities. To varying degrees, previous iterations of these data systems limited regulators' ability to monitor and report BSA-related examination results in a comprehensive and timely manner. For example, before 2001, NCUA manually collected information on BSA-related violations; however, in 2001, NCUA began to redesign its information technology system. NCUA's system now allows it to track more BSA data, including violations and any corrective actions institutions had implemented. Similarly, until the late 1990s, OTS generally tracked BSA data manually, but currently OTS has an Internet-based system that comprehensively tracks BSA examination results. FDIC upgraded its systems to better track violations and the status of corrective actions. OCC has separate systems to track BSA results for large banks and midsize and community banks. OCC's improvements to its system for data on large banks include the increased ability to search the full text of examinations, including BSA reviews. The Federal Reserve for some years has had national supervisory data systems that maintain both data and electronic copies of examination and enforcement documents. These systems were, and continue to be, accessible to all appropriate supervisory staff across the Federal Reserve System. Until recently, the national data system (national examiner database) did not separately track BSA/AML violation data. In 2003, the Federal Reserve began to enhance its national examiner database to capture BSA/AML violations or other BSA examination-related data.

GAO's review of the regulators' data indicated that the number of BSA-related violations generally increased in recent years. Among the frequently cited violations in 2003 and 2004 were violations issued in connection with currency transaction reporting requirements. Furthermore, some regulators cited more BSA violations with greater specificity in later years. For example, FDIC officials indicated that FDIC's current data system, which was implemented in 2003, now specifies subsections of BSA-related regulations that institutions have violated.

In September 2004, the regulators and FinCEN entered into an MOU under which the regulators provide FinCEN with quarterly reports on the number of BSA-related examinations they have conducted, the number and types of BSA violations they cited, and the institutions they cited for repeat violations. The MOU requires FinCEN, in turn, to provide the regulators with reports and analyses of the data submitted by the regulators. As of February 2006, the regulators had provided FinCEN with five quarters of data and two annual reports.[12] FinCEN provided the regulators with aggregated data, which identified certain compliance issues that the regulators could work to address with the institutions they supervise. FinCEN's longer term goal is to provide BSA compliance analyses across the financial services sector. All of the regulators have begun to analyze for their own purposes the BSA compliance data they receive from FinCEN. FinCEN and the regulators have not yet discussed as a group the implications of the violation data, and whether there was a need for additional guidance to examiners so that they could address problem areas that the regulators have been identifying.

Differences Remain in Regulators' Guidance and Terminology for Classification of BSA Noncompliance

Although the regulators and FinCEN increasingly have been enhancing and coordinating information sharing and reporting, differences in how the regulators classify BSA compliance problems remain. For example, regulators differ in the guidance they provide examiners for determining what constitutes a violation, with one regulator not providing any written guidance and others differing in the degree of guidance provided. Furthermore, the regulators' instructions on BSA enforcement, which also provide guidance for interpreting or classifying BSA problems, do not clearly define the terms—intended as criteria for determining the seriousness or scope of a compliance problem—on which those classifications would be based. When GAO reviewed the regulators' BSA examinations, it generally found that the distinction between violations and deficiencies appeared to be that violations represented some action or inaction prohibited by the BSA and implementing regulations, and deficiencies did not. Additionally, there appears to be no clear consensus among examiners regarding how to distinguish between BSA deficiencies and violations.

FinCEN officials said that, in drafting the terms of the MOU, the issue of different terminology was discussed, and that FinCEN and the regulators agreed not to impose any requirements for standardized terminology in the MOU itself. Instead, the MOU requires the regulators to provide FinCEN with information on instances of "significant" noncompliance, regardless of whether the regulator classified it as a violation or a deficiency—that is, all problems for which the regulator is taking supervisory action are to be reported to FinCEN. FinCEN officials said they had to work with the regulators to determine the appropriate information to be provided.

In GAO's review of the regulators' examinations, examiners appeared to have classified apparently similar BSA problems differently. In some cases, examiners cited institutions with "deficiencies," and, in other cases, they cited institutions with "violations." As a result, examiner judgment likely plays a greater role in classifying BSA problems. In turn, this could increase the potential for inconsistencies in classifying compliance problems and subsequent citations. However, regulators emphasized that other factors, such as an institution's risk profile or the diversity of its operations and products, also help explain the differences in the way BSA compliance problems were cited and classified.

Regulators and FinCEN Increased Coordination on BSA Enforcement, and Criminal Cases against Depository Institutions Were Limited

Although the regulators can use a variety of tools to address BSA-related compliance problems, according to the regulators, most BSA-related problems are resolved during the course of an examination. FinCEN also uses a range of enforcement tools to address BSA noncompliance problems, and FinCEN alone can assess CMPs under the BSA. FinCEN and the regulators have increased coordination on enforcement since their September 2004 MOU. While FinCEN and the regulators pursue a variety of enforcement actions for BSA compliance problems, Justice has pursued a limited number of criminal cases against depository institutions for BSA violations.

Most BSA Noncompliance Is Addressed during Examinations, but Regulators Recently Increased Coordination on Formal Enforcement Actions

Although regulators use a broad range of actions to address BSA compliance, according to the regulators, most problems in BSA-related compliance are corrected within the examination framework through supervisory actions. GAO's review of 138 examinations—which were conducted between January 1, 2000, and June 30, 2004, and contained BSA violations—also indicated that the regulators most frequently addressed BSA compliance problems through supervisory actions. The regulators largely obtained oral commitments to correct identified problems from an institution during meetings with its management or boards of directors. Representatives of some regulators noted that if supervisory actions proved insufficient or problems required stronger action, the regulators generally would use informal enforcement actions, such as commitment letters, reflecting specific commitments to take corrective actions in response to problems or concerns. Informal enforcement actions are exercises of the regulators' authority to supervise financial institutions and generally are used to address BSA noncompliance that is limited in scope and technical in nature. To address significant BSA/AML program and BSA violations, the regulators generally use formal enforcement actions. Formal enforcement actions are written documents that are disclosed to the public and are generally more severe than supervisory and informal actions and generally are enforceable through the assessment of CMPs and through the federal court system.

The regulators are not authorized under the BSA to take formal enforcement actions for violations—that delegated authority rests solely with FinCEN. Title 12 of the *United States Code* authorizes the regulators to take formal enforcement action if they determine that a depository institution is engaging in unsafe or unsound practices or has violated any applicable law or regulation. The regulators have interpreted this authority to include violations of the BSA and its implementing regulations when taking formal enforcement actions aimed at addressing violations of BSA/AML program requirements. FinCEN, the administrator of the BSA, takes enforcement action against BSA compliance problems at financial institutions, including, but not limited to, depository institutions. Unlike the regulators, FinCEN can take such action because it is specifically authorized to do so in the BSA and its implementing regulations. According to officials at FinCEN and the regulators, coordination among these agencies on enforcement issues has improved dramatically in recent years.

Justice Has Pursued a Limited Number of Cases against Depository Institutions for BSA Noncompliance

From 2002 to 2005, Justice, either through its Criminal Division or its U.S. Attorneys' Offices, has pursued investigations of six depository institutions for criminal violation of the BSA.[13] The disposition of the criminal cases has varied, but each case included monetary penalties. Justice officials said that the number of cases in which the depository institution was the criminal BSA offender was limited, and that the department had pursued significantly more cases against individuals for BSA offenses. According to a senior Justice official, egregious failures to perform a minimal level of due diligence over a number of years triggered the cases against the depository institutions. Additionally, Justice officials and investigators said that most investigations of depository institutions' criminal violations of the BSA generally originated during law enforcement investigations of the institutions' customers. In July 2005, Justice amended the *U.S. Attorney's Manual* to direct prosecutors to formalize coordination on cases against financial institutions for money laundering and certain BSA offenses.

Recommendations for Executive Action

This report makes three recommendations to build on the current level of coordination, continue to improve BSA administration, and ensure that emerging compliance risks are addressed. GAO recommends that the Director of FinCEN and the Comptroller of the Currency, the Chairman of the Federal Reserve, the Chairman of FDIC, the Director of OTS, and the Chairman of NCUA, (1) work together to make sure emerging risks in money laundering and terrorist financing are effectively communicated to examiners and the industry through updates of the interagency examination manual and other guidance, as appropriate; (2) periodically meet to review BSA violation data to determine if they indicate a need for additional guidance; and (3) jointly assess the feasibility of developing a uniform classification system for BSA compliance problems.

Agency Comments and GAO Evaluation

GAO provided a draft of this report for review and comment to the Departments of Homeland Security, Justice, and the Treasury; the Board of Governors of the Federal Reserve System; the Federal Deposit Insurance Corporation; the National Credit Union Administration; the Office of the Comptroller of the Currency; and the Office of Thrift Supervision. The Department of Homeland Security, Justice, and the regulators provided technical comments, which were incorporated into this report where appropriate.

FinCEN and the regulators provided written comments on the draft report in a joint letter, which is reprinted in appendix II. In their letter, they said they support GAO's recommendations and are committed to ongoing interagency coordination to address them through the formal processes they have in place, particularly the FFIEC BSA/AML Working Group. They also said that they are committed to their role in ensuring that depository institutions are in compliance with BSA/AML requirements, and that they will continue to devote significant resources to make certain institutions correct deficiencies in their BSA/AML programs as promptly as possible.

Justice also provided written comments, which are reprinted in appendix III. In its letter, Justice said that the draft report provided an instructive perspective where it examined the evolution of the relationship between FinCEN, the regulators, and the banks, but that the draft did not provide the same perspective when examining how the examination process meets the needs of law enforcement as the end users of the information. GAO's objectives were to review how the regulators examine for BSA compliance, track and resolve violations, and take enforcement actions. While a review of the reports that depository institutions produce under the BSA that law enforcement uses in its investigations would be instructive, it was outside of the scope of this review. Justice also said that, as a direct result of the success and efforts by the regulated industry, drug traffickers have been forced to seek alternate methods and means of using those institutions to launder their illicit proceeds. Justice further commented that banking regulator practices and the examination process have historically focused more on the placement of those funds into the financial system, and that current investigative efforts suggest that it may prove beneficial to adapt and focus on the layering of those proceeds. To this end, Justice suggested a need for greater outreach and collaboration between law enforcement and regulators familiar with evolving trends. Finally, Justice said that the draft report reflected the efforts made with the revisions to the examination manual and commented that these are positive developments that should bring continuity to examination practice, which will be welcomed by the industry.

1. Introduction

Since the enactment of the Bank Secrecy Act (BSA) in 1970, the U.S. government's framework for preventing, detecting, and prosecuting money laundering has evolved through amendments to the BSA and the enactment of additional related legislation.[1] The most recent comprehensive amendments to the BSA were made through the Uniting and Strengthening America by Providing Appropriate Tools Required to Intercept and Obstruct Terrorism Act (PATRIOT Act) of 2001.[2] Key legislation has supplemented or amended the BSA, expanding its reporting, record-keeping, and enforcement provisions. Federal financial regulators and other federal agencies work within this framework to carry out BSA requirements. The regulators have responsibility for examining depository institutions for compliance with BSA requirements, while overall responsibility for BSA administration rests with the Department of the Treasury (Treasury), through the Financial Crimes Enforcement Network (FinCEN).[3] The regulators conduct reviews of BSA compliance as part of their regular examination process. They take a risk-focused approach targeted to the institution's key areas of risk or specific problems.

Successive Legislation Has Expanded the Responsibility to Combat Money Laundering

The federal government's framework for preventing, detecting, and prosecuting money laundering has been expanded through additional legislation since its inception in 1970 with the BSA.[4] The BSA required, for the first time, that financial institutions maintain records and reports that financial regulators and law enforcement agencies have determined have a high degree of usefulness in criminal, tax, and regulatory matters. The BSA authorizes the Secretary of the Treasury to issue regulations on the reporting of certain currency transactions. The BSA has the following three main objectives: create an investigative audit trail through regulatory reporting standards; impose civil and criminal penalties for noncompliance; and improve the detection of criminal, tax, and regulatory violations.

The reporting system initially implemented under the BSA was by itself an insufficient response to combat underlying money laundering activity because, before 1986, the BSA contained sanctions for failing to file reports or for doing so untruthfully, but it did not contain sanctions for money laundering. The Money Laundering Control Act of 1986

(MLCA) made money laundering a criminal offense, separate from any BSA reporting violations.[5] The MLCA created criminal liability for individuals or entities that conduct monetary transactions knowing that the proceeds involved were obtained from unlawful activity, and the act made it a criminal offense to knowingly structure transactions to avoid BSA reporting. Penalties under the MLCA include imprisonment, fines, and forfeiture. The MCLA also directed each regulator to prescribe regulations requiring insured depository institutions to establish and maintain procedures reasonably designed to ensure and monitor compliance with the reporting requirements of the BSA. To further assist the effectiveness of the BSA, pursuant to this requirement, the regulators promulgated regulations requiring insured depository institutions to establish and maintain procedures designed to ensure compliance with the requirements of the BSA—a BSA and Anti-Money Laundering (AML) program (BSA/AML program).[6]

The Annunzio-Wylie Anti-Money Laundering Act of 1992 (Annunzio-Wylie) amended the BSA in a number of ways.[7] It authorized Treasury to require financial institutions to report any suspicious transaction relevant to a possible violation of a law. It also authorized Treasury to require financial institutions to carry out AML programs and promulgate record-keeping rules relating to funds transfer transactions. Annunzio-Wylie also made the operation of an illegal money-transmitting business a crime.

The Money Laundering Suppression Act of 1994 (MLSA) sought to improve the BSA in at least two notable ways.[8] First, to ensure that bank examiners use the most effective means through the examination process to identify and report money laundering, the MLSA directed the regulators, in consultation with the Secretary of the Treasury and the appropriate law enforcement agencies, to enhance the regulators' training and examination procedures to improve their identification of money laundering schemes. To assist the regulators in this process, the MLSA also required each appropriate law enforcement agency to regularly share information with the regulators regarding emerging money laundering schemes. Second, the MLSA sought to improve the timeliness with which BSA civil penalty cases were processed. Before the enactment of the MLSA, Treasury's Office of Financial Enforcement processed BSA civil penalty cases using a cumbersome process that often prevented the office from pursuing cases because the statute of limitations had expired. Accordingly, the MLSA amended the BSA to direct the Secretary to delegate any authority to assess civil money penalties (CMP) on depository institutions to the appropriate regulators, which already had penalty authority and experience under other banking laws.

As authorized by Annunzio-Wylie, in 1996, FinCEN issued a rule requiring banks and other depository institutions to report, using a Suspicious Activity Report (SAR) form, certain suspicious transactions involving possible violation of law or regulation, including money laundering. During the same year, the regulators issued regulations requiring all depository institutions to report suspected money laundering, as well as other suspicious activities, using the SAR form. The regulators also placed SAR requirements on the subsidiaries, including broker-dealer firms, of the depository institutions and their holding companies under their jurisdiction.

In the wake of the September 11, 2001, terrorist attacks, Congress enacted the PATRIOT Act on October 26, 2001, prompted, in part, by an enhance awareness that combating terrorist financing as part of the U.S. government's overall AML efforts was important because terrorist financing and money laundering both involve similar techniques. Title III of the PATRIOT Act, among other things, expanded Treasury's authority to regulate the activities of U.S. financial institutions; required the promulgation of regulations; imposed additional due diligence requirements; established new customer identification requirements; and required financial institutions to maintain AML programs. In addition, title III defined new money laundering crimes and increased penalties for previously established crimes.

Regulators and Other Federal Agencies Carry Out BSA Requirements

Implementation of the BSA's regulatory and enforcement structure involves many different federal agencies. The Secretary of the Treasury delegated overall authority for enforcement of, and compliance with, the BSA and its implementing regulations to the Director of FinCEN. In addition, FinCEN has the authority to issue regulations; collects, analyzes, and maintains the reports and information filed by financial institutions under the BSA; makes those reports available to law enforcement and regulators; and ensures financial institution compliance through enforcement actions aimed at applying the regulations in a consistent manner across the financial services industry. FinCEN also plays a role in analyzing BSA information to support law enforcement.

Although FinCEN is responsible for ensuring compliance with BSA regulations, FinCEN does not examine financial institutions, including depository institutions, for compliance. Rather, in 1994, the Secretary of the Treasury delegated BSA examination authority to the regulators. The five regulators that oversee financial institutions and examine them for compliance with the BSA and implementing regulations are the Board of Governors of the Federal Reserve System (Federal Reserve), the Office of the Comptroller of the Currency (OCC), the Office of Thrift Supervision (OTS), the Federal Deposit Insurance Corporation (FDIC), and the National Credit Union Administration (NCUA). The specific regulatory configuration depends on the type of charter the depository institution chooses. Banks are regulated at the federal level alone if they are chartered by a federal regulator, such as OCC or OTS, or by federal and state banking departments if they are state-chartered institutions. State banking departments supervise commercial and savings banks with state bank charters, while the Federal Reserve or FDIC serve as the primary federal regulator for these institutions. OTS is the supervisor for state-chartered savings associations.

In August 2004, FinCEN created an Office of Compliance to oversee and work with the federal financial regulators on BSA examination and compliance matters. FinCEN signed a memorandum of understanding (MOU) with the banking regulators in September 2004 that laid out procedures for the exchange of certain BSA information. The MOU requires that the regulators provide information on examination policies and procedures and on significant BSA violations or deficiencies that have occurred at the financial institutions they supervise, including relevant portions of examination reports and information on follow-up and resolution. The MOU also requires FinCEN to provide information to the regulators, including information on FinCEN enforcement actions and analytical products that will identify various patterns and trends in BSA compliance.

Furthermore, agencies under the Departments of the Treasury, Justice, and Homeland Security are to coordinate with each other and with federal financial regulators in combating money laundering and terrorist financing. In addition to FinCEN, the Internal Revenue Service (IRS), through its Criminal Investigation division, uses BSA information and investigates possible cases of money laundering. Justice components involved in efforts to combat money laundering and terrorist financing include the Criminal Division's Asset Forfeiture and Money Laundering Section and Counterterrorism Section; the Federal Bureau of Investigation; the Bureau of Alcohol, Tobacco, Firearms, and Explosives; the Drug Enforcement Administration; the Executive Office for U.S. Attorneys; and U.S. Attorneys' Offices. The Department of Homeland Security's Bureau of Immigration and Customs Enforcement (ICE) also investigates cases involving money laundering and terrorist-financing activities.

Regulators Generally Address BSA Issues through Safety and Soundness or Targeted Examinations

The regulators conduct reviews of BSA compliance as part of their safety and soundness examinations or as targeted examinations focused on BSA compliance.[9] Safety and soundness examinations are periodic on-site examinations conducted to assess an institution's financial condition; policies and procedures; and adherence to laws and regulations, such as the BSA. Generally, these examinations are performed every 12 to 18 months for institutions, including community banks, midsize banks, savings associations, and credit unions, among others, based on the institutions' risk.

More specifically, the frequency of safety and soundness examinations is dependent on the CAMELS rating assigned by the regulator to the institutions.[10] For example, if institutions are rated low risk, a rating of "1" or "2," examinations would be performed every 18 months. If rated as a higher risk, institutions would be examined at least annually. Examination frequency can also be affected by alternate-year examination program arrangements between the regulators and state banking departments.[11] At large complex banking organizations and large banks, some regulators conduct on-site targeted examinations on a continuous basis in cycles of 36 months.

Additionally, the regulators perform targeted (BSA/AML-focused) examinations of banks. The regulators may perform targeted examinations on an "as-needed" basis, because of an unforeseen risk requiring more immediate attention, or to determine whether the institution had taken corrective actions to address problems identified during regular examinations.

The regulators take a risk-focused approach to BSA examinations, which are targeted to the institution's key areas of risk or specific problems. This approach recognizes that attempts to launder money, finance terrorism, or conduct other illegal activities through a bank can come from many different sources, and certain products, services, customers, and geographic locations may be more vulnerable or have been historically abused by money launderers and criminals. In BSA examinations, the risk-focused approach enables regulators to apply the appropriate scrutiny and devote examination resources to business lines or areas within depository institutions that pose the greatest risk for BSA noncompliance, such as funds transfers, private banking, international correspondent banking, and large cash transactions. According to some regulators, the risk-focused approach promotes a more efficient and effective manner of conducting BSA examinations and provides other benefits. In addition to focusing on the major areas of risk, this approach enables examiners to identify risks proactively, determine how well risks are managed over time, and streamline documentation to support areas of risk. It also reduces the regulatory burden on institutions by limiting examinations of institutions to specific areas of risk and allows regulators to schedule examinations according to the institutions' level of risk, thereby resulting in less frequent examinations for lower risk institutions. The risk-focused approach further encourages compliance of institutions by factoring the institutions' risk mitigation or management of risks or corrective actions into the institutions' risk level.

Objectives, Scope, and Methodology

As requested by the Senate Committee on Banking, Housing, and Urban Affairs, we conducted a review of the examination and enforcement programs of the federal banking, thrift, and credit union regulators that was directed at compliance with the BSA by depository institutions in the United States. Specifically, our objectives were to determine how (1) the regulators examined for BSA compliance by the depository institutions they supervise, (2) the regulators have updated examination procedures and trained examiners since the passage of the PATRIOT Act, (3) the regulators identify and track BSA violations to ensure timely corrective actions at the institutions they examine, and (4) enforcement actions are taken for violations of the BSA.

To determine how the regulators assess BSA compliance, we conducted structured interviews with examiners and policy officials from each of the regulators as well as several state banking departments.[12] Additionally, we reviewed the results of an inquiry of the BSA-related examination and enforcement practices of state banking departments conducted by an industry organization. We also reviewed BSA amendments and other relevant federal banking statutes and collected data on the number of examinations that included a BSA-related violation and that were conducted by each regulator between January 1, 2000, and June 30, 2004. In general, the regulators produced these data from their respective information systems and reporting processes used to collect and track information on examinations and violations. Because there was some variability in how the regulators defined examinations and violations, these data were not comparable.

From May 2004 through July 2004, we conducted reliability assessments of most regulators' BSA-related data and related information systems and determined that they were generally reliable for our purposes. Our data reliability assessments generally involved the testing of data relating to BSA violations and enforcement actions for completeness and accuracy, and interviewing and obtaining written responses from officials about the management of these data. Through the data reliability assessments, we determined that for our purposes, the data from OCC, FDIC, OTS, and NCUA were complete and accurate. However, we could not complete our assessment of the Federal Reserve's systems because Federal Reserve officials were unable to provide us, in a timely manner, with the system-related information that we requested.[13] Although the Federal Reserve collected summary information about BSA-related examinations and violations from January 1, 2000, to January 1, 2003, at the time of our request, the Federal Reserve did not track certain specific BSA data in its systems. Therefore, Federal Reserve officials were unable to provide us with certain information in a manner that would have allowed us to complete our testing.

We selected 30 examinations each from OCC, FDIC, OTS, and NCUA that identified BSA-related violations. The Federal Reserve identified 26 examinations, conducted between January 1, 2000, and June 30, 2004, that involved a BSA-related violation. We initially selected all 26 examinations for our review, but reviewed only 18 of the 26 examinations. We eliminated 6 examinations from the review because they involved multiple reviews of individual institutions that covered different examination target areas but shared common examination documentation, which complicated our ability to isolate different events within examinations. We eliminated an additional 2 examinations because they took place before our sample time frame. In total, we reviewed 138 examinations.

Although we randomly selected individual examinations from each regulator, the number of sampled examinations is small and is not representative of the universe of total examinations that each regulator conducts annually. Therefore, we could not use the results of our sample review to generalize about the regulators' application of examination procedures. However, our review of the examinations allowed us to describe how regulators applied their respective BSA/AML examination procedures in the sampled examinations. Table 1 shows the sample size for each regulator that we reviewed.

Table 1. Data Collection Instrument Sample

Regulator	Number of BSA examinations with one or more BSA violations from which we sampled	Sample size
FDIC	713	30
Federal Reserve	26	18
NCUA	873	30
OCC	624	30
OTS	703	30
Total		**138**

Source: GAO.

After selecting our sample of examinations, we requested from each of the regulators the examination reports and related work papers associated with each examination. To review the examination documentation, we developed a data collection instrument by reviewing the BSA requirements and the examination procedures developed by the regulators. We used the data collection instrument to collect information on several aspects of BSA examinations, including the BSA activities reviewed and tested by examiners as well the nature of the violations identified in each examination. The conclusions that we made about the sampled examinations were based solely on what examiners identified and documented during their examinations. Because we did not interview the examiners who conducted the sampled examinations or conduct additional examinations of these depository institutions, we made no judgments about whether examiners properly identified BSA noncompliance during the examinations. After one GAO analyst reviewed each examination using the data collection instrument, an additional GAO analyst reviewed the same examination using the data collection instrument a second time to ensure the reliability of our coding of the review questions and the accuracy of data entry.

To determine how BSA violations were resolved, we performed additional analysis of a subset of our sample examinations with repeat BSA violations. We selected a small number of institutions with repeat violations for additional analysis. As part of this analysis, we (1) reviewed, to the extent available, reports of examination and supporting documentation provided by the regulators in which the violations were initially identified and (2) attempted to track them to the most current report of examination available, to determine the status of corrective action. However, the documentation we reviewed did not allow us to reach any conclusions on how the repeat violations in our sample were resolved; therefore, this analysis is not included in the report.

To determine the extent to which the regulators updated examination procedures and trained examiners, we reviewed the regulators' examination policies, guidance, and procedures. We also collected information on examiner training courses related to AML and the number of examiners trained in 2004 and 2005. We interviewed examiners and policy officials on their examination guidance and training programs, including the newly issued Federal Financial Institutions Examination Council's (FFIEC) *Bank Secrecy Act Anti-Money Laundering Examination Manual* (FFIEC *Examination Manual*). We observed one AML training course taught by FFIEC and also participated in the FFIEC *Examination Manual* outreach events that were provided to industry and examination staff in August 2005.

To determine the extent to which the regulators monitored their respective BSA/AML examination programs, we reviewed the regulators' documentation relating to their systems, interviewed policy officials on their monitoring policies, and reviewed Inspectors General (IG) reports. We followed up on issues raised by the IGs, and obtained written responses from and interviewed data management personnel.

Additionally, we reviewed the MOU adopted by FinCEN and the regulators and interviewed examiners and policy officials from each of the regulators and FinCEN on the MOU requirements, on case referrals to FinCEN, and on the different terminologies the regulators use to describe noncompliance with the BSA.

To determine how enforcement actions are taken for violations of the BSA, we reviewed relevant BSA amendments, Treasury regulations and guidance, banking statutes, and documentation of selected closed examinations involving BSA violations. To determine how action is taken against criminal violation of the BSA by depository institutions, we reviewed public documentation on the associated investigations and case dispositions. In certain cases, we interviewed investigators involved in selected closed cases. We also interviewed officials at FinCEN, ICE, Justice, and the regulators regarding depository institutions' criminal BSA violations.

We conducted our work in New York, New York; San Francisco, California; and Washington, D.C., between January 2004 and March 2006 in accordance with generally accepted government auditing standards. We requested comments on a draft of this report from the heads, or their designees, of the Departments of Homeland Security, Justice, and the Treasury; the Board of Governors of the Federal Reserve System; the Federal Deposit Insurance Corporation; the National Credit Union Administration; the Office of the Comptroller of the Currency; and the Office of Thrift Supervision. FinCEN and the regulators provided written comments in a joint letter, which is reprinted in appendix II. Justice also provided written comments, which are reprinted in appendix III. The Department of Homeland Security, Justice, and the regulators provided technical comments, which we incorporated where appropriate.

2. Regulators Used Similar Procedures for BSA Examinations, but under Pre-2005 Guidance, Their Application Could Vary Widely

Before 2005, the regulators used separate examination guidance to review BSA compliance at depository institutions, although the examination procedures generally were similar. Examination activities included planning and scoping; creation of risk profiles; and supervisory consultation, reporting, and corrective actions. In addition to undertaking these procedures, examiners also exercised professional judgment in determining the manner or extent to which certain procedures were conducted. Although the basic examination procedures were similar for all of the regulators, under pre-2005 guidance, documentation requirements and documentation of certain procedures could vary widely. In addition, most state banking departments that review state-chartered depository institutions for BSA compliance generally use federal BSA examination procedures. In recent years, more state banking departments have conducted BSA examinations and increased their coordination with the regulators and FinCEN.

Examiners Took Similar Steps to Prepare for, Determine Scope of, and Report on BSA Examinations

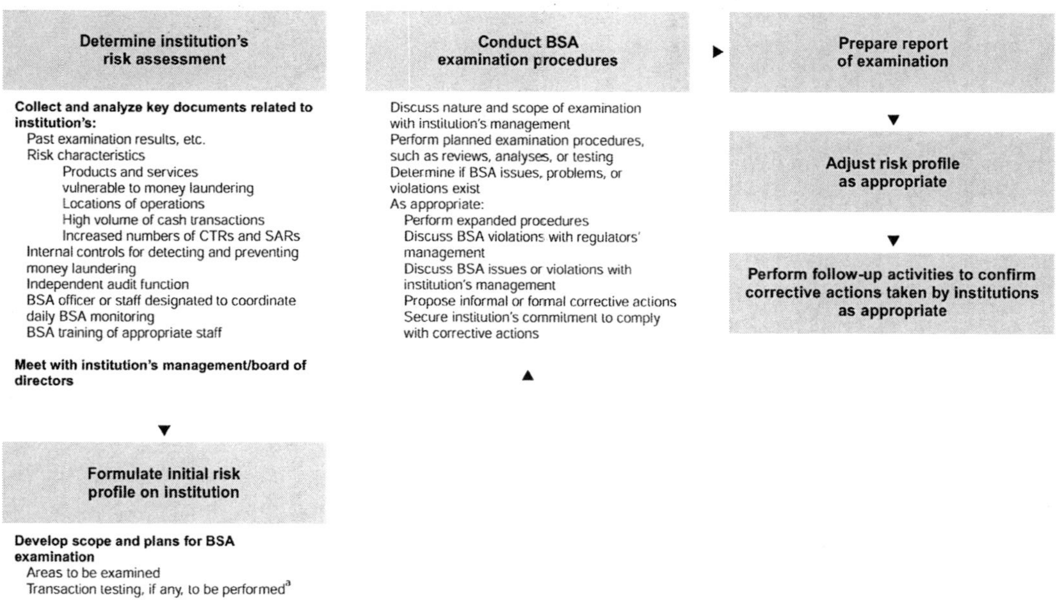

Source: GAO.
[a]As of June 30, 2005, transaction testing was required in all BSA examinations.

Figure 1. BSA Examination Procedures.

In general, the procedures that examiners have used (and continue to use) to prepare for and report on examinations were similar (see fig. 1).[1] For example, guidance called for planning and scoping activities to result in the creation of a risk profile for the institution to be examined. Examiners also were to draw on similar sources of information to create the risk profiles, including the institution's internal assessments and information from other federal agencies. Examiners were then to use the profiles to determine the scope of the examinations. Finally, in concluding the examinations, guidance called for examiners to consult with their supervisors on examinations findings, include recommendations in examination reports, and confer with institutions' management about any corrective actions.

Planning Activities for Examinations Culminate in a Risk Profile

In planning, guidance called for examiners to conduct risk-assessment procedures to evaluate an institution's potential for BSA noncompliance, money laundering, or terrorist financing. To perform the risk assessments, examiners were to gather and analyze information from the institutions or other sources about operational procedures or activities that might expose the institutions to risk in these areas. More specifically, the examiners could use other sources, such as prior examination reports and related work papers. Examiners also gathered information from the institutions themselves, such as documents on BSA/AML policies and programs, audit reports, and products and services offered. Finally, examiners were to draw upon information, such as SARs and Currency Transaction Reports (CTR), which financial institutions filed with the IRS.[2]

In evaluating the information, examiners were to focus on certain products, services, or activities of the institution where the risks for BSA noncompliance, money laundering, or terrorist financing might be higher. These included products, services, or activities such as (1) international wire transfers, monetary instruments, trusts, or private banking;[3] (2) large or increased volumes of cash transactions; (3) operations located in offshore areas that are at high risk for money laundering activities or in high-intensity financial crimes areas (HIFCA);[4] (4) large or increased numbers of CTR and SAR filings; (5) customers found on the Office of Foreign Assets Control's (OFAC) specially designated list;[5] or(6) international correspondent banking.

In addition to analyzing information from the previously discussed sources, examiners were to assess the adequacy of an institution's compliance or risk management systems for identifying, measuring, monitoring, and controlling BSA risks that might stem from banking operations. This assessment entailed a review of the institution's internal controls, and independent audit function, as well as the institution's BSA program, officer, and training. For example, OCC's BSA examination procedures for community banks required examiners to review the bank's quality of risk management, consisting of its policies, processes, personnel, and control systems (including internal/external audit programs). Specifically, examiners were to validate the two fundamental components of any bank's risk management system—internal controls and audits. Federal Reserve examiners also were required to assess the adequacy of the institution's controls over BSA risks and, as such, evaluate the institution's internal controls; audit function; BSA program officer; and training. FDIC required examiners to review the institution's internal controls and audit procedures as part of its risk management assessment. OTS's examination manual required examiners to determine whether the institution implemented an internal audit or conducted a management review or self-assessment of its BSA program.

According to the regulators' procedures, evaluating the adequacy of the independent audit function was a major factor in assessing the institution's risk. To do so, examiners were to assess the auditor's independence, competency, and experience; the scope or coverage of

BSA risk areas; the frequency of audits and transaction testing; audit results; and other factors as required by the regulators' examination guidance. Furthermore, according to examiners, their assessments of the independent audit function could be a factor in determining whether to perform additional procedures, such as transaction testing. For example, according to NCUA examiners, they might interview the credit union's internal auditor to determine the auditor's independence, competency, and knowledge of BSA compliance. The examiners also would use their professional judgment to assess the adequacy of the coverage given by the independent auditor to the BSA compliance review. If examiners determined that the independent audit function or audit report was inadequate or unreliable, they might decide to perform transaction testing or additional testing.

Finally, as a result of the risk-assessment process, examiners then would formulate an initial risk profile on the institution; this initial assessment might be adjusted during or after the examination. The institution's BSA risk profile could be expressed in terms of risk level, such as high, moderate or satisfactory, or low. Examiners exercised professional judgment throughout this process to weigh the factors considered and determine the institution's level of risk.

Examiners Used Risk Profiles to Determine the Scope of Examinations

Examiners were to use an institution's risk profile to determine the nature and extent of procedures to be performed during the examination. If the institution's risk profile was low, examiners generally were to conduct what are variously referred to as basic, core, or limited examination procedures. These procedures included reviews of an institution's

- written, approved BSA/AML program, policies, and procedures to ensure that the institution's BSA/AML program adequately covered all of the BSA-required program elements;
- BSA officer or designated staff to coordinate day-to-day BSA monitoring;
- BSA training provided to the appropriate staff;
- OFAC compliance procedures;
- correction of a deficiency of a BSA program requirement noted in a previous report of examination;[6]
- product lines and services, including wire transfers, deposit-taking facilities, sales of monetary instruments, and exemptions from reporting procedures;
- internal controls for detecting, preventing, and correcting BSA/AML violations;
- Know Your Customer program;[7]
- Customer Identification Program;[8] and
- compliance with record-keeping and reporting requirements, such as CTRs and SARs.

In addition to the basic procedures previously discussed, examiners could perform transaction testing, depending on the regulator's examination requirements. Transaction testing could cover the institution's cash transactions, monetary instruments, wire transfers, SARs, CTRs, exemptions, or samples of the institution's accounts previously tested by its independent auditor. Examiners also could deem transaction testing necessary on the basis of the institution's risk profile or examination results. For example, examiners might discover that an institution failed to file CTRs or that the institution's independent audit was inadequate; as a result, they would perform transaction testing to determine the nature and extent of potential BSA issues or problems.

If an institution's risk profile was high or examiners identified BSA compliance problems (e.g., with the institution's BSA/AML policies, procedures, programs, or internal controls), examiners generally were to conduct expanded procedures in high-risk areas or the areas of identified deficiencies. Expanded procedures generally involved (1) more in-depth reviews of the institution's compliance with BSA, AML, and OFAC requirements and (2) transaction testing. Such reviews or testing might cover various areas, including record keeping and retention, exemptions, sales of monetary instruments, funds transfers, transactions that are payable upon proper identification, international brokered deposits, foreign correspondent banking, pouch activity, and private banking.

Examinations Concluded with Supervisory Consultation, Reporting, and, When Needed, Corrective Actions

As a result of applying BSA examination procedures, examiners might identify BSA compliance deficiencies or violations.[9] Using the regulators' guidance on BSA corrective actions and enforcement, examiners were to determine whether an institution's actions or inactions should be classified as BSA deficiencies or violations. Examiners then were to consult with their supervisors concerning their findings of BSA violations, particularly violations that were deemed to warrant formal enforcement actions, such as written agreements, cease-and-desist orders, and CMPs (for more information, see ch. 5). Examiners were to submit recommended findings of BSA violations and proposed corrective actions to their supervisors and then discuss the results of the examination with the institution's management and board of directors. In these discussions, examiners generally were to secure management's commitment to comply with the proposed corrective actions.

Subsequently, guidance called for examiners to prepare the report of examination, detailing the scope, compliance risk, findings, corrective actions, and management's commitment to take corrective action; the corrective actions taken by management before the end of the examination; or the proposed enforcement actions. During the examination and at the conclusion of the examination, examiners were to enter examination data and results of the examination into the regulators' respective automated reporting systems (see ch. 4). Examiners were to perform follow-up activities between examinations, or at the next scheduled examination, to verify compliance with corrective actions. Finally, regulatory management was to notify FinCEN of significant BSA violations found as a result of the examination. Examiners sometimes recommended or provided input into the decision to notify FinCEN of significant BSA compliance problems.

Under Pre-2005 Guidance, Documentation Requirements Varied Widely

The regulators' pre-2005 requirements for documentation of examination procedures and their documentation of those procedures could vary widely. From each regulator, we reviewed approximately 30 BSA examinations that were conducted under guidance current between January 1, 2000, and June 30, 2004. Because the sample was small, we could not generalize the results of our analysis to make conclusions about how regulators applied the examination procedures to all BSA examinations conducted during this period. However, when coupled with our review of regulator guidance and examination manuals, the results of the examination review illustrated instances where the regulators' documentation of examination procedures varied widely. Individual regulator guidance issued prior to June 2005, required documentation of "major" procedures and conclusions, and our review indicated more documentation of examination planning procedures at larger institutions.

Under pre-2005 guidance, the regulators did not consistently require or document transaction testing. The regulators required transaction testing in examinations of larger institutions with higher asset levels, but not always at smaller institutions. The OCC BSA examination manual for large banks required transaction testing, at a minimum, to form conclusions about the integrity of the bank's overall control and risk management processes and of its overall quantity of risk. OCC examiners stated that transaction testing was required for all high-risk areas of large banks, and we found documentation of transaction testing in 3 of 4 large bank examinations. The Federal Reserve's BSA examination manual required that some transaction testing be performed in all examinations, and the nature and extent of transaction testing could vary, depending on the institution's level of risk. For example, if the institution engaged in high-risk areas, such as private banking, foreign correspondent banking, or international banking, Federal Reserve examiners were required to perform transaction testing in those areas. Our review of Federal Reserve examinations indicated that examiners performed extensive transaction testing at most of the banks. We found documentation of transaction testing in 17 of 18 Federal Reserve examinations we reviewed, including those of large and smaller institutions.

Our examination review found less documentation of transaction testing in examinations at smaller institutions with lower assets, such as the community banks, savings associations, and credit unions supervised by OCC, OTS, FDIC, and NCUA. These regulators' examination guidance permitted examiners to exercise their professional judgment in determining whether to perform transaction testing. See appendix I for more information from our examination review.

Since 2004, State Banking Departments Have Become More Involved in BSA Reviews and Increased Information Sharing with FinCEN

As recently as 2004, about one-third of state banking departments reported not examining for BSA compliance; however, state banking departments have since taken a more active role in conducting these reviews. According to state banking department officials, the increased attention to AML and terrorist-financing issues after September 11, led state banking departments to begin examining for BSA compliance or to expand the scope of their reviews. The state banking departments examining for BSA compliance generally used the same procedures as the regulators. Lastly, state banking departments, the regulators, and FinCEN have increased their coordination of BSA and AML compliance-related efforts.

In 2004, Many State Banking Departments Reported That They Did Not Examine for BSA Compliance

According to a July 2004 Conference of State Banking Supervisors (CSBS) inquiry of banking departments on BSA and AML practices, 35 state banking departments were examining for BSA compliance, either during joint examinations with federal examiners or independently as part of the alternate-year examination programs.[10] In some states, federal examiners independently reviewed institutions or reviewed institutions jointly with examiners from state banking departments. According to a Federal Reserve official, the frequency of these examinations and the decision of whether to perform the review jointly depended on the institution's risk level. An FDIC official said that FDIC reviewed depository institutions for BSA compliance on average every 36 months. Of the remaining state banking departments, at least 15 were not reviewing for BSA compliance. Similarly, a March 2004 FDIC Inspector General (FDIC IG) report indicated that out of 72 examination reports reviewed from state banking departments, 45 did not specifically address BSA compliance. As a result, depository institutions in some states were not being examined for BSA compliance at each examination.

CSBS officials said that in the past, BSA compliance coverage varied among state banking departments, in part, because of differing philosophies about their responsibilities for determining BSA compliance. Specifically, some state banking departments did not interpret BSA-related supervision as a state-level responsibility. According to CSBS officials, departments in these states interpreted their examination responsibilities as determining depository institutions' safety and soundness and compliance with state laws. CSBS officials said that, in general, this supervisory approach was driven largely by state budget constraints and the allocation of examination fees to states' general funds, rather than to examination programs.

Some State Banking Departments Recently Began Reviewing for BSA Compliance; Others Have Intensified Existing BSA Reviews

According to CSBS officials, although the regulators are the entities that are legally responsible for conducting BSA reviews, state banking departments have become more active in conducting these reviews over the last 2 years. For example, the Virginia Bureau of Financial Institutions began examining for BSA compliance in September 2004. Similarly, the Delaware Office of the State Bank Commissioner began conducting BSA reviews in January 2005.[11] Additionally, officials from some state banking departments noted that the increased attention to AML and terrorist-financing issues following September 11, led some state banking departments to begin examining for BSA compliance or to expand the scope of existing reviews. For example, in late 2004, the Louisiana Office of Financial Institutions began conducting independent BSA reviews as part of its safety and soundness examination. The Florida Office of Financial Regulation intensified its BSA examinations; since September 11, it has been reviewing for BSA compliance as part of every safety and soundness examination. State banking departments also have been independently examining for BSA compliance. For example, the Georgia Department of Banking and Finance began examining depository institutions for BSA compliance in early 2004. According to an official from this state banking department, Georgia is performing BSA reviews with federal examiners on an alternating schedule. Furthermore, officials from other state banking departments said that although their state examiners had reviewed for BSA compliance in filing, reporting, and record keeping for some time, their departments more recently began to devote additional training resources to BSA compliance. For example, one state banking department official said that the agency's examiners were able to review more than the institution's BSA policy for BSA compliance than they did in the past. In response to a

CSBS inquiry of state banking departments, as of November 2005, 45 state banking departments were reviewing for BSA compliance.[12]

In general, whether recently examining for BSA compliance or continuing established procedures, state examiners used the same procedures the regulators used to examine for BSA compliance. State examiners generally described using the key steps that federal examiners take in reviewing for AML compliance, which included reviewing the institution's policies and procedures, recent CTRs and SARs, training efforts, and independent audit reports. Similar to federal examiners, state examiners described performing transaction testing to varying degrees, based primarily on the risk presented by the institution being examined. According to CSBS officials, state examiners reviewed state-chartered banks using FDIC's BSA examination procedures. State examiners and Federal Reserve officials said that state examiners generally used the Federal Reserve procedures for banks that are supervised by the Federal Reserve, but examiners sometimes used FDIC procedures for small institutions supervised by the Federal Reserve.

State Banking Departments, Regulators, and FinCEN Also Have Recently Increased Coordination on BSA-Related Examination Activities

During the course of our work, state banking departments, regulators, and FinCEN increased coordination on BSA-related examination and information-sharing activities. For example, in March 2004, the FDIC IG recommended that FDIC (1) coordinate with state banking departments to cover BSA compliance in state-led examinations of FDIC-supervised institutions and (2) for those states that did not cover BSA compliance, develop an alternative FDIC process to address BSA compliance when relying on alternating state examinations. FDIC agreed with the recommendation and, in May 2004, released a regulatory memorandum,

Policy for Bank Secrecy Act/Anti-Money Laundering Examination Scheduling and Frequency. The memorandum requires FDIC to conduct concurrent BSA/AML examinations at all safety and soundness examinations conducted by state banking departments that do not perform BSA and AML examinations, to avoid additional regulatory burdens on the depository institution. In addition, since the issuance of the memorandum, FDIC has conducted independent BSA examinations when state banking departments had not done so during regularly scheduled safety and soundness examinations.

In addition, the regulators also began training state examiners on reviewing for BSA compliance. According to CSBS, a growing number of states are seeking BSA training, with some states doing on-site training with federal agencies. For example, in September 2004, the Federal Reserve provided 2 days of training for staff at a state banking department. In addition, officials from another state banking department said that examiners shadowed federal examiners on BSA reviews as part of their training. A Federal Reserve official further explained that both the Federal Reserve and FDIC recently had provided on-the-job training for the state examiners during joint examinations.

Finally, on June 2, 2005, FinCEN announced the signing of MOUs with 30 state banking departments and the department in Puerto Rico to further improve coordination of BSA and AML activities.[13] According to FinCEN officials, as of March 2006, banking departments from 36 states and the Commonwealth of Puerto Rico, have signed MOUs. The MOUs set forth information-sharing agreements with FinCEN that are similar to the information-sharing agreement between FinCEN and the regulators. According to FinCEN, these agreements provide the framework for enhanced collaboration and information sharing between federal and state agencies that will allow FinCEN to better administer the BSA, while simultaneously assisting state agencies to better fulfill their roles as financial institution departments. Furthermore, a CSBS official said that the MOUs provide a clearer understanding of the role of state banking departments. According to a CSBS official, in the post-September 11 environment, state banking departments also wanted a viable supervisory role in the BSA area because they perceived BSA issues as affecting all regulators. In March 2006, FinCEN was receiving data for the fourth quarter of 2005 from the states.

3. Regulators Have Promoted Consistency in BSA Examinations through Interagency Procedures and BSA Training

During the course of our work, the regulators took steps that promoted consistency of BSA examinations, including issuing new interagency procedures and revising and expanding examiner training. In particular, the new examination procedures describe risk assessments and link them to the creation of risk profiles. The procedures also introduce more uniformity into the assessment of independent audit functions and, for the first time, require transaction testing in all examinations, regardless of the institution's risk profile. As a result, the new procedures provide a framework for greater consistency in BSA examinations across the regulators. To disseminate new information and increase knowledge of BSA and related issues, the regulators have increased training on BSA and the PATRIOT Act and coordinated efforts to educate staff on the interagency procedures. Moreover, some regulators have focused on developing more BSA/AML specialist examiners.

New Interagency Procedures Create Framework for Consistent BSA/AML Examination Processes

As previously discussed, the regulators generally followed the same steps for BSA examinations but differed in the application of some procedures, such as documentation, and in what procedures they left to examiner judgment, such as transaction testing. However, as statutory requirements (e.g., the PATRIOT Act) changed in response to concerns about anti-money laundering and terrorist-financing issues, the regulators also recognized the need to enhance their guidance. On June 30, 2005, the regulators, in collaboration with FinCEN and OFAC, issued a new BSA/AML examination manual through FFIEC, an interagency body prescribing uniform standards for federal examinations. In addition, they committed themselves to updating the manual at least once a year. In the regulators' view, the FFIEC BSA/AML *Examination Manual* is the product of best practices among the regulators and aims to promote procedural consistency in the conduct of BSA/AML examinations at all depository institutions. While both the former and new examination procedures require examiners to evaluate the institution's risk management systems and formulate a risk profile of the institution, the FFIEC procedures provide a uniform process for performing risk assessments. As a result, the manual provides examiners with more focused guidance to follow in performing BSA/AML examinations. Furthermore, in contrast to the previous procedures, the FFIEC procedures also provide uniform factors for assessing the adequacy of an institution's independent audit function and require transaction testing in all examinations.

New Examination Procedures Organize Information on BSA Risk Assessments and Link Assessments to Scoping and Planning

In contrast to previous guidance, the FFIEC *Examination Manual* organizes guidance on risk-assessment procedures primarily in one place, the scoping and planning section for core examinations procedures. The manual also comprehensively describes risk assessments for BSA examinations, taking examiners from the planning stages to using conclusions to develop risk profiles. Formerly, the BSA examination manuals of most of the regulators did not describe the risk-assessment process with the same degree of information or BSA-specificity. For example, two regulators did not have a discrete description of the BSA-risk assessment process, but incorporated it with the risk- assessment process for financial examinations. Other regulators did not explain what conclusions examiners were to draw from their risk-assessment process, such as determining that an institution's risk level was high, moderate, or low.

Additionally, some of the regulators' former BSA examination procedures focused on different aspects of the risk-assessment process, such as the institution's risk assessment of its product lines or services, or its risk management systems, or quality of audit and internal controls, to develop risk profiles of institutions. However, the FFIEC manual emphasizes that all banks must have BSA/AML programs tailored to their particular risks, and that planning and scoping for examinations should be guided by those assessments. That is, examiners should review the institutions' self assessments of their programs to determine if the program (and, thus, risk management systems or controls) are commensurate with all of the risks the institutions undertook.

In presenting guidance on how to link risk assessments to other examination procedures, the new manual also provides a framework for examiners to follow (see fig. 2). For example, according to an OTS official, it provides one "road map" for everyone. A senior Federal Reserve official referred to the manual as a "significant step toward consistency" in the area of AML examination. Additionally, an OCC official stated that the FFIEC procedures provide a minimum threshold for performing examination procedures.

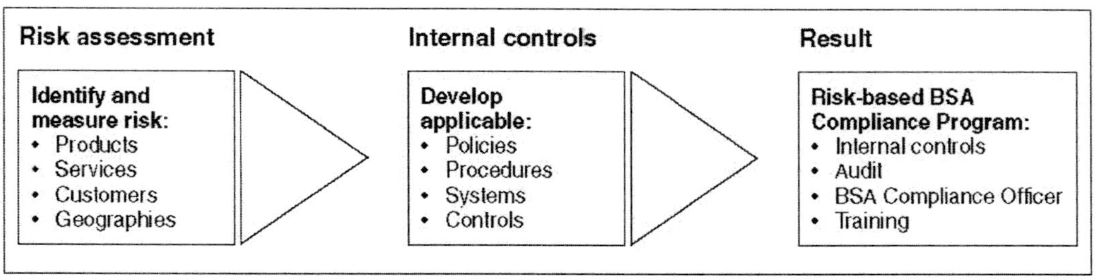

Source: GAO (based on FFIEC's Bank Secrecy Act Anti-Money Laundering Examination Manual).

Figure 2. FFIEC Manual Links Components Necessary for BSA Compliance.

The manual recognizes that, depending on the specific characteristics of the particular product, service, or customer, the risks are not always the same. Various factors, such as number and dollar volume, geographic location, and customer versus noncustomer, should be considered when making a risk assessment. Because of these variables, risks will vary from one institution to another. In formulating a risk-based BSA/AML program, the manual states that institution management should identify the significant risks to its institution and develop a risk assessment tailored to its circumstances. Furthermore, as new products and services are introduced, as existing products and services change, or as the institution expands through mergers and acquisitions, institution management's evaluation of the money laundering and terrorist- financing risks should evolve. The expanded sections of the manual provide guidance and discussions on specific lines of business or products that may present unique challenges and exposures for which institutions should institute the appropriate policies, procedures, and processes.

New Examination Procedures Add Uniformity to Assessment of Independent Audit Function

To confirm that institutions are complying with independent audit requirements, examiners, under former and new procedures, assess the adequacy of the institution's independent audit function during the scoping phase of the BSA examination or later. However, the regulators' former procedures were not uniform; that is, while each regulator considered multiple factors when assessing the independent audit function, none of the regulators used the same set of factors.

In contrast, the FFIEC core examination procedures provide uniform guidance for examiners to follow when validating the independent audit as part of the planning and scoping of the BSA examination. Examiners are required to determine whether the

- BSA/AML testing (audit) was independent;
- qualifications of the person(s) performing the independent testing would allow the institution to rely on the findings and conclusions;
- auditor's reports and work papers were valid; that is, whether the independent testing was comprehensive, accurate, adequate, and timely;
- audit reviewed the institution's suspicious activity monitoring systems for the ability to identify unusual activity;
- bank's audit review procedures confirmed the accuracy of management information systems used in BSA/AML compliance;
- audit tracked previously identified deficiencies and ensured that management corrected them; and
- audit was adequate on the basis of a review of the audit's scope, procedures, and work papers.

By providing a comprehensive and uniform set of factors to consider in assessing the independent audit, examiners could validate the independent audit on a more uniform basis. Additionally, since the independent audit is a factor in determining the institution's risk profile, the interagency procedures for validating the audit also may contribute to more consistent determinations of an institution's risk profile.

New Examination Procedures Require Transaction Testing, Regardless of the Institution's BSA RiskLevel

The FFIEC *Examination Manual* requires transaction testing at each examination, regardless of the institution's BSA risk level. Under some of the regulators' former procedures, transaction testing was not always required; rather, this decision was left to examiner judgment, taking into consideration the institution's BSA risk level. The FFIEC *Examination Manual* emphasizes the importance of transaction testing for making conclusions about the integrity of the institution's overall controls and risk management processes. The manual also requires that transaction testing be performed to evaluate the adequacy of an institution's compliance with regulatory requirements, and the effectiveness of its policies, procedures, processes, and suspicious activity monitoring systems. According to the FFIEC *Examination Manual,* examiners perform transaction testing to evaluate the adequacy of an institution's compliance with regulatory requirements, or to determine whether its policies and procedures and suspicious activity monitoring systems are effective.

More specifically, the manual provides examiners with two options for performing transaction testing. Transaction testing may be performed within the independent audit section of the examination, or it may be completed in procedures contained elsewhere within the manual's core or expanded sections. If transaction testing is performed within the independent audit section, examiners are required to select a judgmental sample that includes transactions other than those tested by the independent auditor. Under previous guidance, examiners for some of the regulators told us that they could choose whether to sample transactions tested by the independent auditor. However, the new procedures do allow examiners to determine the extent of transaction testing to be performed, on the basis of factors such as the examiner's judgment of risks and controls and the adequacy of the independent audit.

If transaction testing is performed within the core or expanded sections of the examination, the FFIEC *Examination Manual* delineates the specific areas under the core and expanded procedures where transaction testing must be performed and specifies the nature of transaction testing that must be performed. For example, the FFIEC core examination procedures describe transaction testing of customer due diligence, currency transaction reporting and CTR exemptions, the purchase and sale of monetary instruments, and funds transfers. The new manual's expanded examination procedures are similar to the regulators' former examination procedures in that they describe transaction testing or reviews of specific areas, such as foreign correspondent accounts, payable through accounts, pouch activities, funds transfers, and foreign branches and offices of U.S. banks.

Regulators Revised Examination Tools for Documenting BSA Procedures to Conform to the FFIEC *Examination Manual*

As previously discussed, the regulators' pre-2005 requirements for documentation of examination procedures and their documentation of those procedures varied widely. The FFIEC *Examination Manual* requires that transaction testing be performed on all examinations and provides some guidance for documenting BSA examination procedures, including scoping, planning, and risk assessments.

According to the regulators, after the new procedures were issued, they revised their examination formats for capturing and documenting BSA examination procedures to conform to the requirements of the FFIEC *Examination Manual*. For example, the Federal Reserve and FDIC revised the examination work programs that their examiners use to document examination procedures, which are entered into the regulators' automated examination reporting system. Our review of these work programs showed that the formats provided for documentation of scoping, planning, risk assessments, and transaction testing. OTS officials said that they had revised their BSA examination work program to conform to the requirements of the manual and require documentation of scoping, planning, risk-assessment, and transaction-testing procedures. NCUA officials stated that NCUA had revised its examination questionnaire to incorporate instructions for documenting transaction-testing and other procedures. The questionnaire, according to our review, provides for documentation of scoping, planning, and transaction-testing procedures. OCC officials told us that they modified their automated examination reporting system, to provide for examiner documentation of scoping, planning, risk-assessment, and transaction-testing procedures in examinations of large, midsize, and community banks. These new formats and tools for documenting transaction-testing and other procedures likely will result in more documentation of these procedures on future BSA/AML examinations, and will make it easier to track BSA/AML examination results as well.

In Recent Years, Regulators Have Intensified Focus on BSA-Related Skills and Issues in Examiner Training

In tandem with an increasing focus on BSA-related issues, regulators also revised examiner training, and some regulators have increased the number of specialized examiners. For example, the regulators have adjusted or expanded their training to incorporate the latest mandates and standards, such as the PATRIOT Act and the FFIEC *Examination Manual*. Some regulators also trained more examiners to specialize in BSA/AML issues.

Each Regulator Provides BSA/AML Training to Its Examiners

Although each regulator provides BSA/AML training to its examiners, each regulator approached training differently (see table 2). For example, OTS and NCUA require all new staff to attend a basic training course on AML compliance. According to OTS officials, OTS hosted a number of regional conferences for examiners that were solely dedicated to the BSA and the PATRIOT Act. NCUA also used regional conferences to train examiners on BSA issues. For example, in its annual report to FinCEN, NCUA stated that BSA compliance was addressed at the regional conference training provided to all examiners in 2002 and 2004. The Federal Reserve requires all staff seeking to obtain an examiner commission to successfully complete a BSA/AML proficiency test.[1] FDIC requires all examination staff to obtain BSA/AML training through classroom and Web-based training. Finally, OCC offers four different training schools, which all provide live, instructor-led training in AML requirements. Additionally, OCC offers specialized BSA/AML training on a voluntary basis to commissioned staff who participate in the Examiner Specialized Skills Program.

Table 2. BSA/AML Training, by Regulator (2004–2005)

Regulator	Training description
FDIC	To increase its level of BSA expertise, FDIC required all examination staff to complete formal training on AML requirements by the end of 2004. FDIC trained every examiner on staff (1,721) in AML requirements by establishing a curriculum comprised of several Web-based components, including externally provided courseware, internally developed presentations, and exercises to strengthen knowledge of topics covered. FDIC examiners also receive AML training through FDIC's formal examiner school, "Introduction to Examinations." In 2005, 38 examiners received AML training through the examiner school. Furthermore, FDIC offered specialized AML training at outside seminars and conferences, such as industry-sponsored events and regulatory conferences. For example, in 2005, 72 subject matter experts attended the FFIEC AML workshop. Also, from November 29 to December 2, 2005, 336 individuals, primarily BSA/AML subject matter experts and other persons with BSA/AML assessment responsibility, attended the FDIC-sponsored "BSA/AML Subject Matter Expert Conference." The purpose of the training conference was to provide guidance on higher-and-emerging-risk topics to ensure a more efficient and consistent BSA/AML examination process. FDIC also provided additional FFIEC *Examination Manual* training to examiners and supervisors during 2005. FDIC also conducts training during examinations. This training is targeted to the individual examiner and addresses the unique business lines and practices at the bank being examined.
Federal Reserve	The Federal Reserve's BSA/AML Risk Section, formerly the Anti-Money Laundering Compliance Section, interacts on a daily basis with the examination staff engaged in AML examinations at the 12 Reserve Banks. Section staff offer case-specific guidance regarding AML requirements. The BSA/AML Risk Section holds monthly systemwide calls and semiannual fora with BSA/AML supervisory staff to provide them with policy updates, training focused on BSA/AML issues, and discussions of recent examination experiences. In addition, examiners from the section participate in select examinations throughout the country to provide on-the-job training to Federal Reserve examiners. Each Reserve Bank also provides ongoing training to supervision staff to keep them informed of changes to regulations, laws, and examination procedures. Typically, BSA/AML training is offered at each Reserve Bank's annual examiner conference. These training sessions provide an opportunity for the Reserve Bank's BSA/AML contacts and the subject matter experts to alert the examination staff of recent changes to legislation and policy directives, updates to examination procedures, and various BSA/AML concerns noted both locally and nationwide. For example, in March 2005, a Reserve Bank trained eight new BSA specialists in AML requirements through a series of workshops. According to a Federal Reserve official, the training that these new specialists received was in addition to and more intense than the online course that all examiners must take. Specialized AML training also has included outside seminars and conferences, such as industry-sponsored events and regulatory conferences. For example, in 2005, 143 examiners attended FFIEC's BSA/AML workshop. Furthermore, as part of the Federal Reserve's entry-level training, examiners are required to complete an online training course. The Federal Reserve's comprehensive training plan for staff members seeking to obtain an examiner commission requires the individual to master a core curriculum and to successfully pass a proficiency test in each core area. For the BSA/AML proficiency test, an individual must demonstrate an understanding of the concept of money laundering, the purpose of the BSA, and the minimum requirements of regulations on BSA/AML programs and requirements for filing SARs.

Table 2. (continued)

Regulator	Training description
NCUA	All new examination staff are required to complete a year-long training curriculum that includes instructor-led training classes and on-the-job training in AML compliance. Seasoned examiners are trained on an ongoing basis using a combination of instructor-led training sessions and regional conferences. During 2005, NCUA provided classroom training to 89 examiners on AML requirements. During August and September 2005, NCUA provided to staff training material addressing the FFIEC *Examination Manual* and the updated NCUA work paper used to document review of the BSA, in accordance with the manual.
OCC	OCC offers instructor-led classroom AML training for its examiners at its Consumer Compliance: Basic, Anti-Money-Laundering, Bank Supervision, and FinCEN Database Training Schools. As part of OCC's entry-level training, all examiners complete 1 week of classroom training and 1 week of course preparation in the Consumer Compliance: Basic School that includes BSA modules. The Anti-Money Laundering School is designed to train participants to recognize money laundering risks and ensure compliance with regulatory requirements. The course heightens awareness of how financial institutions are used in money laundering through hands-on training based upon actual examination results. The Bank Supervision School includes classroom and computer-based training that contains a BSA/AML module, which provides a review of the regulatory requirements. The FinCEN Database Training course trains examiners to access and use the FinCEN database. As of December 2005, 166 examiners attended the Consumer Compliance: Basic School, 89 attended the Anti-Money-Laundering and Terrorist-Financing School, 27 attended the Bank Supervision School, and 21 attended the FinCEN Database Training School. Additionally, OCC provided BSA training targeted to the FFIEC *Examination Manual* to all compliance specialists in September 2005. Approximately 230 examiners were in attendance. Also in 2005, 16 sessions of extensive BSA training that incorporated the FFIEC *Examination Manual* was provided to examiners engaged in community and midsize bank supervision. Approximately 567 examiners attended this training in 2005. The training will continue in 2006. In addition to formal course offerings, OCC periodically provides training in the form of agencywide teleconferences and finances external training opportunities and the industry Certified Anti-Money Laundering Specialist certification as appropriate.
OTS	OTS requires all examiners administering AML exams to complete 3 weeks of classroom training courses, called "Compliance I" and "Compliance II," which include modules on the BSA and the PATRIOT Act. In addition to formal course offerings, OTS provides Web-based AML training. During 2005, OTS recorded 1,483 participants in AML training sessions. Sources: FDIC, Federal Reserve, NCUA, OTS, and OCC.

In addition to their own training, regulators also use interagency or outside venues to train staff. For example, the regulators sent staff to conferences sponsored by trade associations that offered multiday courses and provided informal resources for self-training, such as subscriptions to online newsletters. Regulators also send examiners to interagency AML workshops offered by FFIEC. OTS, in its annual report to FinCEN, stated that in early 2003, FFIEC updated the workshop to incorporate PATRIOT Act requirements. According to FDIC, the workshop objectives focused on recognizing potential money laundering risks, assessing the adequacy of BSA/AML programs, and maintaining up-to-date knowledge of the rules and requirement of BSA/AML statutes and regulations. The workshop generally ran approximately 27 hours and included speakers and presentations by the regulators, FinCEN, IRS, OFAC, and the Federal Bureau of Investigation. FDIC said that providing this training in an interagency forum allowed the regulators to take a more consistent approach to BSA/AML supervisory efforts.

Furthermore, according to the regulators, they updated their AML training to cover of all the relevant provisions of the PATRIOT Act. As mentioned in our May 2005 report, the regulators began offering PATRIOT ACT training for BSA examination staff in 2002 and 2003.[2] This training, provided through instructor-led and Web-based courses, introduced BSA and PATRIOT Act requirements and provided for theoretical and hands-on training. The regulators' AML training curricula included various techniques designed to help the examiners recognize potential money laundering risks facing financial institutions and helped examiners learn procedures for assessing the soundness of an institution's AML program.

Regulators Participated in Joint Efforts to Train Examiners on New Interagency Procedures

Since the issuance of the new procedures on June 30, 2005, FFIEC has coordinated a far-reaching effort to train examiners and the industry on the new procedures, by holding a series of training events across the country. Table 3 provides more information about the training offered since the issuance of the interagency examination procedures.

Table 3. 2005 FFIEC *Examination Manual* Training

Date	Description	Type/Format	Audience	Participation
July 28, 2005	Overview of FFIEC *Examination Manual*	Videoconference	Federal/State examination staff	1,200
August 2-4, 2005	Overview of FFIEC *Examination Manual*	Teleconference (Nationwide) Banking industry	Financial services representatives	8,200
August 15-24, 2005 San Francisco-8/15 Dallas-8/17 Chicago-8/19 New York-8/22 Miami-8/24	Interagency BSA/AML Regional Banker Outreach and Examiner Training Events (manual overview, guidance on risk Assessments, and BSA/AML Q&A)	Group sessions (Event also was subsequently available through the Web for 90 days)	Bankers and examiners	2,000 (bankers) 1,000 (examiners) 12,434 (Web-cast viewers as of August 23)

Sources: Federal Reserve and FDIC

Senior examination and management staff from the regulators attended a nationwide videoconference, hosted by the Federal Reserve, on July 28, 2005. According to an NCUA official, a focus group of NCUA field examiners and office staff participated in the July 28 videoconference. This group, in turn, participated in updating NCUA examinations forms to incorporate the FFIEC *Examination Manual* requirements, identified key sections of the manual and related concepts applicable to credit unions for discussion with staff, and recommended training to be conducted through standard regional processes. For instance, because credit unions do not operate foreign correspondent accounts, staff will be notified that information on BSA risks and transaction testing for these accounts is available, but

NCUA will not incorporate information on those accounts into the agencywide training program.

Additionally, the Federal Reserve, FDIC, OCC, OTS, and FinCEN conducted 2-hour nationwide conference calls, hosted by FDIC, regarding the new examination manual for the banking industry on August 2 to 4, 2005. Furthermore, these four regulators and FinCEN conducted regional outreach meetings aimed specifically at personnel responsible for a financial institution's BSA/AML program. The regulators held half-day sessions in five cities for the banking industry and examination staff.

State banking departments also participated in training on the FFIEC *Examination Manual*. More specifically, according to a CSBS official, CSBS and state banking departments participated in the FFIEC discussions and provided feedback as the procedures were being developed. Furthermore, another CSBS official said that state banking departments are using the manual to conduct BSA reviews. According to a CSBS official, state banking departments participated in the rollout and field testing of the interagency procedures. In addition, state examiners are scheduled to have more formalized BSA coursework through FFIEC, FDIC, and the Federal Reserve as a result of the interagency procedures.

Some Regulators Are Developing More BSA/AML Expert Staff to Serve in a Variety of Roles

Although safety and soundness and compliance examiners primarily perform BSA/AML examinations, some regulators use examiners with specialized skills to provide training, serve as a resource to other examiners, or assist on complex examinations. All of the regulators offer career paths and options for becoming a BSA subject matter expert (see table 4).[3] More recently, some regulators have planned to train or increase substantially the number of subject matter experts they have to help meet PATRIOT Act requirements and address the increasing complexity of BSA examinations. While the regulators prescribe no criteria for BSA/AML specialization, regulatory officials stated that specialization could be achieved through a combination of on-the-job training, classroom training, and industry certification.

Table 4. Examiner Career Path to BSA Specialization, by Regulator

Regulator	Examiner career path
FDIC	Examiners • become commissioned after several years of instruction, examination experience, and successful completion of a commissioning examination; • may specialize in a variety of areas, including the BSA, once they are commissioned; and • receive specialized BSA training, both in the classroom and on the job, and gain experience through BSA examinations. Additionally, FDIC encourages and offers industry designations, such as the Certified Anti-Money Laundering Specialist and Certified Fraud Examiner.

Table 4. (continued)

Regulator	Examiner career path
Federal Reserve	Examiners • must go through the Federal Reserve's examiner commissioning process to become a commissioned examiner; • take two tests, one a midpoint examination taken after 18 months and the other a pass/fail examination, to be commissioned; • can become specialized and work on a specialized team by showing an aptitude for a specialized area and asking for training opportunities; and • attain specialization through a combination of on-the-job and BSA training. The Federal Reserve does not have a requirement for BSA specialists to obtain industry certification.
NCUA	Examiners • are promoted to the principal examiner level after completing a series of training courses and on-the-job training; • after supervisors and examiners jointly demonstrate to regional management that the examiners are competent to handle complex assignments, provide on-the-job training, and conduct team examinations; and • who receive additional training on compliance issues, including AML, become Consumer Compliance Subject Matter Examiners.
OCC	Examiners • are required to take and successfully complete the commissioned examiner test after 5 years of experience as safety and soundness examiners and • can qualify to pursue specialization in various areas, such as capital markets, once they are commissioned. OCC supports a range of certification and licensing for its examiners that are related to the BSA, such as the Certified Anti-Money Laundering Specialist and the Certified Fraud Expert. Additionally, OCC provides a national mentoring program, Examiner Specialized Skills Program, for more experienced staff to mentor staff with less experience. In 2005, there were six "coaches" and 14 participants. In total, 39 examiners have participated in the initiative.
OTS	Examiners • receive certification as a Commissioned Thrift Examiner upon successful completion of in-depth training, both in the classroom and on the job, over a 4- to 5-year period; • that are commissioned serve as core safety and soundness examiners or pursue interests in specialty examination functions, such as compliance; • with many years of experience, go through an accreditation process involving successfully passing the technical portion of a comprehensive compliance test called the Certified Regulatory Compliance Manager; and • that have attained this specialization are required to take 40 to 80 hours of additional training annually.

Sources: FDIC, Federal Reserve, NCUA, OTS, and OCC

According to one of its officials, the Federal Reserve has had a longstanding commitment to BSA/AML supervision and over time has expanded resources specifically dedicated to BSA/AML supervision. For example, Federal Reserve staff noted that, in 2002, a separate AML section was formed to manage and oversee the Federal Reserve's ongoing efforts in the area of BSA/AML. Currently, AML examination subject matter experts interact on a daily basis with examination staff engaged in AML examinations to offer case-specific guidance regarding AML requirements. Moreover, according to officials at the Federal Reserve, the growing trend among the Reserve Banks is to set up a BSA/AML structure comprising teams of examiners who possess a mix of advanced and intermediate BSA skills to focus on BSA/AML issues. As of December 31, 2005, 108 examiners were identified as having advanced BSA skills. According to officials at the Federal Reserve, to qualify as a specialized examiner in this area, examiners must show an aptitude for BSA/AML and undergo additional training. Specialization is achieved through a combination of on-the-job and classroom training. The Federal Reserve also centrally tracks the skill levels of examiners with special skill sets (e.g., BSA compliance).

In a previous report, we noted that FDIC and the Federal Reserve both have examiners who are AML subject matter experts and serve as training resources for other examiners.[4] According to FDIC officials, between June 2004 and December 2005, the number of FDIC's AML subject matter experts more than doubled, from 150 to 347. The officials said the increase was due, in part, to the implementing rules of the PATRIOT Act and the importance of BSA compliance in ensuring the safety and soundness of FDIC- supervised institutions. Both agencies also train examiners who are primarily responsible for conducting BSA/AML examinations. Specifically, FDIC's subject matter experts receive specialized training in the classroom and on the job. Furthermore, in 2005, as a pilot initiative within FDIC, 19 individuals from FDIC's Division of Supervision and Consumer Protection and the Legal Division successfully completed an industry-recognized accreditation for AML specialists. Following this pilot initiative, as of yearend 2005, FDIC extended the program to approximately 37 BSA/AML risk management examination personnel.

In response to an internal quality assurance assessment of OCC's BSA/AML compliance supervision, which found that OCC did not direct sufficient resources to BSA/AML compliance, in July 2005, OCC committed to redirect staff to BSA/AML work and apply additional resources to this area. In a November 2005 letter to Chairman Shelby, the OCC Comptroller stated that, to increase OCC's BSA/AML resources, in addition to other actions, OCC was developing a national pool of experienced BSA/AML examiners to be deployed to address OCC's high-priority and high-risk examinations. While, according to OCC officials, OCC does not have specifically designated BSA/AML specialists, the agency has examiners who possess specialized knowledge in performing BSA/AML examinations. In addition, the agency has examiners specialized in other examination disciplines, such as commercial, retail credit, capital markets, and trust, who are also cross-trained to conduct BSA examinations. Furthermore, OCC has a lead compliance expert in each district office and, as of December 2005, had six full-time BSA/AML compliance policy specialists in the Washington office dedicated to developing policy and training and assisting on complex examinations. OCC officials also stated that OCC supports a range of industry certifications and licensing, and it was committed to sponsoring staff who want to obtain professional certification as money laundering specialists through advanced training and testing.

OTS and NCUA differ from the other regulators in that they have developed consumer compliance subject matter examiners or consumer compliance specialists. These examiners received additional training on compliance issues, including BSA/AML compliance, and act as a resource on issues that arise from the examination process. Additionally, OTS's compliance specialists provide on-the-job training and advice during examinations and analyze draft examination reports and reviews. As of December 31, 2005, NCUA had 27 examiners designated as consumer compliance subject matter examiners, and OTS had 15 dedicated compliance specialists.

4. Systems Improvements Help Regulators Track BSA Examination and Violation Data, but Differences in Terminology Remain

The regulators use various internal control mechanisms to monitor BSA examinations, and recent improvements in their automated examination and enforcement data systems have enabled them to better track and report BSA-related information. Until recently, the systems that regulators used to track data on BSA violations and enforcement had serious shortcomings, but they have updated their systems. Moreover, regulators are able to more readily share BSA-related information, which is a particularly important ability in light of the MOU that regulators signed with FinCEN in September 2004. The regulators agreed to provide FinCEN with quarterly reports on the number of BSA-related examinations they conducted, the number and types of BSA violations cited, and the institutions cited for repeat violations. In addition, FinCEN agreed to provide analytical reports to the regulators and has begun to do so. However, the regulators differ on how they classify and define some BSA compliance problems. For example, not all of the regulators provide written guidance on what constitutes a violation, and existing guidance leaves key terms undefined and varies in scope. Furthermore, our limited review of examinations indicated that different terms were used for similar problems. As a result, inconsistencies in recording and reporting BSA compliance problems could occur.

Regulators Use Supervisory and Quality Assurance Reviews and Tracking Systems to Monitor BSA Examinations

Along with quality assurance reviews and automated tracking systems, the regulators use supervisory (or management) reviews as the primary means of monitoring BSA examinations. These mechanisms reflect federal internal control standards for meeting agency objectives. Control activities as described in the federal standards include internal management reviews and documentation. Additionally, federal internal control standards include monitoring to assess the quality of performance over time. For example, most regulators review and approve key BSA examination procedures, including scoping and planning activities and decisions on violations, as follows:

- Examiners and officials from the Federal Reserve and OCC told us that supervisory review and approval were required for scoping and planning activities on BSA examinations of large banks.
- Federal Reserve and OCC officials stated that district management approved examination plans for BSA examinations of community banks.
- FDIC officials noted that examiners were required to discuss scope changes with managers or supervisors.

As managers communicate with examiners to stay abreast of findings and provide guidance and approvals, they also require review or approval of decisions to cite depository institutions with BSA violations or to take enforcement actions. Informal corrective actions are reviewed at the regulators' field offices, but enforcement actions require higher level review and approval (for more information on informal and formal enforcement actions, see ch. 5). For example, supervisors at the Board of Governors review and approve all decisions to take enforcement actions at the Federal Reserve. The regulators further review examination reports and approve recommendations to notify FinCEN of violations.

All of the regulators also use quality assurance reviews to assess and improve the quality of BSA examinations. These reviews are designed to serve a variety of purposes, such as identifying significant or evolving problems, ensuring consistency in the application of examination procedures, and ensuring the accuracy and completeness of examination data and results and the timeliness of supervisory actions. For example, Federal Reserve officials said that the Reserve Banks use their quality assurance programs partly to determine whether BSA examinations were carried out appropriately and consistently. OTS's quality assurance program reviews BSA examinations to determine the reliability and accuracy of examination data. OTS officials said that 2004 quality assurance reviews assessed the accuracy of OTS's input controls over BSA violation data, examination results and reports, and supervisory actions taken as a result of BSA examinations.

Regulators also conduct or use other reviews—operational, peer, and IG—to assess the accuracy, completeness, and quality of BSA examinations. For example, Federal Reserve officials said that they assess the quality of Reserve Banks' supervision function, including BSA examinations, through an operations review program. According to Federal Reserve officials, recent operations reviews evaluated the timeliness of corrective actions, tested information in BSA examination work papers for accuracy and consistency, and evaluated the adequacy of resources devoted to this area. OCC officials also told us that, as part of their peer review program, examiners from OCC regional offices performed quality reviews of each other's examinations, including BSA examinations. Furthermore, most regulators have undergone IG reviews of their BSA-related examination and enforcement activities and have taken steps to implement recommendation actions. For example:

- In 2001, the Treasury IG reviewed OCC's examination coverage of trust and private banking services. The IG recommended that OCC improve its examination monitoring process to ensure adequate oversight of BSA examinations covering trust and private banking services. OCC indicated that it would conduct targeted internal quality assurance reviews of private banking and trust services beginning in 2002.

- In 2003, the Treasury IG also reviewed OTS's enforcement actions for BSA violations and recommended that the agency enhance its regional reviews of examinations to ensure that substantive BSA violations were incorporated into final reports. According to an OTS official, OTS has implemented this recommendation.
- Since 2003, FDIC's IG also has reviewed aspects of the regulator's BSA-related examination and enforcement activities and made several recommendations to FDIC. For example, in 2004, the IG recommended that FDIC coordinate with state banking departments to cover BSA compliance in state examinations. FDIC has agreed with, and responded to, these recommendations by issuing guidance and agreeing to schedule BSA/AML examinations during safety and soundness examinations led by state examiners.[1]

Finally, regulators use automated data systems to collect, store, and make available examination data and information on supervisory and enforcement actions. Federal internal control standards indicate that managers need such relevant and reliable information to carry out their internal control and operational responsibilities. For example:

- FDIC officials said that the agency collects and stores examination data, but it uses a separate system to record and track data on various types of enforcement actions.
- OCC officials said that staff use data systems for large, midsize, and community banks to retrieve information on prior BSA-related violations and enforcement actions and to identify institutions for BSA/AML-targeted examinations.
- Similarly, OTS officials noted that the agency's data system collects and stores examination data, such as examination start and end dates and violations of laws or regulations, and includes BSA-related violations.
- Federal Reserve officials said that the agency's data systems collect and maintain examination and enforcement data, such as examination start and end dates and violations of laws or regulations, and include BSA-related violations and enforcement actions.

Regulators also rely on data from these systems and other software programs to track information on depository institutions' BSA-related compliance problems and to assist them in taking supervisory or enforcement actions in a timely manner. For example, FDIC officials noted that they use FDIC's data system to produce an internal report that, in part, lists all FDIC-supervised institutions with BSA violations, the number and type of violations cited in examination reports, and repeat violations. OCC and OTS officials said that they use their data systems to produce reports on BSA-related violations for FinCEN.

Data System Improvements Have Allowed the Regulators to Better Track BSA-Related Information

Since 2000, the regulators have changed or upgraded the systems they use to record and monitor examination information. As a result, the regulators can now better track BSA-related information. Some regulators also have been citing BSA violations in greater number and detail in recent years—partly as a result of improved systems and partly as a result of factors specific to each regulator, including revised guidance and an increased emphasis on the BSA.

Changes to Regulators' Data Systems Have Improved Tracking Capabilities

According to regulatory officials, since 2000, all of the regulators have changed or upgraded their data systems to improve their recording and monitoring capabilities. To varying degrees, previous iterations of these data systems limited regulators' ability to monitor and report BSA-related examination results in a comprehensive and timely manner. For example, before 2001, NCUA manually collected information on BSA-related violations. According to a senior NCUA official, in response to the need to provide data to external parties, including Congress, NCUA began to redesign its information technology system in 2001. NCUA's current data system became fully operational in 2002, providing NCUA with increased search capability across examination data. Furthermore, it allows NCUA to track more BSA data, including violations and any corrective actions institutions had implemented.

Similarly, OTS generally collected information on BSA violations manually until the late 1990s, which is when it began automating its examination documentation program. Moreover, the Treasury IG determined that material data inaccuracies with OTS's BSA records could adversely affect supervisory decisions to the extent that OTS senior managers and regional supervisors used the system to monitor, plan, or review individual BSA examination results. In 2003, OTS replaced its former system to facilitate storage of examination work papers with related examination reports. According to OTS officials, the new Internet-based system allows greater flexibility in the examination administration process. For example, OTS officials said that the new system tracks comprehensive data on examinations and violations, including data on BSA compliance. OTS also replaced a separate system used to collect information on enforcement actions. OTS officials noted that these current systems also provide the ability to track repeat violations, corrective actions and associated dates of implementation, and enforcement actions—capabilities that OTS's previous systems had lacked.

Before 2003, FDIC's examination data system did not require entry of BSA violation codes or information from examiners' on-site visits that was related to BSA compliance. As a result, FDIC staff lacked information to confirm that institution management had taken corrective actions to address problems identified during examinations. According to FDIC officials, in 2003, FDIC upgraded its examination data system to a Web-based platform, to enhance overall user capabilities. FDIC indicated that although the former examination data system captured BSA program violations as well as financial record-keeping and reporting violations, the upgrade to the system incorporated violations related to the implementing rules of the PATRIOT Act and the FDIC's suspicious activity reporting rule. FDIC indicated that in 2005, the agency also upgraded its enforcement action data system to a Web-based platform to allow for the selection of multiple bases for enforcement actions and for the automated tracking of BSA-related enforcement actions.

OCC has separate systems to maintain the official electronic records of examination and enforcement information, including information on BSA violations and enforcement actions, for large banks, and midsize and community banks. OCC officials said that in 2000, OCC implemented an interim examination data system for large-bank examinations to address a general need to store more descriptive text, such as examiner narrative, comments, and information on contacts and communications with banks. In late 2003, OCC began integrating this interim system into its current examination data system for large banks to store all the information in one system. One advantage of the system conversion was that it provided OCC with the ability to search the full text of examination narratives, including BSA examinations. According to OCC officials, the redesign and systems improvements will be fully implemented in 2006.

The Federal Reserve for some years has used national supervisory data systems that maintain electronic records of examination and enforcement information, including examination reports, enforcement actions, and other relevant documents. Additionally, the Federal Reserve maintains a national database of supervisory data specifically designed to support its banking supervision activities. These systems were, and continue to be, accessible to all appropriate supervisory staff across the Federal Reserve System. However, at the beginning of our review, Federal Reserve officials said that, unlike other examination areas, the Federal Reserve did not collect and track most BSA-related information through its national database. Rather, officials said that the database maintained narrative information on BSA violations data within reports of examination for purposes of ongoing supervision. They noted that the Federal Reserve used a separate mechanism to centralize information on BSA-related examination findings from the 12 Reserve Banks.[2] Furthermore, they noted that this lack of automation and the use of a separate mechanism limited their ability to centrally track and extract in an automated fashion certain aspects of BSA-related supervision across the 12 Reserve Banks. For example, at the time of our data requests in 2004, the Federal Reserve experienced difficulty in generating information on the total number of examinations conducted between 2000 and 2004 that included a BSA review, and the agency was unable to provide the number and nature of BSA-related violations identified during this period.

During the course of our review, Federal Reserve officials said that the Federal Reserve began to improve centralized tracking and analysis of BSA-related data through its national examination database. In 2003, the Federal Reserve began to enhance its national examiner database to capture BSA/AML violations or other BSA examination-related data. Federal Reserve officials noted that as part of those efforts, in 2004 the Federal Reserve expanded the reporting mechanism to track examination data and expand risk categories and, in 2005, integrated these data into the national database. Federal Reserve officials said that the expanded version would assist in collecting more detailed information, including the nature and frequency of BSA-related violations and the nature of institutions' risk of BSA noncompliance. In addition, Federal Reserve officials noted that in 2004, they began merging more detailed BSA-related information collected from the Reserve Banks with existing supervisory data to provide the Federal Reserve with a national view of various BSA-related items, such as commitments from institution management to correct identified problems and different types of enforcement actions. According to Federal Reserve officials, the Federal Reserve finalized the conversion of its database, and, since the last quarter of calendar year 2005, Federal Reserve staff have been able to extract BSA examination and enforcement data collected by the Reserve Banks.

BSA-Related Violations Increased in Recent Years; Violations of Currency Transaction Reporting Requirements Were Frequently Cited

OCC officials attributed the increase in the number of examinations from 2003 to 2004 to a change in the way OCC counted BSA examinations.

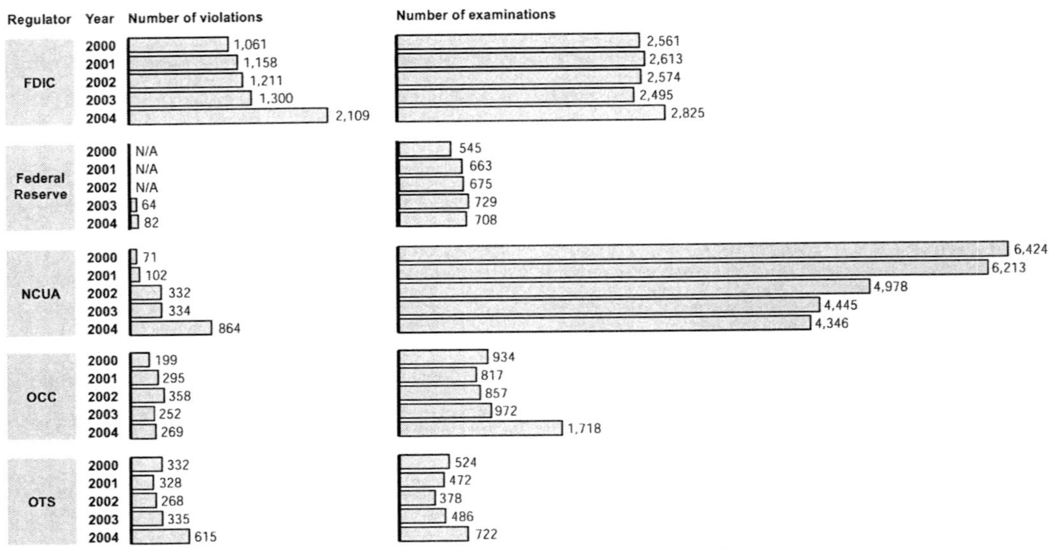

Source: GAO analysis of Federal Reserve, FDIC, NCUA, OCC, and OTS data.

Figure 3. BSA-Related Violations and Examinations, by Regulator (2000–2004).

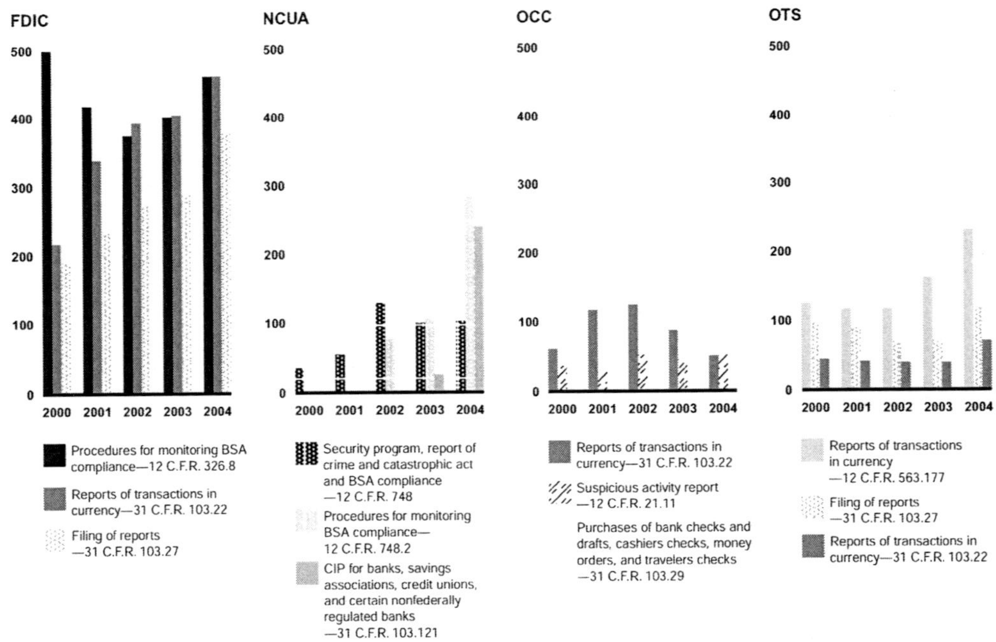

Source: GAO analysis of Federal Reserve, FDIC, NCUA, OCC, and OTS data.

Figure 4. Frequently Cited BSA-Related Violations, by Regulator (2000–2004).

The regulators distinguish between technical violations that are considered minor, such as the late filing of a CTR or failure to fill in certain boxes on a CTR form, and systemic violations, such as failure to have a BSA/AML program. For example, data from FDIC, OCC, and OTS show that in 2003 and 2004, citations issued in connection with CTR requirements (31 C.F.R. §§ 103.22 and 103.27) (see fig. 4) were among the frequently cited BSA-related violations. These violations of the CTR requirements included a failure to (1) file CTRs and

(2) file them in a timely manner. In contrast, NCUA data indicate that in 2003 and 2004, citations issued in connection with procedures for monitoring BSA compliance (12 C.F.R. § 748.2) and the customer identification program (CIP) rule, which was implemented under the PATRIOT Act of May 2003 (31 C.F.R. § 103.121), were among the frequently cited BSA-related violations. Violations of the CIP rule involved improperly verifying the identity of customers at account opening. Other frequently cited violations included violations of the regulators' BSA/AML program rules pursuant to title 12 of the *United States Code.*

In Recent Years, Some Regulators Have Been Citing BSA Violations with Greater Specificity Than Before

NCUA and FDIC cited violations with greater specificity from 2003 to 2004 than from 2000 to 2002. Our review of BSA-related violation data from 2000 through 2001 indicated that NCUA's system generally classified any violation of the BSA/AML program rule regulation under a single broad category. In contrast, from 2002 to 2004, NCUA's violation data identified the particular subsections that institutions violated. In addition, FDIC officials noted that their data quality improved considerably in March 2003 with the implementation of its current examination data system, which can now specify subsections of BSA-related regulations that institutions have violated. In late 2003, FDIC changed the way that it tracked BSA violations. After evaluating how its examination data system generated violation reports, FDIC concluded that it was more useful to review the "number of banks" where specific violations were cited, rather than to record the frequency of each violation cited during each examination. Furthermore, FDIC officials noted that the number-of-banks format is used by FinCEN to ensure a more appropriate comparison from quarter to quarter and among the regulators.

Regulators Now Share More Specific BSA-Related Examination and Violation Data with FinCEN

Under an MOU entered into by the regulators and FinCEN in September 2004, the regulators share more specific BSA-related examination and violation data with FinCEN.[3] Using their examination data systems, the regulators provide FinCEN with quarterly reports on the number of BSA- related examinations they have conducted, the number and types of BSA violations cited, and the institutions cited for repeat violations. According to FinCEN officials, as of February 2006, they had received the aggregate data from the regulators for the fourth quarter of 2004 and the four quarters of 2005. They also had received two annual reports from the regulators, which included the number of financial institutions the regulators examined and descriptions of examination cycles, also as outlined in the MOU.

In turn, the MOU requires that FinCEN provide a compilation that summarizes, by regulator, all of the data provided in the quarterly reports. FinCEN has provided the regulators with these summaries as well as an annual consolidated report.[4] Table 5 summarizes this information for fiscal year 2005.

Table 5. BSA/AML Examinations, Violations, and Enforcement Actions by Regulator(Fiscal Year 2005)

Regulator	Number of examinations[a]	Number of violations[b]	Enforcement actions[c]
FDIC	2,525	2,576	172
Federal Reserve	680	97	52
NCUA	4,715	4,754	1,824
OCC	1,530	405	42
OTS	722	514	29

Source: FinCEN.

[a]The number of examinations conducted within each regulator's established BSA examination cycle, including examinations conducted jointly with state banking departments.

[b]The number of BSA violations cited under title 12 or title 31 of the *United States Code*.

[c]The number of formal and informal enforcement actions taken to address BSA compliance under either title 12 or title 31 of the *United States Code*.

FinCEN officials noted that there are limitations to the aggregate data. These data do not provide insight into the reasons why the violations are occurring; rather, they are indications of issues to follow or act upon through the supervisory process. FinCEN officials said that these data compilations have shown increases in violations of requirements involving CIPs, independent reviews, and BSA training. FinCEN has shared these data with the regulators and given them areas to be aware of for follow-up at their institutions.

According to FinCEN officials, FinCEN provided other analytical products to the regulators as well. For example, FinCEN was directed by the Treasury IG to undertake a SAR data quality review. As part of this effort, FinCEN has identified problems with some SAR filings, which it then shared with the regulators. The regulators told us that they have found these SAR analyses to be useful because they can then direct the specific institutions to address the problems. FinCEN also conducted a systematic review of banking industry compliance with section 314(a) of the PATRIOT Act and identified specific institutions that had not been doing required searches of their accounts.[5] As with the SAR data problems, FinCEN has shared this information with the regulators so that they can conduct follow-up with the institutions to rectify the problem. FinCEN officials noted that these products are intended to help the regulators elicit better BSA compliance. FinCEN plans to provide additional products to the regulators, containing more strategic and tactical analyses, in the future. In addition, FinCEN officials noted that the provision of analysis to determine compliance trends across industry segments and across the financial services sector—that is, banking, securities, insurance, casinos, and others—was a long-term project. Near-term priorities included conducting analyses of cases of significant noncompliance sent in by the regulators. Such analysis would include all known information and BSA-related filings relevant to the institution or customers when considering an enforcement action. FinCEN officials said that its computer system is now operational, and they had begun populating it with case data.

FinCEN officials stressed that they wanted the products they provided to the regulators to be ones that would help the regulators do their job. That is, that the products could help identify emerging areas in BSA compliance that require more guidance, new regulations, or changes to existing guidance. In general, the regulators told us that they were pleased with the analytical products they had received from FinCEN since signing the MOU, and that they were looking forward to receiving additional products from FinCEN in the future, especially those that showed BSA noncompliance trends across financial industries or in specific geographic areas.

The regulators also have begun to analyze the BSA compliance data they receive from FinCEN for their own purposes. For example, OTS officials said the technology upgrades they implemented over the past few years have made analyzing these data much easier. From these analyses, they determined that there were a number of institutions with problems in their BSA training programs. OTS officials in headquarters also analyze examination results on a nationwide basis looking for BSA compliance trends. OCC officials analyze BSA data in two ways. First, OCC identifies common compliance problems and seeks to identify areas needing clarification through new guidance. Second, OCC analyzes BSA compliance data on community banks for money laundering risks to help develop examination strategies and to determine examination scope. According to Federal Reserve officials, since the last quarter of 2005, the Federal Reserve has been able to analyze BSA examination and enforcement data collected by the Reserve Banks and analyze this information at the headquarters level for trends and consistency. Federal Reserve officials also noted that the reports from FinCEN supplement the Federal Reserve's monitoring and analysis of supervisory data. FDIC officials said they have conducted trend analyses of examination data since the issuance of the FFIEC *Examination Manual* and have seen a slight decrease in BSA-related violations overall among FDIC-supervised institutions. According to NCUA officials, NCUA analyzes all of the data collected during the examination and supervisory processes. For example, NCUA analyzes data that examiners must collect, in accordance with NCUA policy, on credit unions' actions to address significant BSA compliance problems. Furthermore, NCUA officials said that NCUA has an initiative under way to create a database of the information contained in the BSA questionnaires that credit unions complete as part of the examination process, allowing NCUA to query this information from NCUA's regions and headquarters. NCUA officials estimated that it would take 3 years to populate the database.

The regulators have been conducting these analyses internally, but they have not yet collectively discussed with FinCEN the implications of the violation data and determined whether there was a need for additional guidance to address problem areas they have been identifying. The MOU states that, by the effective use of information exchanged under its provisions, FinCEN and the regulators will seek to enhance the level of assistance and analysis that can be provided to the banking industry and to law enforcement in the BSA compliance area. Such guidance could provide these additional benefits.

Differences Remain in the Regulators' Guidance and Terminology for Classification of BSA Compliance Problems

Although the regulators and FinCEN increasingly have been enhancing and coordinating information sharing and reporting, differences in how the regulators classify BSA-related compliance problems remain. For example, regulators differ in the guidance they provide to examiners for determining what constitutes a BSA program compliance violation, with some regulators not providing any written guidance and others differing in the degree of guidance provided. Furthermore, the regulators' instructions on BSA enforcement, which also provide guidance for interpreting or classifying BSA-related problems, does not clearly define the terms—intended as criteria for determining the seriousness or scope of a compliance problem—on which those classifications would be based. Additionally, there appears to be no clear consensus among examiners on how to distinguish between BSA-related deficiencies and violations. In our review of the regulators' examinations, examiners appear to have classified apparently similar BSA-related compliance problems differently. In some cases, examiners referred to BSA program compliance problems as "deficiencies"; in other cases, the problems were cited as "violations." As a result, examiner judgment likely played a greater role in classifying BSA-related compliance problems. In turn, this could increase the potential for inconsistencies in classifying BSA-related compliance problems and subsequent citations. However, regulators emphasized that other factors, such as an institution's risk profile or the diversity of its operations and products, also help explain the differences in the way that BSA-related compliance problems were cited and classified.

Regulators' Guidance on How to Cite and Classify BSA-Related Compliance Problems Leaves Key Terms Undefined and Varies in Scope

When we reviewed the regulators' BSA examinations, we generally found that the distinction between BSA/AML program compliance "violations" and "deficiencies" appeared to be that violations represented some action or inaction prohibited by the BSA and implementing regulations, and deficiencies did not. Overall, regulators may cite an institution for a BSA violation if it fails to meet the requirements of BSA/AML programs, which encompass the following four elements:

- internal policies, procedures, and controls to ensure ongoing compliance;
- an independent audit function to test programs;
- a designated individual who is responsible for the day-to-day coordination and monitoring of compliance; and
- an ongoing training program for the appropriate personnel.[6]

Additionally, the regulators may cite institutions for failing to correct a previously cited problem.

Typically, examiners accompanied a description of a violation with a legal citation in examination reports. BSA/AML program compliance deficiencies were not regarded as violations of the laws and regulations, and examination reports generally described the deficiencies as BSA program performance that was faulty or insufficient.

However, the regulators have taken different approaches to providing examiners with guidance on the classification and citation of BSA compliance problems. For example, the Federal Reserve provides no written guidance for determining BSA/AML program compliance violations. Federal Reserve examiners rely on the BSA itself and relevant regulations to classify and cite BSA compliance problems. In addition to the BSA and related regulations, the other four regulators each provide some written guidance for determining BSA violations. Each regulator differs in the nature and amount of guidance provided. FDIC, OCC, and OTS also provide guidance that addresses, to some extent, how examiners are to distinguish BSA/AML program compliance deficiencies from violations.

More specifically, section 8.1 of the FDIC's *Risk Management Manual of Examination Policies* provides some guidance to examiners on the proper citation of apparent violations of the BSA-related regulations in the report of examination. An apparent violation may be cited in situations where deficiencies in the BSA/AML program are serious or systemic in nature, or when weaknesses and deficiencies identified in the BSA program are significant, repeated, or pervasive. The FDIC manual also states that an apparent violation of BSA program requirements should be cited for a specific program deficiency to the extent that the deficiency is attributed to internal controls, independent testing, the individual responsible for monitoring day-to-day compliance, or training.[7] However, if the apparent violation is determined to be an isolated program weakness that does not significantly impair the effectiveness of the overall compliance program, then an apparent violation should not be cited. FDIC's manual also provides examples of specific issues and situations that warrant a citation of an apparent violation.

OCC guidance provides that citing an institution for a BSA violation and taking a subsequent cease-and-desist action are appropriate when a bank "exhibits BSA/AML program deficiencies coupled with aggravating factors, such as highly suspicious activity creating a significant potential for money laundering. . .or other substantial BSA violations." OCC's guidance also lists conditions within BSA/AML programs, including systemic or pervasive BSA record-keeping violations, which can be grounds for citation of a BSA violation. Additionally, OCC's policy guidance on enforcement actions also lists several serious problems for which a citation of a violation and accompanying formal enforcement action might be considered appropriate. OTS specifies that a systemic or other significant failure to file CTRs is a BSA violation. OTS's policy guidance on enforcement actions also lists several serious problems for which a citation of a violation and accompanying formal enforcement action might be considered appropriate. These include situations involving an institution's significant problems or weaknesses with records, systems, controls, or internal audit program. More recently, OTS provided guidance stating that their terms "significant," "material," and "substantive" mean the same thing.

Although NCUA is one of four regulators providing written guidance, it takes a different approach. NCUA does not recognize any difference between program deficiencies and violations, although NCUA officials stated that they regarded a major deficiency as a violation. Instead, NCUA guidance focuses on qualitative factors: BSA violations must be "significant." NCUA provides criteria for determining when a violation is significant, and NCUA's guidance states that consistent assessment of BSA violations is an important part of compliance with the FinCEN MOU. NCUA categorizes significant violations in the following three groups: "pervasive," "systemic," and "repeat." For example, pervasive violations are described as tainting the entire operation of a credit union and include the lack of a written BSA/AML program that adequately covers all required elements. To apply NCUA's guidance, NCUA examiners must first determine if a credit union's activities amounted to significant violations and then classify the activity according to the definitions and examples in the guidance. As a result, NCUA examiners do not report deficiencies. Our review of 30 NCUA examinations identified one deficiency that was described only in work papers. Available information did not indicate whether or how the deficiency was reported in NCUA's automated reporting system. Nevertheless, NCUA examiners told us that they could distinguish deficiencies from violations, and they gave us an example of a deficiency as an institution failing to update a policy but having a procedure in place.

In addition, the regulators often do not clearly define the modifiers or terms used to describe BSA compliance problems. For instance, the regulators frequently use, but do not define or illustrate, the terms “inadequate” and “adequate.” FDIC’s guidance describes as “inadequate” BSA/AML programs with considerable problems, which essentially amount to violations, but the guidance does provide any further explanation or definition. FDIC examiners told us that they did not have standardized criteria for characterizing the adequacy or inadequacy of a BSA program, and that the term “adequate” could mean “satisfactory”; similarly, the term “inadequate” could mean “deficient,” “unsatisfactory,” or “needs improvement.” For example, in our review of FDIC BSA examinations, we found that examiners frequently used the terms “adequate” or “inadequate” to refer to an institution’s level of program compliance and to describe deficiencies or violations.

The different meanings given to these terms also appear to affect how examiners classify BSA problems. For example, NCUA officials said that having an adequate practice but no written policy for the practice would be counted as a BSA violation in NCUA’s data system. However, a Federal Reserve official noted that a violation would not be cited for a practice that was deemed adequate, even though the bank’s policy might not address it. In this example, examiners would direct the institution to take corrective action to ensure that it had a written policy addressing the practice. We also noted that the regulators could use many different terms to refer to the same thing. According to Federal Reserve officials, examiners may use the terms “deficiency,” “weakness,” “inadequacy,” or “exception” to mean the same thing. Furthermore, FDIC guidance refers to violations as “apparent violations.”

FinCEN officials said that, they discussed the issue of different terminology with regulators during the drafting of the terms of the MOU. FinCEN and the regulators agreed not to impose any requirements for standardized terminology in the MOU itself. Instead, they structured the MOU to require the regulators to provide FinCEN with information on instances of “significant” noncompliance, be it a BSA violation under title 12 or title 31 of the *United States Code*, regardless of whether the regulator classified the conduct as a violation or a deficiency. That is, all problems against which the regulator is taking supervisory action are to be reported to FinCEN. This reporting of significant noncompliance is in addition to the quarterly reports the regulators provide to FinCEN under the MOU on the number of BSA-related examinations they have conducted, the number and types of BSA violations cited, and the number of BSA-related enforcements actions put in place or terminated during the quarter.

Examiners Generally Did Not Agree on When a BSA Program Compliance Deficiency Amounted to a BSA Violation

Although four regulators provided some guidance for determining BSA program deficiencies and violations, examiners could not clearly articulate what constituted a deficiency. That is, in our discussions with the examiners, they seemed to agree that a BSA violation amounted to noncompliance with a BSA law or regulation; however, they did not have a uniform definition or understanding of when a BSA program compliance deficiency rose to the level of a violation.

To illustrate, FDIC examiners said that a deficiency was the examiner’s conclusion on the basis of the institution’s lack of compliance with BSA, but a violation was a deviation from or noncompliance with a BSA rule or regulation. NCUA examiners said that a deficiency usually referred to problems with policies; for example, an institution might not have updated a BSA policy for which it had procedures in place. According to OCC examiners, a deficiency was an activity that, although not defined or classified by the statutes as a violation, fell "below standard" and did not reflect sound AML management. OTS examiners stated that there were no clear definitions of BSA violations; however, they regarded a "violation of a regulation" to be a BSA violation. Federal Reserve examiners told us that they had difficulty determining whether a given set of facts amounted to a BSA program deficiency or violation, and that, as a result, a lot of examiner judgment went into determining whether the facts supported a citation of a BSA program deficiency or violation. They also said that they submitted program deficiencies to headquarters for assistance in determining whether deficiencies constituted violations and how problems should be classified.

Examiners Cited Institutions Differently for Apparently Similar Problems, but Regulators Noted Several Factors That Could Have Caused Differences

In our review of 138 BSA examinations, we identified at least 8 instances, involving 17 institutions, in which examiners cited institutions differently for what appeared to be substantially similar problems. For example, different regulators recognized similar substantial or material problems in internal audits, but cited the institutions with either a BSA program deficiency or a violation. In one instance, Federal Reserve examiners pointed out a deficiency to the institution because the internal audit report failed to identify and report material weaknesses that were identified during the examination. But FDIC examiners cited an institution with a BSA violation for its inadequate audit testing that lacked independence and did not test or review certain areas. Similarly, regulators issued different types of citations to institutions that had not adequately tested their systems. Federal Reserve examiners pointed out a deficiency to an institution for not conducting annual independent testing at all of its 15 branches and for failing to perform a regularly scheduled audit. However, OTS and FDIC examiners cited institutions with violations for failing to perform independent testing. Although examiners cited institutions with BSA violations or deficiencies on what appeared to be substantially similar grounds, we did not review the cited violations or deficiencies for correctness and did not conclude that they were incorrect. The lack of uniform, clear guidance for distinguishing between BSA/AML program deficiencies and violations likely increases the examiners' reliance on professional judgment to make findings of deficiencies and violations, which in turn could result in inconsistencies in classifying deficiencies and violations, which was apparent in some of the examinations that we reviewed.

According to most of the regulators, multiple factors could contribute to differences among examiner citations. For example, according to OCC officials, an institution's risk profile, products, or commitment to resolving problems could influence an examiner's determination. The perceived severity of the institution's problem also could influence the decision to issue a violation or a deficiency. One OCC official noted that no two institutions were alike, and that the regulation was not designed to be "one size fits all." Nevertheless, OCC recognized the potential for inconsistent interpretations in citing violations of its BSA regulation. In a May 2005 report sent to the Senate Committee on Banking, Housing, and Urban Affairs, OCC stated that its guidance on citing violations of the regulation was open to multiple and inconsistent interpretations.[8] As a result, OCC revised the guidance in November 2004 to clearly state that there is a statutory mandate that OCC will issue a cease-and-desist order for violations of the regulation, since the OCC's review team had found inconsistent treatment of violations of the regulation.

NCUA officials thought its classifications of BSA problems were consistent, and that it was more important to allow the regulators to have flexibility to interpret and classify BSA compliance problems, given the differences in the institutions they supervised. Federal Reserve officials stated that differences in terms used to describe deficiencies that did not rise to the level of violations were less important, and that consistency in the citation of violations was of primary importance because of the more immediate supervisory consequences of such citations.

5. Regulators and FinCEN Increased Coordination on BSA Enforcement; Criminal Cases Were Limited

Regulators address most BSA-related compliance problems through the examination process. Although the regulators can use tools that range from supervisory actions (such as moral suasion) to informal actions (such as MOUs) and formal enforcement actions (such as the assessment of CMPs), according to the regulators, most BSA-related problems are resolved during the course of an examination. FinCEN also uses a range of enforcement tools, including CMPs; but, according to FinCEN officials, FinCEN must ensure the consistent application of CMPs across all financial institutions, not only those supervised by the regulators. Moreover, unlike the regulators, FinCEN was delegated authority under the BSA to take enforcement actions for violations of the BSA and its implementing regulations. From 2000 to 2005, FinCEN assessed CMPs in 11 cases, with significantly higher penalties in recent years. Although the Secretary of the Treasury has not delegated enforcement authority to the regulators as statute directs, FinCEN officials said there have been no significant consequences of FinCEN and the regulators operating under independent, but overlapping, statutory authorities to assess CMPs. Furthermore, FinCEN and the regulators have increased coordination on enforcement consequent to their September 2004 MOU on information sharing. For example, they have begun to concurrently assess CMPs for significant BSA problems at depository institutions. Criminal cases against depository institutions for BSA violations have been limited. From 2002 to 2005, Justice, either through its Criminal Division or its U.S. Attorneys' Offices, has pursued legal action against six depository institutions for criminal violation of the BSA. The increase in actions has raised some concerns in the banking industry, although Justice officials said that investigations of depository institutions for BSA noncompliance generally have involved only those cases wherein institutions engaged in willful and repeated failures to fulfill their legal duties. Furthermore, in some cases, the alleged criminal conduct of customers revealed to investigators the lapses at the institutions. Most criminal investigations of depository institutions were resolved through deferred prosecution agreements and monetary penalties. Finally, Justice recently formalized coordination on cases where a financial institution would be named as an unindicted coconspirator or allowed to enter into a deferred prosecution agreement.

Regulators Address Most BSA-Related Compliance Problems within the Examination Framework

Each regulator's authority to take supervisory actions and informal enforcement actions lies in its respective general authority to supervise financial institutions and exercise discretion to carry out the purposes of its enabling statute. Supervisory actions generally involve communicating recommendations to institution management during examinations or though the examination report. Although regulators use a broad range of actions to address BSA compliance, according to the regulators, most problems in BSA-related compliance are corrected within the examination framework through supervisory actions. OCC officials noted that such supervisory actions generally are used to correct relatively minor or technical compliance problems. The regulators typically request depository institutions' management and directors to correct problems that were identified during examinations and communicated through the report of examination. OTS officials noted that addressing BSA compliance problems within the examination framework meant that the institutions could correct the problems promptly and the examiners could review the corrections immediately. NCUA encourages examiners to resolve problems informally whenever possible. Representatives of some regulators also noted that if supervisory actions proved insufficient or problems required stronger action, the regulators generally would use informal enforcement actions. Informal enforcement actions are mutual agreements between the regulator and the institution to correct an identified problem. They generally involve written commitments from institution management to correct the problem and are used to address problems that are not critical, and that plausibly could be corrected through a voluntary commitment from the institution's management. For example, OCC issues MOUs or commitment letters, reflecting specific commitments to take corrective actions in response to problems or concerns identified by OCC in its supervision of a bank. The letters are then signed by the institution's board of directors on behalf of the bank and acknowledged by an authorized OCC official. Although informal enforcement actions are not public and are not binding legal documents, failure to honor the commitments could provide the regulator with evidence of the need for formal action. The regulators noted that they generally use informal enforcement actions against BSA noncompliance that is limited in scope and technical in nature. According to representatives of the regulators, the regulators generally require the institutions to inform them after a specified time of their progress in making the corrections, and to verify that the improvements have been made. Furthermore, examiners can conduct verifications before or during subsequent examinations. According to FinCEN data, the regulators took 2,048 informal enforcement actions in fiscal year 2005.

Our review of 138 examinations conducted between January 1, 2000, and June 30, 2004, that contained a BSA-related violation, also indicated that the regulators most frequently addressed BSA problems through supervisory actions. The regulators generally obtained oral commitments from institution management or used informal actions to address problems with components of institutions' compliance programs or limited problems with BSA filings. The regulators mostly obtained oral commitments from institution management to correct identified problems during meetings with management or boards of directors. For example, in a 2002 examination, NCUA examiners identified that a credit union had failed to update its written BSA policy to reflect the name of its new compliance officer. The institution's board of directors agreed immediately to correct the problem. Similarly, in a 2000 examination,

FDIC examiners determined that the bank failed to file four CTRs in a timely manner. The examiners noted that before the examination, bank management already had improved internal practices to avoid such violations in the future. They obtained agreement from the bank president to correct the four instances of CTR-related noncompliance. Our review also identified instances of the regulators' use of informal enforcement actions to address BSA-related noncompliance. For example, in a 2003 examination, NCUA examiners identified a credit union's failure to have written procedures for OFAC compliance. To address this failure and other BSA-related noncompliance, NCUA entered into a written agreement with the institution, called a Document of Resolution, which indicated that the board of directors agreed to develop and approve OFAC procedures after the completion of the examination. In a 2003 examination, OTS examiners addressed an institution's failure to maintain records of a small number of CTR filings by obtaining the institution's written agreement to ensure the appropriate record retention. Federal Reserve officials noted that because all of the Federal Reserve examinations in our sample were of those institutions already under a formal enforcement action, ongoing communication with institution management about the criticisms identified in the reports was particularly important.

Regulators Assess Many Factors in Deciding on Formal Actions against Significant BSA-Related Compliance Problems

In general, the regulators have taken formal enforcement actions against violations of significant BSA/AML program requirements and BSA violations.[1] Formal enforcement actions are written documents that are disclosed to the public, are more severe than informal actions, and generally are enforceable through the assessment of CMPs and through the federal court system. The regulators coordinate formal enforcement actions with state banking departments, where appropriate, and with FinCEN on cases involving significant BSA-related compliance problems. According to FinCEN data, the regulators took 71 formal enforcement actions in fiscal year 2005.

As seen in table 6, the regulators' recent formal enforcement actions for BSA-related compliance problems include consent orders, cease-and-desist orders, written agreements, and CMPs.[2] For example, in two recent and widely publicized cases, OCC and the Federal Reserve, respectively, entered into formal enforcement actions with the Federal Branch of Arab Bank, PLC, and the New York Branch of ABN AMRO Bank, N.V. (ABN AMRO). [3] Through the respective consent orders and CMP assessment, the institutions agreed to the numerous corrective actions outlined by the regulators to remedy the identified BSA-related violations.[4]

Representatives of the regulators noted that they consider a variety of factors when determining whether to pursue formal enforcement action for BSA-related noncompliance. They noted the importance of the specific circumstances of each case when determining the appropriate formal enforcement action for problems within institutions' BSA programs. For instance, a senior FDIC official said that FDIC would consider (1) the extent to which the institution's BSA program failed to detect or deter potential money laundering, (2) the institution's response to previous violation notifications, and (3) the institution's overall risk profile. According to another FDIC representative, Federal Deposit Insurance Act (FDI Act) specifications on enforcement actions do not preclude FDIC from taking different action.

Table 6. Examples of Formal Enforcement Actions Taken against Depository Institutions for BSA-Related Compliance Problems(2004–2005)

Enforcement action	Date	Regulator	Depository institution	Areas of significant BSA-related problems included in actions
Consent order	10/2005	OCC	Key Bank, N.A.	• BSA compliance program • BSA compliance officer function • Suspicious activity reporting • Independent audit • Training
Written agreement	10/2005	Federal Reserve	Deutsche Bank Trust Company	• BSA compliance program • Independent testing • Training • Suspicious activity reporting • Customer due diligence
Written agreement	06/2005	Federal Reserve	First Citizens Bank of Butte	• BSA compliance program
Cease-and-desist order	06/2005	FDIC	First Community Bank of Southwestern Florida	• BSA compliance program • BSA compliance officer function • BSA compliance committee • Customer due diligence
Consent order	05/2005	OCC	InterBusiness Bank, N.A.	• BSA compliance program • Independent testing
Cease-and-desist order	05/2005	FDIC	Muskegon Commerce Bank	• BSA compliance program • Independent testing
Consent order	02/2005	OCC	United Americas Bank, N.A.	• BSA compliance program • BSA compliance officer function • Suspicious activity reporting
Consent order of civil money penalty	02/2005	OCC	City National Bank	• BSA compliance program • Customer due diligence • Suspicious activity reporting
Consent order	02/2005	OCC	Federal Branch of Arab Bank, PLC	• BSA compliance program • Suspicious activity reporting • Monitoring third-party wire transfers
Supervisory agreement	01/2005	OTS	First Federal Savings and Loan Association of Edwardsville	• BSA compliance program • Customer identification • OFAC compliance • Training
Cease-and-desist order	12/2004	OTS	Guaranty Bank	• Suspicious activity reporting • Suspicious activity monitoring • Training

Table 6. (continued)

Enforcement action	Date	Regulator	Depository institution	Areas of significant BSA-related problems included in actions
Civil money penalty	12/2004	OTS	Anchorbank, fsb	• CTR filing • Customer identification program • Training • Independent testing • Suspicious activity reporting
Written agreement	07/2004	Federal Reserve	ABN AMRO Bank, N.V.	• BSA compliance program • Correspondent accounts • Independent audit • Suspicious activity reporting • Customer due diligence

Source: GAO

Thus, if FDIC determines that a bank has a positive compliance history and the bank's management demonstrates a desire and ability to cooperate with FDIC, the regulator might not automatically take a formal action against a failure in a component of the institution's BSA program. Guidance on formal enforcement actions for BSA-related compliance problems issued separately by OCC and OTS in November 2004 and March 2004, respectively, also noted such factors and identified other factors, such as the regulator's confidence in the ability of the institution to correct the problem and whether the institution independently identified and corrected the problem. Finally, Federal Reserve officials said that they issue cease-and-desist orders to institutions that have violated some aspect of the BSA program requirement, but that they sometimes enter into written agreements with the institutions for such violations.

Regulators Do Not Derive Authority for Formal Enforcement Actions Including CMPs, from the BSA

Section 8(s) of the FDI Act also authorizes the regulators to enforce compliance with BSA program requirements. Specifically, in the event that an insured depository institution fails to establish or maintain a BSA program or has failed to correct any previously identified deficiency in its BSA program, the appropriate regulator shall issue an order requiring the institution to cease-and-desist from its violation.[5] Should the institution violate a cease-and-desist order, the regulators are authorized to assess a CMP or file an action for injunctive relief in the appropriate federal district court.[6] Additionally, the regulators may impose CMPs for violations of conditions imposed by a regulator in connection with granting an application or request; violations of written agreements between the institution and the regulator, or any law or regulation; unsafe or unsound practices; and breach of fiduciary duties.

However, the regulators currently do not have delegated authority under the BSA to take formal enforcement actions for violations of the BSA. Title 12 of the *United States Code* authorizes the regulators to take certain formal enforcement actions if they determine that a depository institution is engaging in unsafe or unsound practices or has violated any applicable law or regulation.[7] The regulators have interpreted this authority to include violations of the BSA and its implementing regulations when they take formal enforcement actions aimed at addressing violations of the BSA/AML program requirement.

Critical Reviews of Regulators' BSA Oversight Have Prompted Some Regulators to Change Examiner Procedures and Guidance

Some regulators have changed procedures and examiner guidance related to enforcement in response to weaknesses identified by internal and IG reviews. A 2005 internal quality assurance review at OCC, conducted in the wake of significant BSA failures at Riggs Bank, N.A. (Riggs Bank), determined that among the sampled banks, stronger action was warranted at 8 of 24 community banks, 1 of 6 midsize banks, and 1 of 6 large banks. Furthermore, according to the review findings, OCC's initial supervisory actions were not always severe enough to ensure timely correction of the BSA/AML problems for 22 percent of the sampled institutions. The review also determined that OCC had given banks multiple opportunities and extended periods of time to implement effective BSA/AML programs. In a July 2005 response to the review, a senior OCC official stated that, over the past 18 months, one of the actions OCC had taken to address this problem was to institute a process where OCC staff, including experts at OCC headquarters, would review any proposed citation relating to a BSA/AML program requirement and an OCC Senior Deputy Comptroller would make the final decision to cite a violation.

In 2003, the Treasury IG found that OTS's reliance on moral suasion and thrift management assurances to comply with the BSA was not effective in compelling thrift management to correct their BSA violations in 21 of the 68 sampled thrifts. Furthermore, the Treasury IG indicated that the reports of examination and underlying examination work papers supported OTS taking more forceful and timely enforcement actions against these thrifts. In a detailed review of 9 of 11 cases where OTS issued written enforcement actions in response to substantive BSA violations, the Treasury IG found that in 5 cases, the enforcement documents either were not taken in a timely manner or did not address all of the substantive violations found by the examiners. According to the Treasury IG, the BSA violations continued for years or BSA compliance worsened. To address the report's findings and recommendations, OTS management agreed to make a number of corrective actions, including implementing enhanced supervisory review over the examination process to better ensure that substantive violations identified in an examination would be incorporated into the report of examination. OTS also agreed to issue supplemental examiner guidance (1) on when to initiate stronger enforcement action when substantive BSA violations were found and (2) on time frames for expecting corrective action to avoid repeated violations of the BSA and deteriorating BSA compliance. OTS agreed to improve regional reviews to ensure that substantive BSA violations were identified in the report of examination. OTS officials told us that the improvements made to its examination and enforcement data systems allow for easier monitoring of the timeliness of institutions' corrective actions. According to an OTS official, OTS has implemented all of the Treasury IG recommendations made in connection with this report, including the issuance of guidance on enforcement actions specifically for BSA-related compliance problems.

Other reviews also identified weaknesses in how some regulators followed up on BSA compliance problems. According to the 2005 internal quality assurance review, in the past, OCC did not effectively follow up on BSA/AML violations and/or Matters Requiring Attention among sampled institutions; however, because of OCC's increased emphasis on BSA/AML supervision in 2004 and 2005, follow-up had improved in all areas of BSA/AML supervision.[8] Similarly, a 2004 FDIC IG review indicated that FDIC needed to strengthen its follow-up processes for BSA violations. The FDIC IG determined that there was a wide range of follow-up actions and identified a number of weaknesses in FDIC follow-up processes through reviews of sampled institutions, relevant procedures of FDIC regional offices, and information from FDIC's data systems.[9] The FDIC IG recommended that FDIC reevaluate and update examination guidance to strengthen monitoring and follow-up processes for BSA violations, and take or conduct, among other things,

- prompt, appropriate, and consistent regulatory action in cases where management action is not timely, including cease-and-desist orders for repeat violations, as appropriate, and
- consistent and timely follow-up of BSA violations between examinations to ensure management is taking corrective action.

According to the FDIC IG, FDIC had initiatives under way to reassess and update its BSA policies and procedures, and the agency agreed with the recommendations. An FDIC IG official noted that FDIC has implemented corrective action that addresses the recommendations.

Unlike the Regulators, FinCEN Has Delegated Enforcement Authority under the BSA

FinCEN, the administrator of the BSA, takes enforcement action against BSA compliance problems at financial institutions, including, but not limited to, depository institutions. Unlike the regulators, FinCEN can take such action because the implementing regulations of the BSA specifically delegated authority for it to do so.[10]

While the regulators have examination authority and deal most directly with depository institutions, FinCEN receives information on specific cases of depository institutions' BSA-related compliance problems through referrals of specific cases from the regulators or through reports from institutions filed as a result of the examination process.[11] In 1990, FinCEN's predecessor, the Office of Financial Enforcement, issued guidance on referrals to the regulators that described situations and types of violations that would warrant referral for further action beyond any enforcement actions that the regulators might take. OCC, FDIC, OTS, and NCUA subsequently summarized the guidelines in their respective BSA examination policies and procedures.[12] According to FinCEN officials, each regulator has referred cases for further action, but to varying degrees (see table 7).

Table 7. Number of Referrals from the Banking Regulators to FinCEN (2001–2004)

Agency	Number of referrals to FinCEN, by year			
	2001	2002	2003	2004
FDIC	6	13	2	13
Federal Reserve	3	1	0	4
OCC	0	0	1	1
OTS	0	0	0	1
NCUA	0	1	0	0

Source: FinCEN

In addition to referrals, FinCEN could become aware of BSA compliance problems through examination-related reporting. For example, according to FinCEN officials, if examiners discover that BSA forms have not been filed in a timely manner, the regulators often instruct depository institutions to contact FinCEN or the IRS for a determination on whether BSA forms must be filed late. If such matters rise to a significant level of noncompliance with the BSA, FinCEN reviews the facts to determine what action to take.

FinCEN takes enforcement actions against significant BSA compliance problems by issuing letters of warning or imposing CMPs. According to a senior FinCEN official, such enforcement actions are intended to yield greater compliance from the institution that was the target of the action and serve as an example, thereby resulting in greater compliance from the financial services industry. According to FinCEN officials, FinCEN considers several factors when determining the severity of an institution's violations, including the nature, number, time-span, and rate of reporting failures. Furthermore, FinCEN takes into account whether the violation was willful, repeated, or systemic, and whether the violation was related to a failure in the institution's AML program. FinCEN also considers what corrective actions the institution has taken to address the violations and the effects of actions from other agencies, such as the regulators or law enforcement agencies. FinCEN officials noted that FinCEN issues letters of warning to address cases that involve relatively significant BSA noncompliance, but do not rise to a level that would warrant a CMP.[13] Depending on the nature of the case, CMPs against depository institutions could range from $500 to $1,000,000 per violation.

From 2000 to 2005, FinCEN Imposed CMPs in 11 Cases but, in Recent Years, Assessed Them Concurrently with Relevant Regulators

From 2000 to 2005, FinCEN assessed CMPs against 11 depository institutions.[14] According to FinCEN officials, the use of CMPs has been effective in stopping the violating activities at depository institutions where previous enforcement actions by the regulators had not brought about compliance. FinCEN penalized the depository institutions for significant reporting failures resulting from serious weaknesses in BSA compliance policies and procedures. As seen in table 8, CMPs ranged from $100,000 to $30 million. In 7 of the 11 cases, FinCEN cited willful violation of the BSA.

Table 8. CMPs Assessed Solely by FinCEN and Concurrently with the Regulators (2000–2005)

Year	Depository institution	CMP amount	CMP assessed solely by FinCEN	CMP assessed concurrently by FinCEN and the regulator	Regulator
2005	The New York Branch of ABN AMRO Bank, N.V.	$30 million[a]		√	Federal Reserve
2005	The New York and Miami Branches of Banco de Chile	3 million[b]		√	OCC and Federal Reserve, respectively
2005	The New York Branch of Arab Bank, PLC	24 million		√	OCC
2004	AmSouth Bank	10 million		√	Federal Reserve
2004	Riggs Bank, N.A.	25 million		□	OCC
2003	Korea Exchange Bank	1.1 million	√		FDIC
2003	Banco Popular de Puerto Rico	20 million	√		Federal Reserve
2002	Great Eastern Bank of Florida	100,000	√		FDIC
2002	Sovereign Bank	700,000	√		OTS
2000	Polish and Slavic Federal Credit Union	185,000	√		NCUA
2000[c]	Sunflower Bank, N.A.	100,000	√		OCC

Source: GAO

[a]ABN AMRO Bank, N.V., consented to the assessment of a CMP by FinCEN against the New York Branch of ABN AMRO in the amount of $30 million. The assessment also was concurrent with a $40 million CMP assessed by the Federal Reserve, which included an assessment by OFAC. The federal CMPs were satisfied by one payment of $40 million. In addition, ABN AMRO Bank consented to a separate CMP assessment against the New York Branch by the New York State Banking Department in the amount of $20 million, as well as a $15 million CMP assessment against the Chicago Branch by the State of Illinois Department of Financial and Professional Regulation and a $5 million contribution to an Illinois examiner education fund.

[b]OCC is the primary federal functional regulator of the New York Branch of Banco de Chile, and the Federal Reserve is the primary federal functional regulator of the Miami Branch. FinCEN assessed a $3 million CMP assessment against both branches of Banco de Chile, concurrent with OCC's $3 million CMP assessment against the New York Branch. The Federal Reserve issued a cease-and-desist order against the Miami Branch but did not assess a CMP.

[c]FinCEN's documentation of the CMP assessment indicated that Sunflower Bank, N.A., consented to the assessment on December 27, 1999, and the Director of FinCEN signed the release of the document on January 6, 2000.

In some instances, FinCEN assessed CMPs against depository institutions separate from any enforcement action taken by the relevant regulator. More recently, FinCEN has assessed CMPs concurrently with the regulators.[15] We discuss two examples in more detail in the following sections:

Riggs Bank

In May 2004, FinCEN and OCC concurrently imposed $25 million in CMPs against Riggs Bank for willful and systemic BSA violations.[16] FinCEN determined that Riggs Bank willfully violated the suspicious activity and currency transaction reporting requirements of the BSA and its implementing regulations, and that Riggs Bank willfully violated the AML program requirement of the BSA and its implementing regulations. Riggs' failure to establish and implement a BSA/AML program adequate to meet its suspicious activity and currency transaction reporting requirements constituted systemic violations that demonstrated a reckless disregard of its obligations under the BSA. According to FinCEN, Riggs Bank further demonstrated willfulness by failing to correct the BSA-related compliance problems that OCC previously identified.[17]

The New York Branch of Arab Bank, PLC

More recently, in August 2005, FinCEN and OCC concurrently imposed a $24 million CMP against the New York Branch of Arab Bank, PLC (Arab Bank-New York). According to FinCEN, Arab Bank-New York failed to apply an adequate system of internal controls to the clearing of funds transfers, given the heightened risks of money laundering and terrorist financing posed by the bank's customer base, correspondent institutions, and geographic locations and by the volume of funds it cleared.[18] FinCEN determined that Arab Bank-New York inappropriately limited the scope of systems and controls used to comply with the BSA and manage the risks of money laundering and terrorist financing—for example, by limiting the monitoring and review of transactions to only those entities that the bank viewed as direct customers of Arab Bank-New York. That is, it did not monitor and review transactions for originators and beneficiaries without accounts at Arab Bank-New York for which the bank had served as an intermediary institution. As a result, Arab Bank-New York failed to monitor these funds transfers for potentially suspicious activity. FinCEN also determined that Arab Bank-New York failed to implement procedures commensurate with the risks posed by its U.S. dollar clearing activities. For example, according to FinCEN, the bank did not obtain and use credible publicly available information (which included congressional testimony, indictments in the United States, and well-publicized research and media reports) to monitor and identify funds transfers that warranted further investigation and did not conduct follow-up investigations when it had identified anomalies or potentially suspicious funds transfers.

Furthermore, FinCEN determined, in part, that Arab Bank-New York failed to identify a number of potentially suspicious funds transfers. For example, FinCEN cited funds transfers that the bank cleared from 2001 through 2004 for originators or beneficiaries whom OFAC and the Department of State subsequently declared to be "specially designated terrorists," "specially designated global terrorists," or "foreign terrorist organizations." At the time of the funds transfers, neither OFAC nor State had designated the originators or beneficiaries, and the bank largely complied with the requirement to cease clearing funds transfers once they were designated as such. However, according to FinCEN, once the designation was made, Arab Bank-New York failed to review information in its possession that would have shown it had cleared funds transfers for those individuals and entities, failed to analyze this information, and failed to file SARs. More specifically, Arab Bank-New York did not file the majority of its SARs referencing terrorist financing until after OCC commenced a review of its funds transfer activity in July 2004.

FinCEN Does Not Believe the Lack of Delegated Authority to Impose CMPs under the BSA Has Significantly Affected Enforcement

The Secretary of the Treasury has not delegated to the regulators the authority to assess CMPs under the BSA to address violations. Under the BSA, the Secretary is authorized to assess CMPs against financial institutions, including depository institutions, for violations of the BSA.[19] In 1994, MLSA directed the Secretary to delegate this authority to the regulators and attach terms and conditions deemed appropriate, including a limitation on the dollar amount of penalty authority. The Secretary has delegated this authority to the Director of FinCEN. In 1995, the director established an interagency group consisting of representatives from the regulators and FinCEN to implement the delegation by developing common guidance for the assessment of CMPs. A subgroup of the interagency group developed a draft delegation of CMP authority, a matrix of penalties and decision factors, and guidance for using the matrix. However, according to FinCEN and OCC officials, the agencies could not reach agreement. Further complicating the matter, the statutory mandate for delegation of CMP authority to the regulators did not include NCUA or the Securities and Exchange Commission, which examines broker-dealers for BSA compliance.

More recently, according to FinCEN officials, the challenges in crafting a delegation that would result in consistent and accountable BSA enforcement have increased substantially. For example, FinCEN officials cited the addition, under the PATRIOT Act, of an additional regulator, the Commodity Futures Trading Commission, to the BSA compliance examination process.[20] They also noted the expanded scope of BSA regulation as more types of institutions became subject to BSA compliance. FinCEN officials said that since 1994, FinCEN repeatedly has evaluated the benefits and potential consequences of delegating its CMP authority to the regulators, but currently has no plans to pursue this delegation.

Furthermore, citing the regulators' authority to assess CMPs under the FDI Act, FinCEN officials said that they were not aware of any significant enforcement ramifications caused by the lack of delegated authority. As previously mentioned, the regulators have interpreted their authority under the FDI Act to impose CMPs for violations of any law or regulation to include violations of the BSA. In addition, FinCEN officials noted that through the MOU, FinCEN and the regulators have achieved the coordination on enforcement issues, including CMP issuance, which was intended to occur through the delegation of the authority. For example, if pursuant to the MOU, FinCEN learns from a regulator of a significant BSA violation or deficiency by a financial institution, and FinCEN determines that the imposition of administrative enforcement remedies under the BSA may be warranted, FinCEN is to notify the institution's regulator no later than 30 days after the determination, and before taking any public enforcement action. Similarly, to the extent that FinCEN is not already a party to a regulator's formal enforcement action involving a significant BSA violation or deficiency, under the terms of the MOU, the regulators are to notify FinCEN of formal enforcement actions no later than 30 days after the regulator's decision to pursue the action and before such action is made public.

According to officials at FinCEN and the regulators, coordination among these agencies on enforcement issues has improved dramatically in recent years. FinCEN officials noted that the regulators have involved FinCEN in BSA supervisory and enforcement issues at earlier stages than in the past. For example, as indicated in the MOU, the regulators now inform FinCEN when they have recommended that an institution file CTRs that previously had not been filed as required or inquire of FinCEN's processing center about the need to file.

FinCEN officials also pointed out that the regulators previously notified FinCEN that they were referring cases of noncompliance to FinCEN for potential further action shortly before they separately took formal enforcement actions under banking statute. According to officials from some regulators, in the past, FinCEN sometimes would take enforcement action against an institution on the basis of a referral from a regulator long after the institution had come into compliance with the regulator's formal enforcement action.

More recently, the regulators and FinCEN have been working more closely on enforcement issues. According to Federal Reserve, FDIC, and OTS officials, earlier communication between the regulators and FinCEN has resolved the difference in timing of enforcement actions. As previously described, in 2004 and 2005, FinCEN jointly issued several enforcement actions with OCC and the Federal Reserve. Furthermore, under the MOU, the regulators are to notify FinCEN of the resolution of any action involving a significant BSA violation or deficiency, to the extent not otherwise known to FinCEN, no later than 30 days after the resolution of the action. The regulators also are to provide FinCEN with any materials relevant to the resolution. The MOU also directs the regulators to provide FinCEN with a quarterly assessment of the institutions that have failed to comply with formal enforcements actions requirements, such as requirements to take corrective measures, develop and implement an action plan, or submit progress reports to the regulator. FinCEN officials pointed out that situations could arise in the future where the regulators and FinCEN would pursue different courses of enforcement action, but as directed in the MOU, FinCEN and the regulators would inform one another of any impending action.

Justice Has Pursued a Limited Number of Criminal Cases against Depository Institutions for BSA Noncompliance

Since 2002, Justice, either through its Criminal Division or its U.S. Attorneys' Offices, has pursued investigations of six depository institutions for criminal violation of the BSA (see table 9). Justice officials said that cases where the depository institution was the criminal BSA offender were limited, and that the department had pursued significantly more cases against individuals for BSA offenses. According to a senior official at Justice, egregious failures to perform a minimal level of due diligence over a number of years triggered the cases against the depository institutions.

For instance, in January 2005, Justice announced that Riggs Bank pled guilty to a federal criminal violation of the BSA in connection with repeated and systemic failure to accurately report suspicious transactions associated with bank accounts owned and controlled by Augusto Pinochet of Chile and the government of Equatorial Guinea.[21] Justice cited Riggs Bank's involvement in transactions for Pinochet and his wife from 1994 to 2002 (multiple accounts, investments, and certificates of deposits at Riggs Bank in the United States and at its London branch). This involvement occurred despite an outstanding 1998 attachment order issued by a Spanish magistrate to freeze all of Pinochet's assets worldwide and despite warrants against Pinochet that were issued for human rights crimes by numerous countries, including Spain, Switzerland, Belgium, and France. Additionally, from 1996 to 2004, Riggs Bank opened more than 30 accounts for the government of Equatorial Guinea, numerous Equatorial Guinean government officials, and their family members.[22] Riggs Bank also opened multiple personal accounts for the Equatorial Guinean president and his relatives and assisted in establishing offshore shell corporations for the president and his sons. For both the Pinochet and Equatorial Guinean government accounts, Justice determined that Riggs Bank knew or had reason to know that these transactions were suspicious, but failed to file any SARs until congressional investigators, banking regulators, or law enforcement discovered the transactions.

Similarly, in 2003, Justice and ICE investigators determined that from 1995 through 1998, Banco Popular de Puerto Rico (Banco Popular) allowed a drug dealer to launder approximately $32 million in cash drug proceeds. Law enforcement officials determined that the bank failed to visit the business location, which was within a short walking distance from the bank branch, to verify the customer's purported source of income. Furthermore, the bank neither reported the customer's large cash deposits—at times more than $500,000—nor filed a SAR until February 1998, after $21 million of narcotics proceeds had been laundered at one branch.

In another example, in 2002, the U.S. Attorney's Office for the Southern District of New York determined (through investigations by various law enforcement agencies) that during the 1990s, Broadway National Bank became the institution of choice for narcotics money launderers and other individuals who wanted to shield their financial activities from government scrutiny. According to sentencing documentation, from January 1996 to March 1998, approximately $123 million in cash deposits were laundered and/or structured through a series of highly suspicious transactions, involving approximately 107 accounts.

Table 9. Depository Institutions against Which Justice Has Pursued Charges for Criminal Violation of the BSA (2002–2005)

Year	Depository institution	BSA-related violations or investigations	Disposition	Monetary penalty amount
2005	The Bank of New York	• Failure to file SARs in a timely and complete manner with respect to a company that presented sham escrow agreements to other banking institutions in support of loan applications, while aiding and abetting the fraudulent activity by executing the sham escrow agreements (31 U.S.C. § 5318(G)(1); 31 U.S.C. § 5322)[b] • Failure to implement an effective AML program (31 U.S.C. § 5318(h)) • Aiding and abetting the operation of an unlicensed money-transmitting business (18 U.S.C. § 1960) • Money laundering (18 U.S.C. § 1956)	Nonprosecution agreement	$26 million forfeiture[a]
2005	Riggs Bank, N.A.	• Failure to file timely SARs (31 U.S.C. §§ 5318(g) and 5322(b))	Guilty plea agreement	16 million criminal fine

Table 9. (continued)

Year	Depository institution	BSA-related violations or investigations	Disposition	Monetary penalty amount
2004	AmSouth Bank	• Failure to file timely and complete SARs (31 U.S.C. §§ 5318(g)(1) and 5223(b))	Deferred prosecution agreement	40 million forfeiture
2003	Delta National Bank & Trust Company	• Failure to file a SAR (31 U.S.C. §§ 5318(g) and 5322)	Guilty plea agreement	950,000 forfeiture
2003	Banco Popular de Puerto Rico	• Failure to file timely and complete SARs (31 U.S.C. §§ 5318(g)(1) and 5322(b))	Deferred prosecution agreement	21.6 million forfeiture
2002	Broadway National Bank	• Failure to establish an adequate AML program (31 U.S.C. §§ 5318(h) and 5322(b)) • Failure to file criminal referral forms and SARs (31 U.S.C. §§ 5318(g) and 5322(b)) • Aiding and abetting structuring by customers who Broadway knew were seeking to avoid CTR filing requirements (31 U.S.C. §§ 5324(a)(3) and 5324(d)(2), and 18 U.S.C. § 2)	Guilty plea agreement	4 million criminal fine

Source: GAO

[a]These charges have not been brought against The Bank of New York in any charging document, but are listed in the nonprosecution agreement as having been under investigation by the U.S. Attorneys' Offices in the Eastern and Southern Districts of New York. The bank admitted that it did not have an effective AML program and other BSA-related failures that are discussed later in this chapter. The bank also admitted to unlawful conduct that was unrelated to BSA compliance, including aiding and abetting the unlawful operation of a foreign bank (12 U.S.C. § 3105(d)) and supplying a bank customer with unauthorized, materially false, and misleading escrow agreements that The Bank of New York had no intention of performing and that were submitted in support of loan requests totaling tens of millions of dollars.

[b]The Bank of New York also agreed to pay $12 million in restitution to its victims.

According to Justice officials, evidence that a depository institution willfully violated the law is a key element in proving criminal violations of the BSA. One official said that in the six recent criminal cases against depository institutions, prosecutors sought to demonstrate evidence of the institutions' continued disregard of the spirit of the requirement to implement and maintain a BSA program, and willful and flagrant indifference to a known legal duty. However, the officials also noted that in some cases, there likely was no "smoking gun," or single source of evidence that specifically indicated the institution knew it was in violation of the BSA and continued the violating conduct. In most of these cases, and in accordance with Justice guidelines, federal prosecutors relied, in part, on the institutions' BSA policies and procedures to demonstrate that the institution had corporate knowledge about the violations. A Justice official said that corporate knowledge could be individually or collectively derived—for example, as in situations where individual employees knew about certain aspects of the activity, or where the institution should have known about the activity.

The recent actions brought by Justice have raised concerns in the banking industry that institutions routinely would be targeted for criminal investigation and prosecution for failure to properly implement the requirements of the BSA, such as the failure to file a SAR. For example, some banks are avoiding customers, such as money transmitters and check cashers, who are perceived as presenting heightened risks for BSA noncompliance. According to a senior Federal Reserve official, some banks thus are deciding that the revenues garnered from such customers do not cover the necessary costs of compliance or provide an acceptable return on legal and reputational risks. However, Justice and FinCEN officials noted that such concerns could result from not fully understanding the actions taken in these cases. Justice officials said that investigations of depository institutions for criminal BSA violations generally have not involved negligence in reporting a limited number of suspicious transactions. Furthermore, depository institutions that have repeated BSA violations generally would not face law enforcement investigation or charges of criminal violation of the BSA if they were operating within the spirit and letter of their BSA program. Rather, the institutions likely would face administrative action from their regulators or FinCEN.

Finally, Justice officials and investigators said that most investigations of depository institutions' criminal violations of the BSA generally originated during law enforcement investigations of the institutions' customers. For example, in the AmSouth Bank case, investigation documentation indicated that the U.S. Attorney's Office for the Southern District of Mississippi (along with the IRS and other federal and state agencies) began an investigation of a fraudulent promissory note scheme perpetrated by AmSouth Bank customers in 2002. Investigators and prosecutors learned of AmSouth Bank's BSA failures through the investigation and grand jury subpoenas related to the customers' criminal activity. In November 2003, AmSouth formally was advised that it was a target of a criminal investigation. Similarly, ICE investigators involved in the Broadway National Bank and Banco Popular cases said that the respective undercover narcotics investigations of the banks' customers led law enforcement to open investigations of the banks' BSA failures. In the case of Delta National Bank and Trust Company, ICE investigators also began a financial investigation of the bank after they concluded an undercover money laundering investigation involving a currency exchange business. Justice officials noted that the Riggs Bank case was the exception; the law enforcement investigations initially focused on Riggs Bank itself.

In Some Cases, Law Enforcement Investigations First Identified BSA Failures

In some instances, law enforcement investigations first identified significant BSA failures at depository institutions, rather than examinations conducted by the regulator. For instance, according to ICE and Federal Reserve officials, law enforcement officials informed the Federal Reserve about their investigation of a Banco Popular customer and the compliance problems identified during their investigations.[23] During 1995 and 1998, the Federal Reserve conducted four examinations of Banco Popular, but these examinations did not contain any criticism of the bank's BSA compliance policies or procedures. In 1999, the Federal Reserve expanded the scope of its regularly scheduled examination of the bank and identified significant BSA compliance problems, which resulted in a written agreement with the institution. Law enforcement officials also said that investigations of AmSouth's customers revealed the institution's BSA compliance failures within its wealth management area, while a Federal Reserve examination did not detect these problems. In another example, in October 2003, the New York District Attorney's Office notified FDIC of its money laundering investigation of certain customers of an FDIC-supervised bank. According to the FDIC IG, a 2002 examination of the institution provided little coverage of the high-risk banking activities involved in the New York District Attorney's Office investigation. In December 2003, FDIC initiated an already-scheduled examination of the bank and identified significant BSA violations and a failure to ensure BSA compliance.[24]

Justice officials said that because investigators and prosecutors have a different perspective on BSA enforcement than the regulators, they sometimes identify problems that might not be identified during an examination. One investigator noted that examinations generally do not involve the investigative approach used in law enforcement investigations, which are aimed at identifying underlying offenses, such as narcotics trafficking. Representatives from the regulators said that, through regular examinations, they seek to ensure that depository institutions have systems and controls in place to prevent their involvement in money laundering and to identify and report suspicious transactions to law enforcement. For example, an OCC official explained that the purpose of transaction testing, a key procedure in BSA examinations, is not necessarily to detect structuring or other evidence of criminal wrongdoing on the part of a customer. Rather, according to the interagency procedures, its purpose is to evaluate the adequacy of the bank's compliance with regulatory requirements; determine the effectiveness of its policies, procedures, and processes; and evaluate suspicious activity monitoring systems. Furthermore, the procedures note that if a suspected violation—such as an ongoing money laundering scheme—requires immediate attention, the depository institution should notify the appropriate regulator and law enforcement agencies and must also file a SAR.[25] Our review of sampled BSA reviews identified a number of instances where examiners identified suspicious activity and directed the institutions to file SARs.

Disposition of Criminal Cases against Depository Institutions Has Varied but Included Monetary Penalties in Each Case

According to Justice officials, prosecutors sought to obtain the appropriate dispositions of the cases against depository institutions for criminal violation of the BSA, taking into account factors such as the institutions' willingness to admit misconduct and cooperate with prosecutors. Two of these cases resulted in deferred prosecution agreements (see table 9). That is, prosecutors agreed to defer prosecution of the institution for a specified time, while the institution agreed to admit publicly the facts of its misconduct, cooperate fully with prosecutors, and implement certain corrective actions. The institutions also made payments, generally structured as fines or forfeitures. In one case involving a deferred prosecution agreement, Justice dismissed the charges once the agreement expired because the institutions had complied with its obligations under the agreement. However, if the institution had not complied with the agreement, Justice could have taken the case to trial, using the admission of the violation from the institution and the evidence prosecutors obtained in cooperation with the institution (making conviction highly probable).

For example, in January 2003, Justice and Banco Popular entered into a deferred prosecution agreement to allow the bank to demonstrate its good conduct. The bank agreed to waive indictment and the filing of one count of failing to file SARs in a timely and complete manner. Justice deferred prosecution for 1 year, taking into account the bank's remedial actions at the time of the agreement and its willingness to

- acknowledge responsibility for its actions,
- continue to cooperate with prosecutors,
- demonstrate future good conduct and full compliance with the BSA,
- settle pending civil claims of $21.6 million, and
- consent to the concurrent CMP imposed by FinCEN.

In November 2005, the U.S. Attorneys' Offices for the Eastern and Southern Districts of New York entered into a nonprosecution agreement with The Bank of New York. The bank admitted to

- failure to have an effective AML program;
- intentional failure to take steps to report known evidence of suspected criminal conduct by a bank customer and bank employees;
- repeated failures on the part of the bank's senior executives and legal counsel to perform the institution's legal duty to file a SAR about the suspected criminal activity until the arrest of a bank customer by federal investigators; and
- the untimely, inaccurate, and incomplete filing of the SAR.

The Bank of New York agreed to forfeit $26 million for its illegal conduct and implement numerous remedial actions in response to the misconduct, including

- creating a new senior-level position responsible for coordinating the preparation of SARs;
- training staff on detecting and reporting suspicious activities;
- implementing policies and procedures for auditing retail branches and identifying, investigating, and reporting illegal or suspicious activity; and
- appointing an independent examiner (to serve for 3 years) to monitor and report on the bank's AML procedures and its compliance with the nonprosecution agreement.

As they did in the deferred prosecution agreements, federal prosecutors took several factors into account when determining the disposition of the case. The U.S. Attorneys' Offices for the Eastern and Southern Districts of New York agreed not to prosecute The Bank of New York because of the bank's acceptance of responsibility for the unlawful conduct of its executives and employees, its cooperation in the law enforcement investigations, and its willingness to make restitution to victims of the misconduct and take significant corrective action. The nonprosecution agreement also was contingent upon the bank complying with all terms of the agreement for 3 years. If the bank were to violate the agreement, or commit other crimes, it would be subject to prosecution, including prosecution for the criminal conduct described in the agreement.

Although disposition varied among the six cases, Justice assessed fines or forfeitures on each institution. According to Justice officials, the department's goal was to determine a financial penalty that the depository institutions would perceive as a sanction, rather than an overly punitive penalty that would force the institution to close. The officials also cited another goal—that is, a penalty amount that would elicit good "corporate citizen" conduct from the institution. Justice officials said that in these cases, prosecutors considered several factors (listed in prosecutorial guidelines) when determining whether to pursue such cases. For example, prosecutorial guidelines indicated that prosecutors could consider collateral consequences when determining whether to investigate or take other action against criminal corporate misconduct. According to Justice officials, prosecutors considered the potential effects on the banking market and job losses in the communities that the institutions served. They said that Justice obtained relevant regulatory information, such as the institutions' capital levels and other financial analyses, through the appropriate legal channels to assist them in determining penalty amounts that the institutions could sustain.

Change to the U.S. Attorneys' Manual *Formalized Practice of Obtaining Centralized Approval before Pursuing Cases against Depository Institutions*

During the course of our review, a senior Treasury official also said that discussions had begun with Justice regarding coordination on cases involving prosecuting depository institutions for BSA violations. In July 2005, Justice amended the *U.S. Attorneys' Manual*, which governs the rules of operation of the 93 U.S. attorneys, to require prosecutors to obtain approval from the department's Criminal Division before taking action against financial institutions for money laundering or certain BSA offenses.[26] More specifically, the manual was amended to include section 5322 of title 31 in the requirement that prosecutors obtain approval from the Asset Forfeiture and Money Laundering Section of the department's Criminal Division in cases where a financial institution would be named as an unindicted coconspirator or allowed to enter into a deferred prosecution agreement.

Justice officials said that the change to the manual was a formalization of existing practice. The change was a public way for the department to inform the banking industry about the degree of coordination and consultation between the U.S. attorneys and the Criminal Division on these cases.

6. Conclusions and Recommendations

Because the BSA regulatory structure involves many federal agencies other than FinCEN, which is the administrator of the BSA, coordination among these agencies is critical to effective BSA administration and enforcement. Particularly since the passage of the PATRIOT Act, FinCEN and the regulators have undergone an evolutionary process that has laid the groundwork for more consistent BSA oversight. The initial effects of this closer coordination can be seen in the jointly developed BSA examination procedures for depository institutions, the sharing of more detailed BSA examination information with FinCEN, and the increase in concurrent enforcement of BSA compliance by the regulators and FinCEN. Although these efforts, and their effects, are significant, they also are relatively recent. For example, many of these changes were ongoing during the course of our work for this report. The regulators and FinCEN continue to make refinements to overall BSA examination, monitoring, and enforcement policies and procedures.

Regulators Have Created a Framework for Consistency in BSA Examinations

In particular, the regulators have made notable progress in the area of examinations. Until passage of the PATRIOT Act, each regulator separately developed and used examination procedures to determine depository institutions' compliance with the BSA. In recent years, a number of agency IG and internal quality assurance reviews have identified inconsistencies in BSA examinations. In addition, when we reviewed a sample of examinations from each of the regulators over a 4-year period, we found inconsistent documentation of examination procedures, such as transaction testing, particularly at smaller depository institutions. We stress the importance of adequate, accurate, and consistent documentation in examinations, as in audits.[1] But, we also acknowledge that some variation is inevitable, and examiners need to be able to exercise professional judgment in determining the scope of examinations and to allow for differences among institutions (e.g., complexity and lines of business). Nevertheless, the wide variation in examination policies and procedures among regulators that existed prior to 2005 suggested that the regulators may not have been examining banks consistently—particularly in terms of transaction testing, a procedure that has assumed greater importance in the current environment of increased risk of money laundering and terrorist financing.

In this environment, on June 30, 2005, the regulators issued jointly developed examination procedures, which currently are being used for BSA examinations conducted not only by federal bank examiners but also by state examiners. The interagency procedures represent a genuine step forward in that they provide a framework for greater consistency in BSA examinations across the regulators. At the same time, the procedures retain the risk-focused approach used in former examination procedures, thus allowing the regulators to direct resources to areas deemed higher risk and use examiners' professional judgment in planning, conducting, and concluding examinations. Furthermore, for the first time, FinCEN also participated in the development of the examination procedures. Although the Secretary of the Treasury delegated examination authority for BSA compliance at depository institutions to the regulators, it is through continuing coordination with the regulators that FinCEN works to ensure consistent implementation.

Because the new interagency procedures have been in use for a short period, it is too soon to judge their effect on BSA administration and enforcement. In theory, the procedures should result in more consistency in the conduct and results of BSA examinations. Yet, the interagency procedures cannot be viewed as the only "fix" necessary. BSA examinations, in and of themselves, are designed to verify that systems are robust and function as intended—in compliance with laws and regulations. But, the cumulative effect of AML/BSA-related legislation, especially post-September 11, and some recent high-profile cases of BSA noncompliance have made BSA compliance, and thus examinations, a priority area for oversight and coordination. Congress did not expect the regulators to substitute for law enforcement; rather, the BSA was designed to help create a road map for law enforcement agencies in their AML, and now counter-terrorist financing, work. The FFIEC *Examination Manual*, in turn, recognizes that an effective BSA/AML program requires sound risk management and so it provides guidance on identifying and controlling risks associated with money laundering and terrorist financing. The regulators and FinCEN understand that the risks are not static and that new risks are always emerging as criminals seek to launder their funds or use funds to commit other crimes. The regulators and FinCEN committed to update the manual, as appropriate, to capture developments in the BSA/AML areas. Because of the evolving nature of risk, it is incumbent on them to use the manual or other guidance, as appropriate, to communicate these new risks to the industry and law enforcement so that the industry can take measures to control for these new risks and law enforcement can incorporate them into their investigations.

Regulators Have Improved Their Systems for Monitoring BSA Examination Results

As our work has shown, partly as a result of IG reporting and amid increased attention to BSA compliance and related issues, regulators have improved mechanisms used to track BSA-related information. As a result, the regulators likely will be able to better report on and correct BSA compliance problems. As an example of some of the problems that existed before the regulators made the changes, in our limited review of examination files, we were not always able to track how BSA noncompliance problems were corrected. Furthermore, the regulators increasingly have been using their examination and enforcement data systems to monitor BSA problems at their banks and compile the quarterly data they send to FinCEN. FinCEN and the regulators also helped improve the quality of this information by setting some common standards for reporting in their MOU. While each regulator is responsible for keeping track of compliance problems among the institutions they supervise, it remains FinCEN's responsibility, as the BSA administrator, to (1) analyze the data it receives from all relevant agencies and (2) share trend information with the regulators and industry so that they better understand risks and problem areas within their purview. FinCEN created an Office of Compliance in 2004, in part to work with regulators on BSA examination and compliance matters, and FinCEN has begun to share analytical information with the regulators. The common formats and more detailed data give FinCEN the opportunity to more readily discern those trends and share any concerns with regulators; however, FinCEN only will be able to do this at the aggregate level. It is up to the regulators themselves to undertake the kind of detailed analysis required to understand and track BSA compliance issues among the institutions they supervise, and they have begun to do so. With five quarters of data to review, regulators have begun to see some trends and problem areas. So that others, including examiners, law enforcement, and the banking industry itself, can further benefit from this analysis, it is incumbent upon the regulators to periodically review the BSA violation data to determine whether additional guidance is needed to address problem areas.

Although the new interagency examination procedures and improved systems help banking regulators better understand one another's processes and could facilitate more consistent BSA examinations across regulators, the procedures do not directly address a documentation issue that has implications for BSA enforcement. Because each regulator retained different policies for documenting and classifying BSA problems, the regulators continue to report some compliance problems using different terms. As a result, it is difficult to make qualitative distinctions between compliance problems. Moreover, in their MOU with FinCEN, the regulators agreed to report all "significant" BSA problems, without attempting to address the issue of how the different terms the regulators use might become standardized. When developing the MOU, FinCEN and the regulators discussed the issue of different terminology, but they chose not to address it at that time and agreed to use the umbrella term "significant" and see how the system worked. Although FinCEN and the regulators have reached an accommodation, it is possible that FinCEN is receiving more or less information than it actually needs under the MOU. This variety of terminology can also make it difficult for banking regulators to have a comprehensive overview of BSA compliance at their institutions and for FinCEN to have a comprehensive overview across regulators.

Regulators, FinCEN, and Justice Have ImprovedCoordination on BSA Enforcement Actions

The disparate nature of the BSA regulatory structure also requires coordination in BSA enforcement. While our review of BSA violations showed that the number of violations increased from 2000 to 2004, most of those violations were technical in nature, often resulting from late or incomplete filing of paperwork. Nevertheless, although relatively rare, significant and serious violations of the BSA have had far-reaching consequences. Over the past several years, IG reports, particularly those on FDIC and OTS, identified inconsistencies in BSA enforcement at those agencies. Amid increased media and congressional attention on some depository institutions' BSA compliance failures—such as Riggs Bank, Arab Bank-New York, and ABN AMRO Bank, N.V.—the regulators and FinCEN increasingly have brought formal enforcement actions against depository institutions, including significant CMPs. In the face of separate and sometimes overlapping legal authorities to bring formal enforcement actions against depository institutions for significant BSA compliance problems, the regulators and FinCEN have increased coordination on these actions by issuing them concurrently. In addition, as part of their 2004 MOU, FinCEN and the regulators agreed to notify one another in advance of taking separate formal enforcement actions and sharing information concerning informal and supervisory actions as well.

In a limited number of cases, Justice has taken action against depository institutions for egregious failures to perform a minimal level of due diligence over a number of years. While Justice has resolved most of these cases through deferred prosecution agreements or similar arrangements (where the institution agreed to take significant corrective actions, often in connection with formal administrative action from its regulator; forfeit a monetary penalty; and remain in compliance with the BSA for a specified time), if the institution were to violate the terms of the agreements, federal prosecutors would take the cases to trial. The recent criminal action taken against depository institutions by Justice has raised concerns within the banking industry that their institutions routinely would be targeted for criminal investigation and prosecution for failure to properly implement the requirements of the BSA. However, to better coordinate the actions of federal prosecutors, Justice recently formalized procedures that require U.S. attorneys to obtain approval from Justice's Criminal Division when dealing with cases that allege financial institutions are BSA offenders. Because these changes are recent, it remains to be seen if the new procedures will ease industry concerns and provide the public with the communication of coordinated and consistent federal action that Justice intended.

Concluding Observations

Finally, in our concluding observations on BSA compliance and enforcement, we note that significant work remains to be done with other financial institutions. Our report concentrated on the federal banking regulators, but the PATRIOT Act requires other types of institutions to meet BSA requirements. Consequently, it appears more important than ever for FinCEN to coordinate with other federal agencies charged with examination responsibility for BSA compliance. To that end, FinCEN signed MOUs with many state banking departments and the IRS and has been working to sign MOUs with the securities and futures regulators. However, according to FinCEN officials, the problem of different terminology will be exacerbated when other financial regulators begin reporting examination data to FinCEN on BSA noncompliance problems. Ultimately, only FinCEN can provide a "bird's eye" view of BSA administration—disseminating analysis and information to the regulators and others to ensure consistency in BSA oversight, the identification of trends and patterns in BSA compliance, and developments in money laundering and terrorist financing.

Recommendations for Executive Action

To build on the current level of coordination, continue to improve BSA administration, and ensure that emerging compliance risks are addressed, this report makes the following three recommendations to the Director of FinCEN, the Comptroller of the Currency, the Chairman of the Federal Reserve, the Chairman of the FDIC, the Director of OTS, and the Chairman of NCUA:

- As emerging risks in the money laundering and terrorist-financing areas are identified, FinCEN and the regulators should work together to ensure these risks are effectively communicated to examiners and the industry through updates of the interagency examination manual and other guidance, as appropriate.
- To supplement the analyses of shared data on BSA violations, FinCEN and the regulators should meet periodically to review the analyses and determine whether additional guidance to examiners is needed.
- Because of the different terminology the regulators use to classify BSA noncompliance, FinCEN and the regulators should jointly assess the feasibility of developing a uniform classification system for BSA noncompliance.

Agency Comments and Our Evaluation

We received written comments on a draft of this report in a joint letter from the Board of Governors of the Federal Reserve System, the Federal Deposit Insurance Corporation, the National Credit Union Administration, the Office of the Comptroller of the Currency, the Office of Thrift Supervision, and FinCEN. We also received written comments from the Department of Justice. These letters are reprinted in appendixes II and III. The Departments of Homeland Security and Justice and the regulators provided technical comments, which were incorporated into this report where appropriate.

In their letter, FinCEN and the regulators said they support our recommendations and are committed to ongoing interagency coordination to address them through the formal processes they have in place, particularly the FFIEC BSA/AML Working Group. They also said that they are committed to their role in ensuring that depository institutions are in compliance with BSA/AML requirements, and that they will continue to devote significant resources to make certain institutions correct deficiencies in their BSA/AML programs as promptly as possible.

In its letter, Justice said that the draft report provided an instructive perspective where it examines the evolution of the relationship between FinCEN, the regulators, and the banks, but that it did not provide the same perspective when examining how the examination process meets the needs of law enforcement as the end users of the information. Our objectives were to review how the regulators examine for BSA compliance, track and resolve violations, and take enforcement actions. While a review of the reports that depository institutions produce under the BSA, and that law enforcement uses in its investigations, would be instructive, it was outside of the scope of this review. Justice also said that, as a direct result of the success and efforts by the regulated industry, drug traffickers have been forced to seek alternate methods and means of using those institutions to launder their illicit proceeds. Justice further commented that banking regulator practices and examination process have historically focused more on the placement of those funds into the financial system, and that current investigative efforts suggest that it may prove beneficial to adapt and focus on the layering of those proceeds. To this end, Justice suggested a need for greater outreach and collaboration between law enforcement and regulators familiar with evolving trends. Finally, Justice said that the draft report reflected the efforts made with the revisions to the examination manual and commented that these are positive developments that should bring continuity to examination practice, which will be welcomed by the industry.

Appendix I. Under Pre-2005 Guidance, Regulators' Documentation Requirements Varied Widely

The regulators' pre-2005 requirements for documentation of examination procedures and their documentation of those procedures varied widely. We reviewed approximately 30 Bank Secrecy Act (BSA) examinations from each federal banking regulator (regulator) that were conducted under guidance current between January 1, 2000, and June 30, 2004. Because the sample was small, we could not generalize the results of our analysis to make conclusions about how regulators applied the examination procedures to all BSA examinations conducted during this period. However, when coupled with our review of regulator guidance and examination manuals, the results of the examination review illustrated instances where the regulators' documentation of examination procedures varied widely and where regulators did not consistently require or document transaction testing. For example, we found less documentation of transaction testing in examinations at smaller institutions, such as the community banks, savings associations, and credit unions supervised by the Office of the Comptroller of the Currency (OCC), the Office of Thrift Supervision (OTS), the Federal Deposit Insurance Corporation (FDIC), and the National Credit Union Administration

(NCUA), than at large institutions. However, examination guidance permitted examiners to exercise their professional judgment in determining whether to perform transaction testing.

Regulators Required Documentation of "Major" Procedures Planning and Scoping Procedures More Often Were Documented for Large Institutions

Individual regulator guidance issued prior to June 2005 required documentation of "major" procedures and conclusions. Furthermore, our review indicated more documentation of examination planning procedures at larger institutions. For example, OCC's policies and procedures manual instructed examiners to document essential examination information, such as procedures performed, and the manual stated that the documentation must support conclusions about supervisory activities in either paper or digital form. The manual also stated that in most cases, work papers did not need to include all of the data reviewed during a supervisory activity, but that examiners should retain only those documents necessary to support the scope of the supervisory activity, significant conclusions, rating changes, or changes in a risk profile.

- In our review of 30 OCC examination files, OCC documented planning, scoping, or risk assessments in 7 of the 30 examinations. The sample included 4 large, 25 smaller banks, and 1 bank without asset data. The examination files of 3 of the 4 large banks, with assets ranging from about $18 billion to $34 billion, contained documentation of planning, scoping, and risk assessments. In contrast, 3 of the 25 files of smaller banks, with assets ranging from $205 million to $366 million, contained documentation of planning or scoping. OCC officials explained that documentation of planning and scoping procedures for the smaller and community banks was contained in the agency's automated examination system, which we did not review.

The Board of Governors of the Federal Reserve System's (Federal Reserve) commercial bank examination manual provided guidance on documentation of examination procedures, including BSA examinations. [1] This guidance did not explicitly require documentation of specific examination steps, but it specified that work papers, as a whole, should support the information and conclusions contained in the report of examination. The Federal Reserve examination guidance specifically provided that the primary purposes of the work papers were to provide written support of the examination and audit procedures performed during the examination and the results of testing and to formalize the examiner's conclusions. Federal Reserve examiners told us that they documented planning and scoping decisions and risk assessments for examinations of large, complex banking organizations in a scoping memorandum, which describes areas to be reviewed and procedures to be conducted, including transaction testing, examination resources, and the expected product.

- Of the 18 Federal Reserve BSA examination files that we reviewed, all contained documentation of planning or scoping procedures. The file sample included 9 large banks with assets of more than $85 billion and 9 smaller banks with assets of less than $1 billion.

Similar to OCC, FDIC's guidance on documentation of examination procedures focused on documenting major examination procedures or conclusions. FDIC's risk management manual of examination policies stated that work paper documentation for BSA examinations should support the conclusions included in the Examination Documentation module in the automated examination database. At a minimum, the documentation should include the examiner's assessment of the bank's BSA and anti-money laundering (AML) programs and procedures, and related audit or internal review functions. FDIC examiners also told us they used the Examination Documentation module to document examination procedures, but that risk assessments should be documented in work papers.

- In our review of 30 FDIC examination files, the agency documented planning, scoping, or risk assessments in examinations of 17 banks, including 6 large banks, with assets ranging from about $125 million to $264 million, and 11 smaller banks, with assets ranging from about $9 million to $89 million.

NCUA's examiner guidance allowed examiners to determine the extent of documentation of examination procedures. More specifically, the NCUA examiner guide required examiners to document supervision plans for examinations in the scope workbook and material concerns in the examination report, but the guide also stated that examiners' discretion would determine the extent of documentation. Although it gave no specific requirements, NCUA directed examiners to include documentation on the (1) extent of procedures and testing performed, (2) review of applicable regulatory compliance, (3) analysis and assessment of risk areas, and (4) conclusions and recommendations.

- In October 2002, NCUA began using scope workbooks to document planning, scoping, and risk assessments in BSA examinations, according to an NCUA official. This affected 23 of 30 examinations in our review. Our review of a sample of the scope workbooks showed that for each BSA review completed and documented, examiners were required to document BSA scoping information and compliance but not BSA risk assessments. Before October 2002, examiners used a "progress checklist" to document the results of BSA reviews, but the checklists did not explicitly refer to BSA reviews or risk assessments. The assets of the credit unions whose BSA examinations we reviewed ranged from $130,000 to $246 million.

OTS's examination manual provided limited instructions for documenting an institution's BSA program. For example, the manual referred to a preliminary examination response kit, which is a request for a collection of information prior to the examination. The institution must provide information about its BSA officer, policy, and compliance programs and must list filed Currency Transaction Reports (CTR). This information assists examiners in determining the scope of the examination.

- Among the 30 OTS BSA examinations reviewed, 3 files contained documentation of planning, scoping, or risk assessments. Two files contained asset information—the institutions had assets of $92 million and $297 million.

Regulators' Former Examination Guidance Allowed Variation in Documentation of Transaction Testing

Although we found little to no documentation of transaction testing at many institutions of smaller assets sizes, which were supervised by OCC, FDIC, OTS and NCUA, we did not conclude that transaction testing was not performed in all of these instances. The regulators required transaction testing in examinations at larger institutions with higher asset levels, but did not always require testing at smaller institutions. Our review of the regulators' BSA examinations indicated that documentation of transaction testing generally was more extensive for larger institutions with higher assets than for smaller institutions with lower assets. For example, the OCC BSA examination manual used for examinations of large banks required transaction testing. The manual provided that examiners were to conduct limited transaction testing, at a minimum to form conclusions about the integrity of the bank's overall control and risk management processes and its overall quantity of risk. If examiners identified weaknesses or concerns as a result, they were to select a "quantity of risk" procedure and conduct additional targeted testing of specific areas of concern.[2] According to OCC examiners assigned to large banks, transaction testing was required for all high-risk areas of these banks.

- Our review of 30 OCC examinations, including 4 examinations of large banks with assets ranging from about $18 billion to $34 billion, found documentation of transaction testing in 3 of the 4 large banks. The examination file of 1 bank did not have any asset information but contained documentation of transaction testing. One bank was designated as a high BSA risk and another was located in a high-intensity financial crimes area (HIFCA).

In contrast, according to OCC's BSA examination manual for community banks, examiners were to determine at the beginning of the supervisory activity what transaction testing, if any, should be included, and the extent of transaction testing was to reflect the bank's compliance risk profile, audit coverage, and results.[3] The manual also stated that transaction testing was appropriate for banks with higher risk characteristics and weak controls. Moreover, OCC examiners assigned to community banks told us that OCC policy did not require transaction testing of community banks at low risk for money laundering. As a result, OCC examiners assigned to community banks would not have to perform transaction testing if they determined that the banks had a low BSA risk.

- Our review of examinations of 25 banks with assets ranging from $21 million to $440 million, found documentation of transaction testing in examinations of 5 banks. OCC officials provided reasons why a number of examinations might not have documentation of transaction testing. First, they said that their record retention rules required the destruction of examination work papers for examinations 3 years and older. Application of the record retention rule could have affected documentation for 13 examinations in our review. OCC officials also stated that their documentation policy required examiners to document transaction testing only if examiners identified a BSA issue or problem, sometimes referred to as "documentation by exception." Consequently, if examiners did not identify BSA issues or concerns requiring transaction testing, they would not have documented transaction testing. OCC officials further stated that "documentation by exception" was necessary to make the maximum use of its limited resources.

The Federal Reserve's BSA examination manual required transaction testing of several areas to be completed by Federal Reserve examiners or the institution at the direction of Federal Reserve examiners. According to Federal Reserve examiners, Federal Reserve policy required that transaction testing be performed in all BSA examinations, and the nature and extent of transaction testing could vary depending on the institution's level of risk. For example, if the institution was engaged in high-risk areas, such as private banking, foreign correspondent banking, or international banking, Federal Reserve examiners were required to perform transaction testing in those areas and to select a judgmental sample of transactions to test.

- Our review of Federal Reserve examination files found that Federal Reserve examiners performed extensive transaction testing at most of the banks. We found documentation of transaction testing in 17 of the 18 examination files, including 9 large banks with assets ranging from about $1 billion to $85 billion, and 8 smaller banks with assets of less than $1 billion. Of the 18 banks, 8 were designated as having a high BSA risk level and 12 were located in HIFCAs. Examiners performed and documented transaction testing on the 8 high-risk banks and 11 of the 12 banks located in HIFCAs.

According to OTS's examination guidance, transaction testing at the savings associations or thrifts it supervised should be "entirely judgmental." Nevertheless, OTS examiners told us that they were specifically required to document transaction testing of CTR samples.

- Our review of 30 OTS examinations of large and small savings associations found documentation of transaction testing in 9 files. The files for 2 of 8 savings associations, with assets from about $117 million to $370 million, contained documentation of transaction testing, as did 4 of 13 files for savings associations with assets ranging from about $4 million to $98 million. Nine OTS examinations lacked documentation on asset size; however, 3 of these 9 examinations contained documentation of transaction testing. OTS officials also explained that they had a policy of "documenting by exception." That is, examiners were not required to document every procedure, particularly in examinations of low-risk institutions, or to document anything in the work papers that did not relate to the report of examination.

Similarly, our review of FDIC's risk management manual of examination policies did not disclose any explicit requirements that examiners document transaction testing in examinations of FDIC-supervised banks. According to FDIC examiners, transaction testing was based on their judgment and dependent on circumstances. For example, FDIC examiners told us that transaction testing was not done on all lines of business, but that they could sample from the independent auditor's work. FDIC examiners also said they could test CTRs if "red flags" were identified, select a sample of high-risk customers, or select accounts with large volumes of transactions. Examiners also said they would perform additional testing if they determined that the scope of the independent audit was not adequate, or that test areas were not covered by the independent auditor.

- Our review of 30 FDIC bank examination files found documentation of transaction testing in 12 files, including 5 of 10 larger banks with assets ranging from $102 million to $264 million and 7 of 20 smaller banks with assets of less than $90 million. Two of the 5 large banks were rated high risk and located in HIFCAs. One of the 7 smaller banks was rated high risk. According to an FDIC official, examinations files for small community banks might not have contained documentation of transaction testing because the banks have few BSA-related transactions or documents requiring transaction testing. The official gave the example of a CTR, which many small banks may never file because they do not have reportable transactions.

NCUA's examiner guide did not explicitly require transaction testing; however, it stated that the risk-focused examination enabled examiners to perform a process review of a credit union's well-managed areas without extensive transaction testing. According to NCUA examiners, the nature and extent of transaction testing and sampling were based on their discretion. They also cited factors that they considered in deciding to perform transaction testing—these factors included the presence of large cash transactions, CTRs, and the credit union's risk assessment, which might affect the number and types of accounts tested. However, NCUA examiners said they would not perform transaction testing for each of the credit union's risky areas, unless a "red flag" was raised during the examination or the credit union's past examination results indicated a problem area.

- Our review of 30 NCUA BSA examination files of credit unions found no documentation of transaction testing in any of the examinations. An NCUA official explained that documentation of transaction testing could be lacking because the paper copy documenting transaction testing was often destroyed after the procedures were entered into NCUA's automated system.

Appendix II. Comments from FinCEN and the Federal Banking Regulators

Board of Governors of the Federal Reserve System
Federal Deposit Insurance Corporation
Financial Crimes Enforcement Network
National Credit Union Administration
Office of the Comptroller of the Currency
Office of Thrift Supervision

April 11, 2006

Ms. Yvonne D. Jones
Director, Financial Markets and Community Investment
U.S. Government Accountability Office
441 G Street, N.W.
Washington, D.C. 20548

Dear Ms. Jones:

Thank you for the opportunity to review and comment on the Government Accountability Office (GAO)'s draft report entitled, *Bank Secrecy Act – Opportunities Exist for FinCEN and the Banking Regulators to Further Strengthen the Framework for Consistent BSA Oversight (GAO 06-386)*. The report reviews the Bank Secrecy Act (BSA) examination and enforcement programs of the Board of Governors of the Federal Reserve System, the Federal Deposit Insurance Corporation, the National Credit Union Administration, the Office of the Comptroller of the Currency, and the Office of Thrift Supervision (collectively, the "Federal Banking Agencies") for U.S. depository institutions as well as the role of the Financial Crimes Enforcement Network (FinCEN). The report covers a broad scope in an area that has undergone rapid and significant changes. As the report notes, in the past two years, the Federal Banking Agencies have jointly issued the *Federal Financial Institutions Examination Council BSA/AML Examination Manual* (Manual) in coordination with FinCEN, and have made many improvements in their coordinated efforts to address BSA and anti-money laundering (AML) compliance problems at depository institutions.

The Federal Banking Agencies and FinCEN support the GAO's recommendations set forth in the report and are committed to ongoing interagency coordination to address those important recommendations. The GAO recommends:

- As emerging risks in the money laundering and terrorist financing area are identified, we recommend that the regulators and FinCEN work together to make sure these are effectively communicated to examiners and industry through updates of the interagency exam manual and other guidance, as appropriate.
- To supplement the analysis of shared data on BSA violations, FinCEN and the regulators should meet periodically to review the analyses and determine whether additional guidance to examiners is needed.

- In light of the different terminology the regulators use to classify BSA noncompliance, we also recommend that FinCEN and the regulators jointly assess the feasibility of developing a uniform classification system for BSA noncompliance.

The Federal Banking Agencies and FinCEN have formal processes in place to review and implement the recommendations. Specifically, under the auspices of the *FFIEC Bank Secrecy Act/Anti-Money Laundering Working Group*, the Federal Banking Agencies and FinCEN meet to discuss and address Bank Secrecy Act regulations, policy, examination, training, and compliance matters. The Working Group convenes monthly to ensure that these matters are addressed expeditiously.

There are various other formal processes that promote collaboration among the Federal Banking Agencies and FinCEN regarding issues that may affect depository institutions. For example, the Federal Banking Agencies actively participate as members of the *Bank Secrecy Act Advisory Group* (BSAAG), which FinCEN chairs on behalf of the Secretary of the Treasury. Comprised of regulators, law enforcement, and representatives from industries subject to BSA rules, the BSAAG meets semi-annually to elevate and address issues such as BSA examination consistency, suspicious activity reporting, currency transaction reporting, sharing of information, privacy and confidentiality of information, and utility of BSA data.

Emerging risks in the money laundering and terrorist financing area are considered through our participation in the aforementioned groups and will be incorporated, as appropriate, into the interagency Manual. Additionally, the Federal Banking Agencies, in cooperation with FinCEN, are committed to reviewing and evaluating the BSA violation data to determine if additional examiner guidance is necessary. Similarly, the Federal Banking Agencies and FinCEN are currently evaluating the use of terminology when describing noncompliance with the BSA to consider whether uniform guidance for examiners is feasible.

We are strongly committed to our role in ensuring that depository institutions are in compliance with BSA/AML requirements. To this end, we will continue to devote significant resources to make certain that the institutions fully understand our expectations and remediate deficiencies in their BSA/AML programs as promptly as possible.

Thank you for your efforts, and if you have any questions or need additional follow-up information, please do not hesitate to contact us.

Sincerely,

Susan Schmidt Bies, Governor
Board of Governors of the Federal
Reserve System

Martin J. Gruenberg, Acting Chairman
Federal Deposit Insurance Corporation

Robert W. Werner, Director
Financial Crimes Enforcement Network

JoAnn M. Johnson, Chairman
National Credit Union Administration

John C. Dugan, Comptroller
Office of the Comptroller of the Currency

John M. Reich, Director
Office of Thrift Supervision

Appendix III
Comments from the Department of Justice

U.S. Department of Justice

APR - 7 2006

Washington, D.C. 20530

Ms. Laurie E. Ekstrand
Director
Homeland Security and Justice
U.S. Government Accountability Office
Washington, D.C. 20548

Dear Ms. Ekstrand:

Thank you for the opportunity to review and comment on the Government Accountability Office (GAO) draft report GAO-06-386 entitled "BANK SECRECY ACT: Opportunities Exist for FinCEN and the Banking Regulators to Further Strengthen the Framework for Consistent BSA Oversight." The Department provided its technical comments under separate cover to Toni Gillich, Senior Analyst-in-Charge, Financial Markets and Community Investment. The comments below are the Department's formal comments for inclusion in the GAO published report.

The draft report provides an instructive perspective where it examines the evolution of the relationship between FinCEN, regulators, and the banks. The report, however, does not provide the same perspective when examining how and if the examination process meets or adequately addresses the needs of the end-users of the information, i.e., law enforcement.

Examinations tend to be technical in nature, where most of the violations that are cited are of little or no consequence to law enforcement. The fines of financial institutions by regulators are quite frequently the result of a criminal investigation, where the regulators are engaged at the request of the criminal investigators or as an ancillary by-product of the substantive criminal investigation.

The report highlights the regulators' role and obligations to assess risk and BSA compliance in their examinations. Equally, it speaks to the regulators' continuing education responsibilities, yet only highlights very limited anecdotal examples of continuing education among law enforcement elements, citing the Internal Revenue Service and the Federal Bureau of Investigation, in a very limited seminar or conference setting. The Department believes that the GAO may have improved its analysis of continuing education by including a discussion of the expertise and training the Drug Enforcement Administration (DEA) could offer. The DEA has expertise gained from its experience policing the estimated $65 billion a year drug trade within the U.S.

Laurie E. Ekstrand Page 2

As a result of its enforcement and investigative experience, the DEA has developed insight into how drug traffickers have evolved their strategies and techniques for laundering money. Further the DEA has gained an understanding of how traffickers identify and exploit the limitations of the U.S. financial markets. Also, the GAO may wish to include information about how, as a direct result of the tremendous success and efforts by the regulated industry, the traffickers have been forced to seek alternate methods and means of employing those institutions to clean or launder their illicit proceeds.

The DEA has the experience to establish a methodology that may prove more effective than that traditionally used by U.S. banking institutions which focuses on placement in the money laundering scheme. Banking regulator practices and the examination process have historically focused more on placement. This result is due, in part, to the required use of a standard examination checklist by the functional regulators. Current investigative efforts suggest that it may prove beneficial to adapt and focus more on layering. Further, the historical approach does not always effectively account for the changing demographic being served by the institution. The regulated industry, however, is intimately familiar with their customer demographics and, consequently, is capable of detecting, modifying, and adjusting its risk-metrics to reflect changes in anti-money laundering (AML) practices. The use of a technical standardized risk assessment checklist can hinder financial institutions from addressing changes in their customer base. Consequently, the GAO may wish to propose or at least consider a greater outreach and collaboration between law enforcement and functional regulators familiar with evolving trends. It is likely that such collaboration might increase the regulators' awareness and their ability to assess adequate AML practices.

The draft report does reflect the efforts made with the revisions to the examination manual, all of which are positive and should bring continuity to the examination practice, something that will be welcomed by the regulated industry, especially where addressing the refinement of definitions.

If you have any questions regarding our comments, please contact Richard P. Theis, Assistant Director, Management and Planning Staff, Audit Liaison Group.

Sincerely,

Paul R. Corts
Assistant Attorney General
for Administration

cc: EOUSA Audit Liaison
Criminal Division Audit Liaison
DEA Audit Liaison
FBI Audit Liaison

APPENDIX IV
GAO CONTACT AND STAFF ACKNOWLEDGMENTS

GAO Contact

Yvonne D. Jones (202) 512-2717 or jonesy@gao.gov

GAO Acknowledgments

In addition to the contact named above, Barbara I. Keller, Assistant Director; Toni Gillich; M'Baye Diagne; Yola Lewis; Marc Molino; Elizabeth Olivarez; Carl Ramirez; Omyra Ramsingh; Barbara Roesmann; and Adam Shapiro made key contributions to this report.

RELATED GAO PRODUCTS

Terrorist Financing: Better Strategic Planning Needed to Coordinate U.S. Efforts to Deliver Counter-Terrorism Financing Training and Technical Assistance Abroad. GAO-06-19. Washington, D.C.: October 24, 2005.

USA PATRIOT Act: Additional Guidance Could Improve Implementation of Regulations Related to Customer Identification and Information Sharing Procedures. GAO-05-412. Washington, D.C.: May 6, 2005.

Information Security: IRS Needs to Remedy Serious Weaknesses Over Taxpayer and Bank Secrecy Act Data. GAO-05-482. Washington, D.C.: April 15, 2005.

Anti-Money Laundering: Issues Concerning Depository Institution Regulatory Oversight. GAO-04-833T. Washington, D.C.: June 3, 2004.

Combating Terrorism: Federal Agencies Face Continuing Challenges in Addressing Terrorist Financing and Money Laundering. GAO-04-501T. Washington, D.C.: March 4, 2004.

Terrorist Financing: U.S. Agencies Should Systematically Assess Terrorists' Use of Alternative Financing Mechanisms. GAO-04-163. Washington, D.C.: November 14, 2003.

Combating Money Laundering: Opportunities Exist to Improve the National Strategy. GAO-03-813. Washington, D.C.: September 26, 2003.

Internet Gambling: An Overview of the Issues. GAO-03-89. Washington, D.C.: December 2, 2002.

Interim Report on Internet Gambling. GAO-02-1101R. Washington, D.C.: September 23, 2002.

Money Laundering: Extent of Money Laundering Through Credit Cards Is Unknown. GAO-02-670. Washington, D.C.: July 22, 2002.

Anti-Money Laundering: Efforts in the Securities Industry. GAO-02-111. Washington, D.C.: October 10, 2001.

Money Laundering: Oversight of Suspicious Activity Reporting at Bank-Affiliated Broker-Dealers Ceased. GAO-01-474. Washington, D.C.: March 22, 2001.

Suspicious Banking Activities: Possible Money Laundering by U.S. Corporations Formed for Russian Entities. GAO-01-120. Washington, D.C.: October 31, 2000.

Money Laundering: Observations on Private Banking and Related Oversight of Selected Offshore Jurisdictions. GAO/T-GGD-00-32. Washington, D.C.: November 9, 1999.

Private Banking: Raul Salinas, Citibank, and Alleged Money Laundering. GAO/T-OSI-00-3. Washington, D.C.: November 9, 1999.

Private Banking: Raul Salinas, Citibank, and Alleged Money Laundering. GAO/OSI-99-1. Washington, D.C.: October 30, 1998.

Money Laundering: Regulatory Oversight of Offshore Private Banking Activities. GAO/GGD-98-154. Washington, D.C.: June 29, 1998.

Money Laundering: FinCEN's Law Enforcement Support Role Is Evolving. GAO/GGD-98-117. Washington, D.C.: June 19, 1998.

Money Laundering: FinCEN Needs to Better Manage Bank Secrecy Act Civil Penalties. GAO/GGD-98-108. Washington, D.C.: June 15, 1998.

Money Laundering: FinCEN's Law Enforcement Support, Regulatory, and International Roles. GAO/GGD-98-83. Washington, D.C.: April 1, 1998.

Money Laundering: FinCEN Needs to Better Communicate Regulatory Priorities and Timelines. GAO/GGD-98-18. Washington, D.C.: February 6, 1998.

Private Banking: Information on Private Banking and Its Vulnerability to Money Laundering. GAO/GGD-98-19R. Washington, D.C.: October 30, 1997.

Money Laundering: A Framework for Understanding U.S. Efforts Overseas. GAO/GGD-96-105. Washington, D.C.: May 24, 1996.

Money Laundering: U.S. Efforts to Combat Money Laundering Overseas. GAO/T-GGD-96-84. Washington, D.C.: February 28, 1996.

GAO's Mission

The Government Accountability Office, the audit, evaluation and investigative arm of Congress, exists to support Congress in meeting its constitutional responsibilities and to help improve the performance and accountability of the federal government for the American people. GAO examines the use of public funds; evaluates federal programs and policies; and provides analyses, recommendations, and other assistance to help Congress make informed oversight, policy, and funding decisions. GAO's commitment to good government is reflected in its core values of accountability, integrity, and reliability.

REFERENCES

Executive Summary

[1] Bank Secrecy Act, titles I and II of Pub. L. No. 91-508, 84 Stat. 1114 (1970), as amended, codified at 12 U.S.C. §§ 1829b, 1951-1959, and 31 U.S.C. §§ 5311-5322.

[2] The Uniting and Strengthening America by Providing Appropriate Tools Required to Intercept and Obstruct Terrorism Act of 2001, Pub. L. No. 107-56, 115 Stat. 272 (2001). We refer to this act as the "PATRIOT Act."

[3] The Secretary of the Treasury is authorized, after consultation with the appropriate federal regulator, to prescribe minimum standards for AML programs required by section 352(a) of the USA PATRIOT Act. PATRIOT Act, § 352, 115 Stat. 272, 322 (2001) (codified at 31 U.S.C. § 5318(h)).

[4] GAO uses the term "regulators" to refer collectively to the federal regulators of depository institutions, including banks, thrifts, and federally chartered credit unions. The federal banking regulators are the Federal Deposit Insurance Corporation, Board of Governors of the Federal Reserve System, National Credit Union Administration, Office of the Comptroller of the Currency, and Office of Thrift Supervision.

[5] FinCEN, originally established by order of the Secretary (Treasury Order 105-08) on April 25, 1990, was reestablished as a bureau within the Department of the Treasury pursuant to section 361(a)(2) of the PATRIOT Act. In addition to the statutory duties and powers assigned to FinCEN by the PATRIOT Act, the Director of FinCEN has other delegated authorities related to the implementation and administration of the BSA, as outlined in Treasury Order 108-01, dated September 26, 2002.

[6] 31 C.F.R. § 103.56(b)(1)-(5).

[7] We use the term "state banking departments" to refer to state authorities responsible for the regulation and supervision of state-chartered depository institutions in all 50 states, the Commonwealth of Puerto Rico, the District of Columbia, the U.S. Virgin Islands, and the U.S. Pacific Island Territory of Guam.

[8] The Conference of State Bank Supervisors is an organization that represents the interests of the state banking system to federal and state legislative and regulatory agencies.

[9] FFIEC, a formal interagency body comprising one member from each of the regulators, prescribes uniform standards for the federal examination of financial institutions by the regulators.

[10] Commissioned examiners are Federal Reserve, FDIC, and OCC examiners who have received classroom training and on-the-job training over several years and have successfully completed the commissioning examination.

[11] Each regulator uses a different term for those examiners that specialize in BSA compliance. In this report, we refer to these examiners as "subject matter experts."

[12] Some of the data that the regulators provide to FinCEN are confidential supervisory information. Because of the possible use of sensitive information, the MOU restricts the disclosure of the analytical products that FinCEN provides to the regulators. Other parties would need written authorization from FinCEN to obtain these reports.

[13] Justice's Criminal Division develops, enforces, and supervises the application of all federal criminal laws, except those specifically assigned to other divisions within the department. The Criminal Division and the 93 U.S. Attorneys have the responsibility for overseeing criminal matters under more than 900 statutes as well as certain civil litigation. The division attorneys prosecute many nationally significant cases, and the division formulates and implements criminal enforcement policy.

1. Introduction

[1] Bank Secrecy Act, titles I and II of Pub. L. No. 91-508, 84 Stat. 1114 (1970), as amended, codified at 12 U.S.C. §§ 1829b, 1951-1959, and 31 U.S.C. §§ 5311-5322.

[2] The Uniting and Strengthening America by Providing Appropriate Tools Required to Intercept and Obstruct Terrorism Act of 2001, Pub. L. No. 107-56, 115 Stat. 272 (2001). We refer to this act as the PATRIOT Act.

[3] In addition to the duties delegated to FinCEN by the Secretary, FinCEN also has specific statutory duties and powers under the PATRIOT Act to support law enforcement efforts against domestic and international financial crimes. 31 U.S.C. § 310; Treas. Order No. 180-01, September 26, 2002.

[4] Currency and Foreign Transactions Reporting Act (commonly referred to as the Bank Secrecy Act), Pub. L. No. 91-508, 84 Stat. 1114 (1970) (codified as amended in 12 U.S.C. §§ 1829(b), 1951-1959; 31 U.S.C. §§ 5311-5330).

[5] Pub. L. No. 99-570, title I, subtitle H, 100 Stat. 3207-17 (1986).

[6] Such regulations are found in various parts of title 12 of the Code of Federal Regulations: 12 C.F.R. § 21.1–21.21 (Office of the Comptroller of the Currency); 12 C.F.R. § 208.63 (Board of Governors of the Federal Reserve System); 12 C.F.R. § 326.8 (Federal Deposit Insurance Corporation); 12 C.F.R. § 563.177 (Office of Thrift Supervision); and 12 C.F.R. § 748.2 (National Credit Union Administration). The regulations adopted by each regulator generally require depository institutions to establish a written compliance program approved by their boards of directors that, at a minimum, (1) provides for a system of internal controls to ensure ongoing compliance, (2) provides for independent testing for compliance to be conducted by institution personnel or an outside party, (3) designates a compliance person to coordinate and monitor day-to-day compliance, and (4) provides training for the appropriate personnel.

[7] Pub. L. No. 102-550, title XV, 106 Stat. 3672 (1992).

[8] Pub. L. No. 103-325, title IV, 108 Stat. 2247 (1994).

[9] The regulators also are required to review the BSA/AML programs of insured depository institutions during their regular safety and soundness examinations. 12 U.S.C. § 1818(s)(2).

[10] The regulators and state banking departments use the "Uniform Financial Institutions Rating System" to assess the soundness of financial institutions and identify those institutions requiring special supervisory attention. Under the rating system, six essential components of an institution's financial condition and operations are evaluated: Capital, Assets, Management, Earnings, Liquidity, and Sensitivity to interest-rate or market risk (CAMELS). The ratings are assigned on a scale of 1 to 5, with 1 being the highest and 5 the lowest. Other rating systems are used for financial institutions other than banks, such as U.S. operations of foreign banking organizations. NCUA uses a modified version of this rating scale.

[11] In accordance with 12 U.S.C § 1820(d), the appropriate federal banking regulator generally shall, not less than once each 12-month period, conduct a safety and soundness examination of each insured depository institution. The safety and soundness examinations of certain depository institutions may be conducted in alternate years by state banking departments and federal banking agencies. State banking departments conduct independent safety and soundness examinations in accordance with the alternating examination cycle program prescribed within section 10(d) of the Federal Deposit Insurance Act. NCUA conducts joint examinations with the states every 18 months.

[12] We interviewed officials and/or examiners from Florida's Office of Financial Regulation, Georgia's Department of Banking and Finance, Illinois' Department of Financial and Professional Regulation, Louisiana's Office of Financial Institutions, New York's State Banking Department, Utah's Department of Financial Institutions, and Virginia's Bureau of Financial Institutions.

[13] In July 2004, we interviewed Federal Reserve officials involved in managing the Federal Reserve's national examination data system. We received written responses to all of our data reliability questions in April 2005.

2. Regulators Used Similar Procedures for BSA Examinations but under Pre-2005 Guidance, Their Application Could Vary Widely

[1] Before 2005, the regulators had separate BSA examination guidance, but, in June 2005, they issued interagency examination guidance. See chapter 3 for a discussion of the new interagency examination guidance adopted in 2005. The new guidance has not changed the basic procedures.

[2] Examiners may access the IRS's Currency and Banking Retrieval System to obtain CTRs, SARs, and other information, such as Reports of Foreign Bank and Financial Accounts. Examiners also may access FinCEN's Currency and Banking Query System, which is a sophisticated, enhanced query system, to obtain detailed information on SARs.

[3] Most industry participants agree that the primary market for private banking consists of high-net-worth individuals and their business interests. Privacy and confidentiality are important elements of private banking relationships, and banks that act as a fiduciary for such individuals may have statutory, contractual, or ethical obligations to uphold the customers' confidentiality.

[4] Beginning in 2000, Treasury and Justice designated certain areas as HIFCAs: Chicago, Illinois; Los Angeles, California; San Francisco, California; Miami, Florida; San Juan, Puerto Rico; the southwest border (Texas and Arizona); and New York and New Jersey. HIFCA designations were designed to allow law enforcement to concentrate resources in areas where money laundering or related financial crimes were occurring at a higher-than-average rate.

[5] OFAC administers and enforces economic and trade sanctions against countries and groups of individuals, such as terrorists and narcotics traffickers. OFAC publishes a list of individuals and companies owned or controlled by, or acting for or on behalf of, targeted countries. It also lists individuals, groups, and entities designated under programs that are not country-specific. Collectively, such individuals and companies are called "Specially Designated Nationals." Their assets are to be blocked, and U.S. persons generally are prohibited from dealing with them.

[6] 12 U.S.C § 1818(s).

[7] "Know Your Customer" refers to the due diligence institutions are expected to conduct to understand the financial and transaction profiles of their customers so that they can monitor more effectively for unusual or suspicious transactions.

[8] Section 326 of the PATRIOT Act required the Secretary of the Treasury and the federal functional regulators to develop regulations establishing minimum standards for

financial institutions regarding the verification of a customer's identity in connection with opening an account. 31 U.S.C. § 5318(l). These regulations require financial institutions to establish a written customer identification program. See, for example, 31 C.F.R. §§ 103.121–103.123; see also GAO, *USA PATRIOT Act: Additional Guidance Could Improve Implementation of Regulations Related to Customer Identification and Information Sharing Procedures*, GAO-05-412 (Washington, D.C.: May 6, 2005).

[9] We discuss BSA violations and deficiencies in more detail in chapter 4.

[10] CSBS is an organization that represents the interests of the state banking system to federal and state legislative and regulatory agencies. Results of the inquiry showed that CSBS contacted 50 banking departments, the Commonwealth of Puerto Rico, and the District of Columbia. Two of the 52 departments did not respond to the inquiry. On the basis of these results, at least 15 banking departments were not examining for BSA compliance.

[11] According to the CSBS officials, in most states, state laws do not charge banking departments with examining state-chartered depository institutions for BSA compliance or with enforcing BSA compliance. Additionally, some banking departments are pursuing legislative changes to allow them to share information, including BSA examination, with other appropriate entities such as FinCEN.

[12] Results of the inquiry indicated that 49 banking departments, the District of Columbia, the Commonwealth of Puerto Rico, and the U.S. Pacific Island Territory of Guam participated in the inquiry. One of the 52 participants did not respond to the inquiry. On the basis of the results, at least 6 banking departments were not examining for BSA compliance.

[13] The MOUs vary by state and define state banking departments' roles and responsibilities.

3. Regulators Have Promoted Consistency in BSA Examinations through Interagency Procedures and BSA Training

[1] Commissioned examiners are Federal Reserve, FDIC, and OCC examiners who have received classroom training and on-the-job training over several years and have successfully completed the commissioning examination.

[2] GAO-05-412.

[3] Each regulator uses a different term for those examiners specializing in BSA compliance. In this report, we refer to these examiners as "subject matter experts."

[4] GAO-05-412.

4. Systems Improvements Help Regulators Track BSA Examination and Violation Data, but Differences in Terminology Remain

[1] These responses included issuing guidance that (1) outlines how BSA assessment factors are considered in determining the appropriate enforcement actions, (2) develops an internal control process to verify that all BSA violations are promptly included in the systems used to report to Treasury, and (3) establishes procedures to prevent institutions

with inadequate BSA/AML programs from bidding on franchises or failed bank assets. The IG noted that FDIC was making significant improvements in its supervision of BSA/AML programs in response to these recommendations and the agency's own initiatives.

[2] According to Federal Reserve officials, some Reserve Banks have developed mechanisms to collect and store data on BSA-related information, including violations, supervisory actions, and institutions' progress on implementing corrective actions for BSA-related problems.

[3] Officials from FinCEN and the regulators noted that before the adoption of the MOU, in accordance with Treasury regulation, the regulators were required to submit some aggregate data on BSA violations to FinCEN and its predecessor within Treasury.

[4] Some of the data that regulators provide to FinCEN are confidential supervisory information. Accordingly, the MOU restricts the disclosure of analytical products provided by FinCEN to the regulators in the absence of written authorization from FinCEN.

[5] The section 314(a) regulations set forth the process by which law enforcement agencies provide FinCEN with names and identifying information on suspects. FinCEN distributes this information to financial institutions across the country and requires that institutions search their accounts to identify any matches (see GAO-05-412).

[6] 12 C.F.R. § 326.8 (FDIC), 12 C.F.R. § 208.63 (Federal Reserve), 12 C.F.R. § 748.2 (NCUA), 12 C.F.R. § 21.21 (OCC), and 12 C.F.R. § 563.177 (OTS).

[7] Section 326.8 of the FDIC *Rules and Regulations*.

[8] OCC, *Bank Secrecy Act/Anti-Money Laundering Supervision* (May 2005).

5. Regulators and FinCEN Increased Coordination on BSA Enforcement; Criminal Cases Were Limited

[1] According to the September 2004 MOU signed by FinCEN and the regulators, for purposes of the MOU, a significant violation includes a systemic or pervasive BSA/AML program deficiency, systemic or pervasive BSA reporting or record-keeping violations, or a situation where a banking organization fails to respond to supervisory warnings concerning such failures or weaknesses. A significant violation also includes nontechnical, one-time BSA violations that demonstrate willful or reckless disregard for the requirements of the BSA, or that create a substantial risk of money laundering or the financing of terrorism within the institution. The regulators' formal enforcement actions could solely address BSA compliance problems or involve other and unrelated safety and soundness problems at the institution.

[2] OCC uses the term "consent order" for a cease-and-desist order, which has been entered into and becomes final through the board of directors' execution. An authorized OCC official also signs consent orders. Like all orders to cease and desist, the consent order is issued pursuant to 12 U.S.C. § 1818(b). Aside from its title, a cease-and-desist order is identical in form and legal effect to a consent order. However, a cease-and-desist order is imposed on an involuntary basis after issuance of an OCC Notice of Charges, a hearing before an administrative law judge, and a final decision order issued by the Comptroller of the Currency.

[3] The Federal Reserve has delegated authority to the Reserve Banks to enter into written agreements with institutions (with the prior concurrence of senior Federal Reserve officials); however, the authority to take other types of formal enforcement actions remains with the Federal Reserve.

[4] OCC took subsequent action that is discussed later in this chapter.

[5] 12 U.S.C. § 1818(s). NCUA has similar authority under 12 U.S.C. § 1786(q).

[6] 12 U.S.C. §§ 1818(i)(2) and 1786(k)(2).

[7] Section 1818 authorizes the regulators to use several formal enforcement actions.

[8] According to OCC, "Matters Requiring Attention" are informal enforcement actions that document practices that (1) deviate from sound fundamental principles and are likely to result in financial deterioration if not addressed or (2) result in substantive noncompliance with laws and regulations. Matters Requiring Attention also involve a commitment from institution management to take corrective action and a specified time frame for such action.

[9] In its comments on the report, FDIC generally disagreed with this and other conclusions made in the FDIC IG report, but agreed with the report's recommendations.

[10] 31 C.F.R. §103.56(a). Although 31 C.F.R. 103.56 refers specifically to the "Assistant Secretary (Enforcement)," under paragraph 8(c) of Treasury Order No. 180-01, the term the "Assistant Secretary (Enforcement)," as used in the regulations, rules, instructions, and forms issued or adopted for the administration and enforcement of the BSA, is deemed to mean the Director of FinCEN.

[11] BSA regulations allow the regulators to submit evidence of specific BSA violations to FinCEN at any time—not just in the course of examinations. 31 C.F.R. § 103.56(e).

[12] Federal Reserve guidelines only authorize Board of Governors staff to make referrals to FinCEN.

[13] According to FinCEN officials, FinCEN also issues Letters of Caution to address cases involving nonsignificant, often technical, BSA compliance problems.

[14] Since 1999, FinCEN also issued CMPs against 14 other financial institutions, including casinos, check cashers, money exchanges, and money remitters. FinCEN has issued CMPs against two individuals for BSA violations.

[15] According to enforcement documents, payments of concurrent FinCEN and OCC CMP assessments would be satisfied by one payment to the Treasury.

[16] On May 14, 2004, the Board of Governors of the Federal Reserve System issued a consent cease-and-desist order to Riggs National Corporation (then a bank holding company), and Riggs International Banking Corporation, an Edge corporation organized under section 25A of the Federal Reserve Act (12 U.S.C. § 611), which was a wholly owned subsidiary of Riggs Bank, Washington, D.C. Because Riggs International Banking Corporation ceased to exist as a separate entity as of December 31, 2004, and all of Riggs International Banking Corporation's remaining operations, accounts, property, and records were transferred to Riggs Bank, on January 26, 2005, the Board of Governors terminated the May 2004 order, and Riggs Bank consented to the issuance of a new order to cease and desist.

[17] According to its consent order of CMP, OCC determined that Riggs Bank failed to detect or investigate suspicious activities and did not file SARs as required. Among other failures, Riggs Bank did not investigate suspicious activities occurring in accounts related to the countries of Saudi Arabia and Equatorial Guinea. OCC also determined

that Riggs Bank failed to adequately monitor for suspicious activity involving cash, wire, or monetary instrument transactions. Specifically, Riggs Bank failed to identify or monitor potentially suspicious activity pertaining to (1) tens of millions of dollars in cash withdrawals from accounts related to the Saudi Arabian embassy and (2) dozens of sequentially numbered international drafts that totaled millions of dollars that were drawn from accounts related to officials of Saudi Arabia that were returned to the bank. Riggs Bank also did not identify or monitor dozens of sequentially numbered cashier's checks that were drawn from accounts related to officials of Saudi Arabia made payable to the account holder, millions of dollars deposited into a private investment company owned by an official of the country of Equatorial Guinea, hundreds of thousands of dollars transferred from an account of the country of Equatorial Guinea to the personal account of a government official in the country, and more than a million dollars transferred from an account of the country of Equatorial Guinea to a private investment company owned by a Riggs Bank relationship manager. OCC also cited problems with Riggs Bank's BSA/AML program, including seriously deficient internal controls, inadequate independent testing, ineffective management to oversee day-to-day BSA compliance, ineffective training, and systemic problems with Riggs Bank's risk management procedures.

[18] Arab Bank-New York performed the clearing function for members of the Arab Bank Group in foreign jurisdictions and domestic and foreign correspondent institutions independent of the Arab Bank Group. In addition, as a member of the Clearing House Interbank Payments System and other settlement systems in the United States, Arab Bank-New York cleared funds transfers involving major commercial banks in the United States. None of the originators and beneficiaries in funds transfers that Arab Bank-New York cleared as an intermediary institution held accounts at Arab Bank-New York.

[19] 31 U.S.C. §§ 5321 and 5330, 12 U.S.C. §§ 1829b(j) and 1953, and 31 C.F.R. § 103.57.

[20] Section 321(b) of the USA PATRIOT Act amended the definition of "financial institutions" subject to the BSA to include futures commission merchants, commodity trading advisors, and commodity pool operators registered or required to be registered under the Commodity Exchange Act. Accordingly, FinCEN amended the BSA implementing regulations to delegate BSA examination authority to the Commodity Futures Trading Commission with respect to futures commissions merchants, commodity trading advisors, and introducing brokers in commodities. 68 Fed. Reg., 65393, 65399 (2002) (codified at 31 C.F.R. § 103.56(b)(9)).

[21] According to Justice, other federal law enforcement agencies involved in the case included the Federal Bureau of Investigation, the United States Secret Service, and the IRS.

[22] According to Justice, Equatorial Guinea has billions of dollars of oil reserves within its territorial waters, resulting in a significant influx of capital from businesses in the United States and elsewhere. By 2003, these accounts had become Riggs Bank's largest single relationship, with balances and outstanding loans that totaled nearly $700 million. In February 2003, the U.S. Senate Permanent Subcommittee on Investigations of the Committee on Governmental Affairs, at the request of Senator Carl Levin, Ranking Minority Member, and the support of the Subcommittee Chairman, Norm Coleman, initiated a bipartisan investigation to evaluate the enforcement and effectiveness of key AML provisions in the PATRIOT Act, using Riggs Bank as a case history. Following a

July 2004 hearing and report on the results of the investigation, on March 16, 2005, the subcommittee issued a separate report identifying additional accounts connected to Pinochet at other financial institutions.

[23] ICE and IRS-Criminal Investigation division conducted separate investigations into multiple accounts at Banco Popular.

[24] In May 2004, FDIC issued a cease-and-desist order against the bank for BSA violations.

[25] The procedures also indicate that if a depository institution knows, suspects, or has reason to suspect that a customer may be linked to terrorist activity against the United States, the bank should immediately call FinCEN's Financial Institutions Terrorist Hotline.

[26] Justice's Criminal Division develops, enforces, and supervises the application of all federal criminal laws, except those specifically assigned to other divisions within the department. The Criminal Division and the 93 U.S. attorneys have the responsibility for overseeing criminal matters under more than 900 statutes as well as certain civil litigation. The division attorneys prosecute many nationally significant cases, and the division formulates and implements criminal enforcement policy.

6. Conclusions and Recommendations

[1] Examination documentation is essential for supervision of examinations; reviews of examination quality; and, ultimately, regulator oversight of financial institutions. Moreover, the documentation must be of a quality that would support findings and recommendations; constitute a clear record of decision making; and allow internal and external reviewers, auditors, and regulators to understand the examiners' work and analyses.

Appendix I

[1] This manual was still in effect when we issued this report.

[2] OCC specified "quantity of risk" procedures to include the selection and testing of various accounts, such as exemptions, sales of monetary instruments, funds transfers, international brokered accounts, and nonresident alien accounts.

[3] Community banks are those banks that have assets of less than $1 billion.

INDEX

A

acceptance, 20, 128
access, 2, 17, 18, 19, 26, 43, 44, 45, 48, 52, 53, 94, 149
accommodation, 132
accountability, 47, 146
accreditation, 97, 98
accuracy, 5, 37, 48, 78, 79, 90, 100
acquisitions, 90
ADC, 50
affect, 30, 64, 102, 110, 139
agent, 41
aggregation, 47
alternative, 87
amendments, 62, 74, 78, 80
American Stock Exchange, 7
appendix, 73, 80, 85
aptitude, 97, 98
arrest, 128
artificial intelligence, 3
assessment, 50, 63, 64, 66, 72, 78, 82, 83, 88, 89, 90, 92, 93, 98, 109, 112, 114, 120, 122, 123, 136, 150
assessment procedures, 66, 82, 89
assets, 2, 9, 15, 20, 21, 28, 67, 85, 123, 135, 136, 137, 138, 139, 149, 151, 154
association, 14, 57
attachment, 123
attacks, 75
attention, 14, 16, 27, 49, 50, 51, 65, 67, 77, 85, 86, 127, 131, 132, 148
auditing, 80, 128
authority, 3, 5, 6, 7, 20, 21, 27, 37, 63, 65, 72, 75, 76, 112, 113, 116, 118, 122, 130, 152, 153
automation, 103
availability, 9, 16
awareness, 30, 75, 94

B

Bank Secrecy Act, i, iii, v, vii, 1, 29, 49, 50, 51, 52, 55, 57, 59, 61, 62, 68, 74, 80, 87, 89, 134, 145, 146, 147, 148, 151
bankers, 16, 95
banking, 2, 3, 5, 10, 11, 12, 13, 14, 17, 18, 19, 20, 21, 23, 25, 28, 30, 32, 34, 35, 43, 46, 47, 48, 52, 53, 56, 57, 62, 63, 64, 65, 66, 67, 68, 69, 74, 75, 76, 77, 78, 80, 81, 82, 84, 85, 86, 87, 96, 100, 101, 103, 106, 107, 112, 114, 123, 124, 126, 127, 129, 131, 132, 133, 134, 135, 138, 147, 148, 149, 150, 151
banking department, 14, 20, 21, 34, 63, 64, 66, 67, 68, 69, 76, 77, 78, 81, 85, 86, 87, 96, 101, 106, 114, 133, 147, 148, 150
banking industry, 66, 96, 106, 107, 112, 126, 129, 131, 132
banks, vii, 1, 2, 3, 4, 6, 7, 8, 11, 12, 13, 14, 15, 16, 17, 18, 19, 20, 21, 22, 23, 25, 26, 28, 44, 51, 52, 53, 54, 55, 56, 57, 58, 63, 67, 70, 73, 75, 77, 82, 85, 87, 89, 91, 92, 100, 101, 102, 105, 107, 117, 126, 130, 131, 134, 135, 136, 137, 138, 139, 147, 148, 149, 154
Belgium, 123
binding, 113
birth, 39
black market, 25, 42
blocks, 28
body, 53, 88, 147
bonds, 2
Bureau of Alcohol, Tobacco, Firearms, and Explosives, 77

C

California, 80, 149
capital markets, 97, 98
carrier, 16, 37, 43
cartel, 25, 26
cash flow, 2, 20, 29, 34
cast, 95
central bank, 56
certificates of deposit, 123
channels, 129
Chile, 120, 123
classes, 94
classification, 47, 73, 108, 133
classroom, 69, 92, 94, 96, 97, 98, 147, 150
clients, 47
coaches, 97
coding, 79
collaboration, 56, 68, 74, 87, 88, 134
collateral, 3, 4, 12, 18, 129
Colombia, 25, 26
commercial bank, 135, 153
commitment, 4, 51, 65, 67, 72, 84, 98, 111, 113, 146, 152
commodity, 153
communication, 27, 28, 114, 123, 132
community, 50, 63, 67, 70, 77, 82, 85, 92, 94, 100, 101, 102, 107, 117, 134, 135, 137, 139
compensation, 21, 46
competency, 82
compilation, 105
complexity, 64, 69, 96, 130
compliance, vii, 1, 2, 3, 4, 5, 8, 13, 20, 21, 26, 28, 29, 30, 31, 32, 33, 34, 35, 36, 37, 47, 48, 49, 50, 51, 54, 58, 62, 63, 64, 65, 66, 67, 68, 69, 70, 71, 72, 73, 74, 75, 76, 77, 78, 81, 82, 83, 84, 85, 86, 87, 90, 91, 92, 94, 96, 97, 98, 99, 101, 102, 105, 106, 107, 108, 109, 110, 112, 113, 114, 115, 116, 117, 118, 119, 121, 122, 123, 125, 126, 127, 128, 129, 130, 131, 132, 133, 134, 136, 137, 147, 148, 150, 151, 152, 153
components, 76, 82, 93, 113, 148
computer systems, 53
concentration, 12, 19
conduct, 17, 18, 21, 22, 24, 27, 29, 37, 48, 57, 66, 67, 68, 74, 75, 77, 79, 82, 83, 84, 87, 88, 96, 97, 98, 100, 106, 110, 112, 113, 118, 121, 125, 127, 128, 129, 130, 137, 148, 149
confidence, 57, 116
confidentiality, 20, 58, 149
configuration, 76
conformity, 12, 57, 58
consensus, 71, 108
consent, 114, 128, 151, 152
consultants, 50
continuity, 74, 134
control, 4, 13, 19, 20, 22, 28, 29, 36, 42, 45, 50, 69, 82, 85, 99, 101, 131, 137, 150
Controlled Substances Act, 3
conversion, 103
conviction, 127
corporations, 14, 23, 124
costs, 126
counsel, 27, 49, 54, 55, 128
coverage, 37, 82, 86, 100, 127, 137
covering, 19, 100
credit, 2, 3, 11, 14, 15, 19, 20, 21, 25, 28, 30, 34, 40, 43, 45, 48, 62, 63, 77, 78, 83, 85, 95, 98, 107, 109, 113, 134, 136, 139, 147
creditors, 3
crime, 2, 36, 75
criminal activity, vii, 1, 2, 3, 22, 24, 27, 54, 57, 58, 62, 126, 128
criminals, 20, 24, 36, 57, 77, 130
criticism, 126
currency, 2, 4, 6, 7, 8, 10, 12, 16, 23, 24, 26, 32, 34, 37, 38, 39, 43, 50, 52, 70, 74, 91, 121, 126
curriculum, 93, 94
customers, 1, 3, 5, 6, 7, 8, 13, 15, 17, 18, 19, 20, 21, 33, 34, 36, 38, 39, 41, 44, 45, 46, 47, 48, 49, 54, 57, 58, 62, 66, 73, 77, 82, 105, 106, 112, 121, 125, 126, 139, 149
cycles, 63, 77, 105

D

damage, 18
danger, 18
data collection, 53, 79
database, 18, 42, 52, 70, 94, 103, 107, 136
dating, 55
debt, 49
decision making, 154
decisions, 64, 99, 100, 102, 135, 146
deficiency, 65, 71, 83, 109, 110, 111, 116, 122, 123, 151
definition, 19, 28, 38, 110, 153
demand, 16, 29, 56
demographics, 19
Department of Homeland Security, 63, 73, 77, 80
Department of Justice, 63, 133, 143
deposit accounts, 16, 39, 42, 43, 52
deposits, 2, 9, 10, 11, 12, 13, 14, 15, 17, 24, 25, 30, 42, 84, 124
desire, 116
destruction, 137

detection, 15, 22, 35, 62, 74
deviation, 110
directives, 93
disclosure, 147, 151
disposition, 53, 55, 72, 128
disseminate, 65, 68, 88
distribution, 53
diversity, 71, 108
division, 63, 76, 147, 154
draft, 26, 44, 73, 80, 99, 122, 133, 134
drug trafficking, vii, 1, 2, 20, 62
drugs, 23
duties, 5, 35, 112, 116, 147, 148

E

earnings, 20
electricity, 14
embargo, 56
employee compensation, 47
employees, 1, 3, 5, 8, 18, 21, 24, 35, 36, 38, 45, 47, 48, 58, 126, 128
employment, 4, 11, 14, 18, 21, 22, 36, 42
environment, 88, 130
equity, 7
ethical standards, 57, 58
ethics, 46
evidence, 4, 6, 14, 57, 113, 125, 127, 128, 152
evolution, 73, 134
examinations, 2, 3, 21, 22, 35, 51, 52, 62, 63, 64, 66, 67, 68, 69, 70, 71, 72, 77, 78, 79, 80, 81, 84, 85, 86, 87, 88, 89, 91, 92, 93, 95, 96, 97, 98, 99, 100, 101, 102, 103, 105, 106, 108, 109, 110, 111, 113, 118, 126, 127, 130, 131, 134, 135, 136, 137, 138, 139, 148, 152, 154
execution, 40, 151
exercise, 4, 13, 15, 17, 20, 63, 67, 85, 113, 130, 135
expertise, 93
experts, 2, 69, 93, 96, 98, 117, 147, 150
exposure, 49

F

failure, 4, 5, 27, 65, 104, 109, 113, 114, 116, 119, 121, 123, 126, 127, 128, 132
family, 123
family members, 123
federal law, 8, 9, 32, 153
feedback, 96
finance, 43, 45, 77
Financial Crimes Enforcement Network, vii, 2, 26, 55, 61, 62, 74
financial institutions, 1, 2, 5, 6, 16, 19, 24, 43, 45, 46, 53, 56, 57, 62, 72, 73, 74, 75, 76, 82, 94, 95, 105, 112, 113, 118, 122, 129, 132, 133, 147, 148, 150, 151, 152, 153, 154
financial intermediaries, 21, 26
financial planning, 19
financial regulation, 62
financial system, 1, 25, 57, 74, 134
financing, 19, 23, 62, 63, 64, 66, 67, 68, 73, 75, 76, 82, 85, 86, 88, 90, 121, 130, 133, 151
firms, 21, 22, 75
flexibility, 102, 112
focusing, 22, 48, 77
food, 10
foreign banks, 3, 14, 15, 16, 17
foreign exchange, 23
foreign policy, 27, 56
France, 123
fraud, 1, 2, 29
free trade, 25, 42
funding, 146
funds, 2, 5, 7, 9, 10, 11, 12, 13, 14, 15, 16, 19, 21, 24, 25, 26, 28, 30, 33, 35, 40, 41, 43, 45, 46, 47, 48, 56, 57, 74, 75, 77, 84, 86, 91, 121, 131, 134, 146, 153, 154

G

Georgia, 86
goals, 27, 46
government, vii, 1, 3, 6, 45, 46, 47, 80, 123, 124, 146, 153
grand jury, 126
gravity, 4
groups, 25, 44, 109, 149
guidance, 5, 22, 50, 51, 53, 64, 65, 66, 67, 68, 71, 73, 80, 81, 82, 83, 84, 85, 88, 89, 90, 91, 93, 95, 98, 99, 100, 101, 102, 106, 107, 108, 109, 110, 111, 117, 118, 122, 130, 131, 133, 134, 135, 136, 138, 149, 150
guidelines, 20, 118, 125, 129, 152
guilty, 66, 123
Guinea, 123, 152, 153

H

hands, 94, 95
handwriting, 25
hard currency, 23
hip, 14, 33
hiring, 22, 36, 48
holding company, 152

host, 18, 22
House, 16, 153
housing, 25
human rights, 123

I

identification, 1, 10, 11, 14, 24, 30, 33, 35, 39, 40, 41, 42, 44, 49, 57, 58, 75, 76, 84, 105, 115, 116, 133, 150
identity, 6, 13, 16, 20, 21, 39, 40, 41, 42, 57, 105, 150
implementation, 52, 57, 66, 102, 105, 130, 147
imprisonment, 75
incentives, 21, 47
inclusion, 51
income, 20, 33, 124
independence, 82, 111
industrialized countries, 56
industry, 19, 26, 69, 73, 74, 76, 78, 80, 93, 94, 95, 96, 97, 98, 106, 119, 131, 132, 133, 134, 149
influence, 111
information exchange, 107
information sharing, 53, 68, 71, 87, 107, 112
information technology, 33, 70, 102
inheritance, 20
input, 84, 100
insight, 106
institutions, 2, 7, 12, 16, 26, 62, 63, 65, 66, 67, 68, 70, 71, 72, 73, 74, 75, 76, 77, 78, 79, 80, 81, 82, 85, 86, 87, 88, 89, 90, 98, 99, 100, 101, 102, 105, 106, 107, 108, 111, 112, 113, 114, 116, 117, 118, 119, 120, 121, 122, 123, 124, 125, 126, 127, 128, 129, 130, 131, 132, 133, 134, 135, 136, 137, 138, 147, 148, 149, 150, 151, 152, 153
instruction, 96
instruments, 6, 9, 10, 16, 17, 24, 25, 26, 32, 39, 43, 46, 52, 82, 83, 84, 91, 154
insurance, 106
integration, 31
integrity, 5, 22, 29, 35, 69, 85, 91, 137, 146
intensity, 2, 61, 82, 137
interest, 6, 20, 28, 37, 148
intermediaries, vii, 1, 20, 57, 62
internal controls, 4, 13, 22, 27, 29, 30, 32, 34, 41, 45, 46, 48, 49, 66, 67, 82, 83, 84, 89, 109, 121, 148, 153
Internal Revenue Service, 52, 61, 63, 76
international trade, 15
internet, 58
interview, 79, 83
investment, 12, 15, 19, 20, 21, 23, 46, 47, 153

J

job training, 87, 93, 94, 96, 97, 99, 147, 150
judgment, 54, 63, 66, 67, 71, 81, 83, 85, 88, 91, 108, 111, 130, 135, 138
jurisdiction, 6, 21, 23, 28, 75

K

knowledge, 5, 6, 16, 34, 35, 36, 40, 41, 68, 83, 88, 93, 94, 98, 125
Korea, 120

L

law enforcement, vii, 1, 3, 16, 17, 52, 53, 57, 58, 62, 73, 74, 75, 76, 107, 119, 124, 126, 127, 128, 130, 131, 134, 148, 149, 151
laws, 2, 5, 7, 8, 11, 16, 20, 21, 22, 28, 29, 30, 31, 32, 34, 35, 36, 47, 51, 56, 58, 62, 63, 75, 77, 86, 93, 101, 108, 130, 147, 150, 152, 154
lawyers, 23
layering, 31, 74, 134
lead, 29, 58, 98
legislation, 27, 74, 93, 130
lending, 5, 19, 35, 49
liability, 21, 45, 75
lifestyle, 12
likelihood, 13
limitation, 122
links, 11
litigation, 147, 154
loans, 2, 3, 4, 47, 48, 49, 153
location, 10, 11, 12, 14, 21, 33, 37, 48, 89, 124
Louisiana, 86
low risk, 77, 137

M

management, 4, 5, 13, 18, 19, 22, 23, 27, 29, 30, 31, 32, 34, 35, 36, 37, 41, 42, 43, 46, 47, 48, 49, 50, 51, 57, 58, 65, 67, 69, 72, 78, 80, 82, 84, 89, 90, 95, 97, 99, 100, 102, 103, 111, 113, 116, 117, 118, 126, 152, 153
mandates, 28, 92
market, 19, 43, 129, 148, 149
marketing, 46
markets, 30
matrix, 50, 122
meanings, 110
measures, 8, 47, 49, 123, 131

media, 121, 132
mentor, 97
mentoring, 97
mentoring program, 97
mergers, 90
messages, 16
Mexico, 25, 26
Miami, 95, 120, 149
modules, 94
money, vii, 1, 2, 3, 5, 6, 9, 11, 12, 13, 14, 15, 16, 17, 18, 19, 20, 21, 22, 23, 24, 25, 26, 27, 30, 31, 35, 36, 43, 44, 46, 47, 48, 49, 50, 54, 57, 58, 61, 62, 63, 64, 66, 68, 73, 74, 75, 76, 77, 82, 88, 90, 93, 94, 95, 98, 107, 109, 114, 115, 116, 121, 124, 126, 127, 129, 130, 133, 136, 137, 149, 151, 152
money laundering, vii, 1, 2, 3, 5, 9, 13, 14, 15, 16, 17, 18, 19, 20, 21, 22, 24, 25, 26, 30, 31, 35, 36, 43, 44, 47, 48, 49, 57, 58, 61, 62, 63, 64, 66, 68, 73, 74, 75, 76, 82, 88, 90, 93, 94, 95, 98, 107, 109, 114, 121, 126, 127, 129, 130, 133, 136, 137, 149, 151
Money Laundering Control Act, vii, 1, 3, 61, 74
monitoring, 4, 13, 16, 18, 22, 30, 32, 34, 35, 36, 38, 46, 47, 50, 69, 70, 80, 82, 83, 90, 91, 99, 100, 102, 105, 107, 108, 109, 115, 117, 118, 121, 127, 129
movement, 23
multiple factors, 90, 111
murder, 1

N

narcotics, 10, 11, 27, 124, 126, 127, 149
narratives, 103
Nasdaq Stock Market, 7
national identity, 33
national security, 27, 56
needs, 25, 35, 50, 73, 110, 132, 134
neglect, 21
network, 16
New York Stock Exchange, 7

O

observations, 133
offenders, 132
oil, 153
omission, 24
organ, 68, 89
organization, 46, 78, 147, 150, 151
organizations, 14, 27, 63, 77, 135, 148
outline, 57
oversight, 50, 62, 100, 129, 130, 133, 146, 154
ownership, 20, 42, 56, 57

P

Pacific, 147, 150
Panama, 16, 25, 26, 42
partnership, 14, 20, 22, 33
pass/fail, 97
peer review, 100
penalties, 4, 18, 27, 36, 50, 55, 62, 63, 65, 72, 74, 75, 76, 112, 122
performers, 47
permit, 7, 23
personal accounts, 33, 123
perspective, 73, 127, 134
planning, 19, 63, 66, 68, 81, 82, 85, 89, 90, 91, 92, 99, 100, 130, 135, 136
preparation, 43, 94, 128
prevention, 15, 49, 62
primary data, 52
private investment, 30, 46, 153
production, 23
program, 3, 4, 5, 8, 22, 28, 29, 30, 31, 32, 46, 47, 48, 50, 51, 54, 62, 63, 66, 72, 75, 77, 82, 83, 89, 90, 92, 95, 96, 98, 100, 102, 104, 105, 107, 108, 109, 110, 111, 114, 115, 116, 117, 119, 121, 124, 125, 126, 128, 130, 136, 148, 150, 151, 153
progress reports, 123
Puerto Rico, 87, 120, 124, 125, 147, 149, 150

Q

qualifications, 35, 42, 90
quality assurance, 98, 99, 100, 117, 118, 130
query, 53, 68, 107, 149

R

range, 1, 65, 71, 72, 97, 98, 112, 113, 118, 119
rating scale, 148
ratings, 148
real time, 16
reconcile, 45
reconciliation, 41
regulation, vii, 1, 6, 9, 16, 49, 51, 72, 75, 105, 110, 111, 116, 117, 122, 147, 151
regulations, 1, 4, 5, 6, 7, 8, 9, 13, 20, 24, 25, 28, 29, 30, 31, 32, 34, 35, 36, 47, 51, 52, 55, 56, 58, 63, 70, 71, 72, 74, 75, 76, 77, 80, 93, 94, 101, 105, 106, 108, 109, 112, 117, 118, 121, 130, 148, 149, 151, 152, 153

regulator gene, 148
regulators, vii, 1, 8, 16, 52, 53, 62, 63, 64, 65, 66, 67, 68, 69, 70, 71, 72, 73, 74, 75, 76, 77, 78, 79, 80, 81, 84, 85, 86, 87, 88, 89, 90, 91, 92, 94, 95, 96, 99, 100, 101, 102, 104, 105, 106, 107, 108, 109, 110, 111, 112, 113, 114, 116, 117, 118, 119, 120, 122, 123, 124, 126, 127, 129, 130, 131, 132, 133, 134, 137, 147, 148, 149, 151, 152, 154
regulatory oversight, 21
regulatory requirements, 5, 18, 69, 91, 94, 127
relationship, 16, 18, 19, 21, 73, 134, 153
relationships, 2, 11, 13, 15, 17, 18, 19, 20, 21, 31, 33, 34, 35, 149
relatives, 123
reliability, 50, 78, 79, 100, 146, 149
reproduction, 37
reputation, 18, 50
reserves, 153
resolution, 76, 123
resources, 5, 36, 63, 64, 73, 77, 86, 94, 98, 100, 130, 134, 135, 138, 149
responsibility, 5, 35, 47, 53, 57, 63, 74, 86, 93, 128, 131, 133, 147, 154
restitution, 125, 128
retail, 9, 10, 23, 42, 98, 128
retention, 6, 36, 41, 84, 114, 137
risk, vii, 2, 3, 4, 5, 13, 15, 16, 17, 18, 19, 20, 21, 22, 25, 29, 30, 31, 32, 35, 36, 37, 39, 41, 42, 43, 44, 45, 46, 47, 48, 49, 50, 51, 58, 63, 64, 66, 67, 68, 69, 71, 74, 77, 81, 82, 83, 84, 85, 86, 87, 88, 89, 90, 91, 92, 93, 95, 98, 103, 108, 111, 114, 127, 130, 135, 136, 137, 138, 139, 148, 151, 153, 154
risk assessment, 21, 50, 64, 66, 68, 82, 88, 89, 90, 91, 92, 135, 136, 139
risk management, 16, 29, 30, 31, 50, 51, 69, 82, 85, 88, 89, 91, 98, 130, 136, 137, 138, 153
risk profile, 30, 63, 64, 66, 67, 68, 71, 81, 83, 84, 88, 89, 90, 108, 111, 114, 135, 137
rubber, 12

S

safety, 63, 69, 77, 86, 87, 96, 97, 98, 101, 148, 151
sales, 3, 15, 26, 39, 83, 84, 154
sample, 30, 34, 36, 37, 38, 39, 40, 41, 42, 43, 44, 45, 47, 48, 49, 64, 79, 84, 91, 114, 130, 134, 135, 136, 138
sampling, 139
sanctions, 27, 28, 56, 74, 149
Saudi Arabia, 152
savings, 63, 67, 76, 77, 85, 134, 138
savings banks, 76
school, 69, 92, 93
search, 22, 53, 70, 102, 103, 151
searches, 18, 42, 53, 106
Secretary of the Treasury, 28, 53, 63, 65, 74, 75, 76, 112, 122, 130, 147, 149
securities, 6, 21, 37, 48, 106, 133
security, 28, 33
seizure, 3, 18
selecting, 49, 79
self, 55, 82, 89, 94
self-assessment, 82
Senate, 62, 78, 111, 153
sentencing, 124
September 11, 68, 75, 85, 86, 88, 130
series, 2, 21, 24, 56, 64, 69, 93, 95, 97, 124
service provider, vii, 1, 12, 21, 23
services, 5, 10, 11, 14, 15, 16, 17, 18, 19, 20, 21, 30, 33, 34, 35, 36, 46, 57, 58, 64, 68, 70, 76, 77, 82, 83, 89, 90, 95, 100, 106, 119
severity, 111, 119
shares, 20
sharing, 68, 87, 129, 132
sign, 21, 133
single currency, 24
skills, 35, 64, 69, 96, 98
smoking, 125
social security, 11, 39, 40
software, 30, 33, 101
sole proprietor, 14, 33, 38
Spain, 123
specialization, 64, 96, 97
specificity, 70, 89, 105
stages, 68, 89, 122
standards, 14, 21, 54, 74, 80, 88, 92, 99, 101, 131, 147, 149
statutes, 1, 28, 78, 80, 94, 111, 147, 154
stock, 7
storage, 102
strategies, 46, 107
stress, 130
structuring, 24, 25, 26, 34, 39, 48, 125, 127
summaries, 27, 51, 53, 105
supervision, 16, 22, 27, 30, 56, 86, 93, 94, 98, 100, 103, 113, 118, 136, 147, 151, 154
supervisor, 18, 44, 76
supervisors, 53, 57, 67, 82, 84, 93, 97, 100, 102
suppliers, 15, 25, 33
suppression, 57
suspects, 9, 151, 154
suspense, 19
suspicious activity reports, 2
Switzerland, 123
symbols, 13

systems, 1, 4, 5, 12, 13, 15, 16, 22, 25, 27, 30, 34, 36, 46, 47, 53, 64, 69, 70, 78, 80, 82, 84, 88, 89, 90, 91, 99, 101, 102, 103, 105, 109, 111, 117, 118, 121, 127, 130, 131, 148, 150, 153

T

technology, 107
telecommunications, 16
telephone, 14, 33, 34
terrorism, 1, 27, 77, 151
terrorist organization, 121
theory, 130
threshold, 10, 13, 19, 24, 34, 89
thrifts, 63, 117, 138, 147
time, 8, 11, 13, 29, 34, 37, 39, 41, 51, 74, 77, 78, 79, 86, 88, 98, 99, 103, 113, 117, 119, 121, 127, 128, 130, 132, 151, 152
time frame, 8, 34, 37, 41, 51, 79, 117, 152
timing, 123
tracking, 64, 99, 102, 103
trade, 15, 26, 27, 28, 94, 149
trading, 153
training, 1, 5, 18, 35, 36, 48, 57, 58, 64, 66, 68, 69, 75, 80, 82, 83, 86, 87, 88, 92, 93, 94, 95, 96, 97, 98, 99, 106, 107, 108, 109, 128, 147, 148, 150, 153
training programs, 5, 35, 48, 80, 107
transactions, 1, 2, 5, 6, 7, 8, 9, 10, 11, 12, 13, 15, 16, 17, 18, 19, 20, 22, 23, 24, 25, 28, 30, 34, 35, 37, 38, 39, 41, 42, 43, 44, 45, 46, 47, 48, 49, 50, 52, 53, 57, 58, 63, 74, 75, 77, 82, 83, 84, 91, 121, 123, 124, 126, 127, 138, 139, 149, 153
transport, 16
transportation, 23, 52
trend, 98, 107, 131
trial, 127, 132
trust, 3, 5, 12, 14, 19, 20, 21, 28, 30, 34, 35, 42, 46, 47, 48, 98, 100
turnover, 12

U

U.S. Department of the Treasury, 27
U.S. Treasury, 29
uncertainty, 65
uniform, 64, 68, 73, 88, 90, 110, 111, 133, 147
unions, 63, 77, 85, 95, 107, 134, 136, 139, 147
United Nations, 28, 58
United States, 3, 6, 7, 8, 12, 16, 17, 24, 25, 26, 28, 37, 38, 45, 62, 72, 78, 105, 106, 110, 116, 121, 123, 153, 154
universe, 79
updating, 32, 88, 95

V

values, 25, 146
variability, 78
variables, 90
variance, 11, 34
variation, 130
victims, 125, 128
voice, 29, 56
vulnerability, 21

W

walking, 124
warrants, 14, 123
weakness, 65, 109, 110
wealth, 20, 126
web, 14, 15, 23, 58
wetlands, 1
wholesale, 25
wires, 39, 42
withdrawal, 6, 10, 24, 52
words, 4
work, 35, 37, 51, 63, 67, 68, 70, 71, 73, 74, 76, 79, 80, 82, 87, 88, 90, 92, 94, 97, 98, 100, 102, 109, 117, 129, 130, 131, 133, 135, 136, 137, 138, 154
World Wide Web, 28
writing, 52
wrongdoing, 127

Y

yield, 119